The Complete Idiot's Reference Card

Chronology of Shakespeare's Works

Work	Probable Date of Composition
King Henry VI, Part I	1589–1590
King Henry VI, Part II	1590–1591
King Henry VI, Part III	1590–1591
King Richard III	1592–1593
Venus and Adonis (poem)	1592–1593
The Comedy of Errors	1592–1594
Sonnets	1593–1609
The Rape of Lucrece (poem)	1593–1594
Titus Andronicus	1593–1594
The Taming of the Shrew	1593–1594
Two Gentlemen of Verona	1594
Love's Labor's Lost	1594–1595, revised 1957
King John	1594–1596
King Richard II	1595
Romeo and Juliet	1595–1596
A Midsummer Night's Dream	1595–1596
The Merchant of Venice	1596–1597
King Henry IV, Part I	1596–1597
The Merry Wives of Windsor	1597, revised 1600–1601
King Henry IV, Part II	1598
Much Ado About Nothing	1598–1599
King Henry V	1599
Julius Caesar	1599
As You Like It	1599
Hamlet	1600–1601
The Phoenix and the Turtle (poem)	1601
Twelfth Night	1601–1602
Troilus and Cressida	1601–1602
A Lover's Complaint (poem)	1602–1608
All's Well That Ends Well	1602–1603
Measure for Measure	1604
Othello	1604
King Lear	1605
Macbeth	1606
Anthony and Cleopatra	1606–1607
Coriolanus	1607–1608
Timon of Athens	1607–1608
Pericles	1607–1608
Cymbeline	1609–1610
The Winter's Tale	1610–1611
The Tempest	1611
King Henry VIII	1612–1613

tear here

alpha
books

Timeline for Shakespeare's Age

1520	Bowling becomes popular in London.
	(The shirts, fortunately, came later.)
1531	Church of England established; Henry VIII is the supreme head.
	Halley's Comet arouses a wave of superstition.
1533	The future Queen Elizabeth I born.
1547	King Henry VIII dies.
	First prediction by astrologer Nostradamus.
1553	Queen Mary I ("Bloody Mary") assumes throne.
1558	Queen Mary I dies; Elizabeth I assumes throne.
1564	Shakespeare born.
	Over 20,000 people killed by plague in London.
1572	Writers John Donne and Ben Jonson born.
	Pigeons first used to carry letters.
1577	Holinshed publishes *The Chronicles of England, Scotland and Ireland*, Shakespeare's primary source for the history plays.
	Francis Drake sets sail around the world.
1582	Shakespeare married.
	First known life insurance in England.
1586	Mary Queen of Scots tried for treason.
1587–1592	Shakespeare established in London as an actor/playwright.
	Forks used for the first time in French courts.
1588	Great Britain defeats the Spanish Armada.
1594	Shakespeare is a founding member of the Lord Chamberlain's Men acting company.
1599	The Globe Theater built; Shakespeare is a shareholder.
1603	Queen Elizabeth dies, James VI of Scotland becomes James I of England.
	The plague once again ravages London.
1605	The Gunpowder Plot—Guy Fawkes and accomplices arrested.
1607	The founding of Jamestown in America.
1612–1616	Shakespeare probably retires from London life to Stratford.
	Pocahontas (American Indian princess) marries John Rolfe.
1616	Shakespeare dies. His wife Anne gets the "second-best" bed.
1620	Plymouth colony founded in America.
1623	Publication of Shakespeare's *First Folio*.
1625	James I (James VI of Scotland) dies.
	Charles I (son of James I) assumes throne.
1635	Speed limit established for London coaches: 3 mph.
1649	Charles I (son of James I) executed.

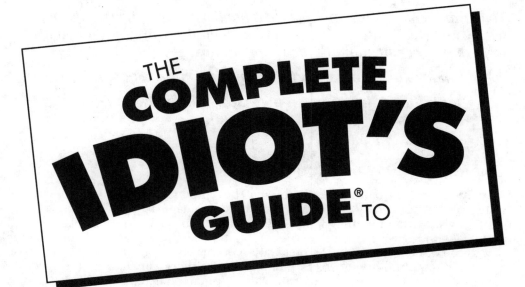

THE COMPLETE IDIOT'S GUIDE® TO

Shakespeare

by Laurie Rozakis, Ph.D.

alpha
books

A Division of Macmillan General Reference
A Pearson Education Macmillan Company
1633 Broadway, New York, NY 10019-6785

To Gardi Ipema Wilks, my treasured publicist. "Your heart's desires be with you!" (As You Like It). My deepest thanks, Gardi, for all your hard work on my behalf...and for believing in me.

Special thanks to Carol Mann Lash, my photo researcher and best friend.

> *"But if the while I think on thee, dear friend,*
> *All losses are restored and sorrows end."*

—"Sonnet 30"

Macmillan General Reference books may be purchased for business or sales promotional use. For information please write: Special Markets Department, Macmillan Publishing USA, 1633 Broadway, New York, NY 10019.

International Standard Book Number: 0-02862905-1
Library of Congress Catalog Card Number: 98-89733

01 00 99   8 7 6 5 4 3 2 1

Interpretation of the printing code: the rightmost number of the first series of numbers is the year of the book's printing; the rightmost number of the second series of numbers is the number of the book's printing. For example, a printing code of 99-1 shows that the first printing occurred in 1999.

Printed in the United States of America

Alpha Development Team

Publisher
Kathy Nebenhaus

Editorial Director
Gary M. Krebs

Managing Editor
Bob Shuman

Marketing Brand Manager
Felice Primeau

Acquisitions Editor
Jessica Faust

Development Editors
Phil Kitchel
Amy Zavatto

Assistant Editor
Georgette Blau

Production Team

Development Editor
Amy Zavatto

Production Editor
Christy Wagner

Copy Editor
Cliff Shubs

Cover Designer
Mike Freeland

Photo Editor
Richard H. Fox

Illustrator
Jody P. Schaeffer

Book Designers
Scott Cook and Amy Adams of DesignLab

Indexer
John Jefferson

Layout/Proofreading
Angela Calvert
Mary Hunt

Contents at a Glance

Contents

Foreword

In 2001, as we enter the new millennium, Shakespeare would have his 437th birthday. He ages gracefully. Romeo and Juliet are still perennial young lovers; Hamlet's angst still enacts our own; we continue to be awed by Lear's descent into madness, charmed by Beatrice and Rosalind, mystified and appalled by Iago, and delighted (and a tiny bit appalled as well) by Falstaff. We still say "Et tu Brute" and "Love is blind" and "Let's kill all the lawyers" and many other quotable lines that come from the treasure house of Shakespeare's plays and poems.

The twentieth century has been particularly rich in presentations of Shakespeare. Productions of his plays abounded in a spectacular range of modes, from attempts at reproducing the Elizabethan theatrical experience, to such oddities as *Swinging the Dream*, a 1939 film version of *A Midsummer Night's Dream* featuring Louis "Satchmo" Armstrong as Bottom; and an adaptation of *Othello* to *kabuki*, the traditional, highly stylized Japanese drama form.

All of Shakespeare's plays have been produced within the last 50 years, some of them many times; complete cycles of the entire canon have been performed on stage on several occasions, both in England and the United States. Film and television have adopted the Swan of Avon with enthusiasm. *Hamlet* has been filmed scores of times. Adaptations of the plays have also been widely produced, testifying to the timeless relevance of Shakespeare's themes. Perhaps best known are the Broadway musical and film versions *West Side Story* (from *Romeo and Juliet*); the great Japanese film director Akira Kurosawa's *Throne of Blood* (from *Macbeth*); and *Forbidden Planet*, a famous science-fiction film of the 1950s, based on *The Tempest*. And, as was true in earlier centuries, numerous operas have been based on the plays as well.

The rich production history reminds us that the plays of Shakespeare were written as popular entertainment and have continued their mass appeal. We have no reason to think they will not continue to enthrall audiences in the twenty-first century. The sonnets, too, are republished regularly, in editions ranging from scholarly annotated texts to illustrated pocket-sized volumes. The best known of these love poems are often featured in contemporary wedding ceremonies (including my own: "Sonnet 116").

But the treasure house of Shakespeare can be hard to get into—indeed, warnings of Shakespeare's difficulty are likely to loom larger for the student beginning his or her acquaintance with the Bard than the familiar accolades. Shakespeare's language, while brilliantly lucid, is the English of another, very different age, which can be obscure and hard to read. Moreover, though he addresses the quintessential elements of human life common to everyone's experience—love, longing, honor and deceit, age, death—he often does so in terms that were familiar to his original audiences but are less so to us. In short, it's true: Shakespeare *can* be hard to get into. Certainly, many of even the most enthusiastic fans can recall feeling somewhat baffled at first encounter. But the difficulties are usually overcome with a little coaching, and as Shakespeare's centuries-long, inextinguishable popularity attests, it is well worth overcoming them.

Fortunately, there are keys to the treasure houses of art and literature, and you have a fine one in your hands. Laurie Rozakis has combined a humorous and accessible format with her considerable knowledge of the material to produce an excellent introduction to the man, his world, and his works.

—Charles Boyce

Charles Boyce, author of the internationally acclaimed reference *Shakespeare A to Z*, grew up in Baltimore, Maryland. He attended Dartmouth College, where he majored in English Literature, and Columbia University, where he studied modern South Asian History and Literature. He is currently a freelance writer, contributing articles on art and literature to various magazines, as well as a published poet. He lives in New York with his wife and daughter.

Introduction

The Top 10 Plays Shakespeare Chose Not to Publish:

10. *Henry VIII, I Am, I Am*
9. *Fast Times at Verona High*
8. *Om'let*
7. *Romeo and Steve*
6. *Twelfth Night, Children Stay Free*
5. *Six Degrees of Francis Bacon*
4. *Stratford-upon-Avon, 90210*
3. *Romeo and Michelle's High School Reunion*
2. *Henry VIII Was a Big Fat Idiot*

And the #1 Play Shakespeare Chose Not to Publish:

1. *Big Macbeth and Fries*

Which ones *did* make the cut? Well, you remember murderous *Macbeth*, indecisive *Hamlet*, and those cute kids *Romeo and Juliet*. But what about *Coriolanus*, *Timon of Athens*, and *Titus Andronicus*? And all those histories—all 10 of them. For your entertainment, ladies and gentlemen, this book has it all: tragedy, comedy, history, pastoral, pastoral-comical, historical-pastoral, tragical-historical, tragical-comical-historical-pastoral, scene individable, or poem unlimited [*Hamlet*, II, ii, 323–376].

It's time to belly up to the Bard, so sit back and relax. You're in good hands. By the time you finish *The Complete Idiot's Guide® to Shakespeare*, you'll understand why William Shakespeare is the greatest writer the world has ever known. But even better, you'll join the millions and millions of people who love Shakespeare and his works.

What You'll Learn in This Book

In *The Complete Idiot's Guide® to Shakespeare*, I'll teach you everything you need to know about the Bard, from his life and times to his plays and poetry. You'll get summaries of every plot, descriptions of key scenes, a list of famous quotations, and even the low-down on Shakespearean plays, movies, and actors. Here's what you'll find in each part of this book:

Part 1, "Shakespeare's Life and Times," surveys Shakespeare's life, including his childhood, education, marriage, family, and fame in London. Then you'll learn what life was like for Shakespeare and his contemporaries by exploring the social, political, religious, and cultural realities of the age. Next, hop aboard the theater tour and find out all about Renaissance actors and the repertory system. No survey would be complete without a chronology of Shakespeare's works, basic dramatic terms, and the secret of Shakespeare's plots—it's all here, too. Then comes a review of Shakespearean English, so you can talk the talk as well as walk the walk! The section ends with a discussion of the authorship question: Who *really* wrote Shakespeare's plays? Get the evidence on the Earl of Oxford, Sir Francis Bacon, Christopher Marlowe, and the incumbent, William Shakespeare.

**Part 2, "The Comedies (or "Love Makes the World Go 'Round")," explores Shakespeare's comedies: *The Comedy of Errors, Two Gentlemen of Verona, The Taming of the Shrew, Love's Labor's Lost, A Midsummer Night's Dream, The Merchant of Venice, As You Like It, Much Ado About Nothing, Twelfth Night,* and *The Merry Wives of Windsor.* Enjoy Shakespeare's humor and see whether or not his characters *do* live happily ever after!

Part 3, "Problem Plays," covers *All's Well That Ends Well, Troilus and Cressida,* and *Measure for Measure.* You'll learn why these three works are classified as "problem plays" as you read excerpts, plot summarizes, and critical analysis.

Part 4, "Tragedies," surveys the headliners: *Titus Andronicus, Hamlet, Romeo and Juliet, Julius Caesar, Othello, The Moor of Venice, King Lear, Macbeth, Antony and Cleopatra, Coriolanus,* and *Timon of Athens.* Enjoy murder, mayhem, and magic as you read Shakespeare's bloodiest play, visit with the world's most celebrated star-crossed lovers, and thrill to tragic tales of power, ambition, and ruthlessness.

Part 5, "Romances," covers four plays: *The Tempest; The Winter's Tale; Pericles, Prince of Tyre;* and *Cymbeline.* I'll take you on a tour of the magical world of the Shakespearean romance, where wild things can—and do—happen.

Part 6, "Histories," summarizes the 10 history plays: *King Henry VI, Part I; King Henry VI, Part II; King Henry VI, Part III; King Richard III; King Richard II; King John; King Henry IV, Part I; King Henry IV, Part II; King Henry V;* and *King Henry VIII.* You'll take an armchair survey through a wide swath of English history, from the deposition of Richard II in 1399 to the defeat of Richard III at Bosworth Field to the coronation of Henry VII in 1485. I'll show you how the Masters of the Medieval Universe played power politics.

Part 7, "Poems and Sonnets," covers Shakespeare's four famous long poems: "Venus and Adonis," "The Rape of Lucrece," "A Lover's Complaint," and "The Phoenix and the Turtle," as well as his 154 sonnets. Today Shakespeare is celebrated for his drama, but in his day, William was king for his verse. Here, find out why. You'll also discover why the sonnets have sparked more commentary and stirred up more controversy than any other Shakespearean work besides *Hamlet.*

More for Your Money!

In addition to all the explanation and teaching, this book contains other types of information to make it even easier for you to learn about Shakespeare's works and the Renaissance. Here's how you can recognize these features:

Star Quality

Stars of the page, stage, and silver screen will all be found here. Want to know who else was a star during Shakespeare's time? Want to find the best Shakespeare films and the top Shakespearean actors? Mel Gibson, Patrick Stewart, Laurence Olivier, James Earl Jones, Richard Burton, Meryl Streep, Kevin Kline, Kenneth Branagh—all the Shakespearean stars shine here!

Will Power

These are interesting, useful bits of background information that give you the "inside edge" when it comes to understanding and appreciating Shakespeare and the time in which he lived. You could skip these tidbits, but you won't want to because they're much too tasty!

Sweets to the Sweet

Use these hints to make it easier to bridge the gap between Shakespeare's day and our own. That's because these sidebars point out Shakespeare's word play and language changes. Here, you'll find facts, figures, and critical analysis that can make you feel like a Shakespearean expert—or just sound like one!

Forsooth!

English has changed somewhat in the past 400 years! Here's where I define the vocabulary you'll encounter in Shakespeare's plays and poems.

Fire at Will

These warnings help you stay on track and avoid misreading the plays or misinterpreting key plot events.

Special Thanks to the Technical Reviewer

The Complete Idiot's Guide® to Shakespeare was reviewed by an expert who double-checked the accuracy of what you'll learn here to help us ensure that this book gives you everything you need to know about Shakespeare. Special thanks are extended to Michael LoMonico, editor of *Shakespeare* magazine (Georgetown University and Cambridge University Press), English teacher at Farmingdale High School, and a noted Shakespearean teacher and long-time associate of the Folger Shakespeare Library in Washington, D.C. Thank you, Michael, for lending your considerable experience and expertise to this project. It's very much appreciated.

Part 1
Shakespeare's Life and Times

Good name in man and woman, dear my lord,
Is the immediate jewel of their souls.
Who steals my purse steals trash; 'tis something, nothing;
'Twas mine, 'tis his, and has been slave to thousands;
But he that filches from me my good name
Robs me of that which not enriches him
And makes me poor indeed.

—Othello

"The remarkable thing about Shakespeare," Robert Graves said, "is that he really is very good, in spite of all the people who say he is very good."

When anyone asks who is the greatest English playwright of all time, Shakespeare's is the only name that comes to mind. Why? Shakespeare articulated thoughts and emotions with unmatched clarity and beauty.

In this section of the book, you'll get the lowdown on Shakespeare the man. In addition, you'll find out all about Shakespeare's time and place, his theater, and his language.

Chapter 1

Whose Life Is It Anyway?

Throughout Shakespeare's life, his name was variously spelled as Shagsbere, Shaxpere, Shackerpere, Shaxpeare, Shakesspeare, and Shakespeare. In fact, in 1869, George Wise published *The Autograph of William Shakespeare...Together with 4000 Ways of Spelling the Name According to English Orthography* (Scheackespyrr and Schaeaxspierre being two such possibilities).

Now that you know so much about Shakespeare's name, it's time to learn all about his life. First you'll read about his birth and family. Next comes his education, marriage, and children. Then you'll get to the bottom of the mystery of the so-called "Lost Years," when Shakespeare left his hometown of Stratford to make his name as an actor and playwright in London. This chapter concludes with a discussion of his death, last will and testament, and legacy.

Paper Trail

Mark Twain compared piecing together Shakespeare's life to reconstructing a dinosaur from a few bits of bone stuck together with plaster. According to Twain's theory, we know more about the Stegosaurus than we do about Shakespeare.

Actually, Shakespeare's life is no deep mystery; on the contrary, it's unusually well-documented for a normal Tom, Dick, or Will of his time. Unfortunately, the documentation takes the form of drab entries in church registers and city archives rather than torrid love letters and tell-all tabloids. What's a Shakespeare fan to do? Not to worry. Even if we can't dish the dirt on the Bard, we *can* get the facts. Let's start at the very beginning, with his debut on the stage of life.

Happy Birthday to You!

> There was a star danced, and under that was I born.

—Much Ado About Nothing

Shakespeare was born in April, 1564, in Stratford-upon-Avon, Warwickshire, about 100 miles northwest of London. According to the records of Stratford's Holy Trinity Church, the wee William was baptized on April 26. As with most sixteenth century births, the actual day is not recorded. Since it was customary to baptize infants three days after their birth and since Shakespeare died 52 years later on April 23, it has become traditional to assign April 23 as his birthday. (Same birth date, same death date: So far this is easy—see?)

Fire at Will

In Shakespeare's day, players and dramatists were regarded as persons of dubious standing, about whom no one was likely to be very interested, unless they were concerned with some scandal or the victim of a lewd joke. As a result, there was no push to save anecdotal records.

The Dynamic Duo: John and Mary

Shakespeare came from solid, middle-class stock. His father John was an established Stratford glove maker and leather dresser who also sold agricultural commodities—a man on the rise, sort of a Renaissance Rotarian. John Shakespeare served in Stratford government as a member of the Council, moving up the ranks to constable, chamberlain, alderman, and finally high bailiff, the equivalent of town mayor. But the good times weren't to continue.

Mary was equally busy on the home front. When the final count was in, she had eight children with John Shakespeare. William was the third child and the first son.

About 1577, John Shakespeare's fortunes began to decline, although we don't know why. There are records of debts. In 1586, he was replaced as alderman for shirking responsibilities, and in 1592 he was reprimanded for not coming to church for fear of process of debt. To add insult to injury, his application for a coat

Will Power

The first recorded mention of John Shakespeare took place in 1552, when he was fined for keeping a dunghill in front of his house.

of arms was denied. Fortunately, his by-then famous son was able to obtain a coat of arms for his father. But more on that later.

School Daze

There's no record that Shakespeare attended school, but as the son of a prominent businessman, he would have been entitled to free tuition at the local grammar school. As a result, it's logical to assume he did his time with the books.

The books that Shakespeare cracked, however, bear almost no relationship to what we study today. After he learned his letters, the world's most celebrated writer was drilled in Latin grammar, later reading and translating the standard Roman authors. He would have cut his eye teeth on what was considered the relatively easy Latin of *Aesop's Fables* (translated from Greek) before moving on to the tough stuff: Caesar, Cicero, Virgil, Ovid, Horace, Suetonius, Livy, Seneca, Terence, and Plautus.

No one knows how long Shakespeare remained at the Stratford Grammar School, but it seems likely that he was apprenticed to his father's business in the usual way, perhaps some time around 1577, when John Shakespeare's fortunes took a turn for the worse.

Since William did not attend college, he would not have been regarded as a man of learning in the same league as fellow writers Ben Jonson and John Milton. Jonson, in particular, was quite scornful of what he perceived as Shakespeare's educational shortcomings: "He [Shakespeare] has small Latin and less Greek," he sniffed. By our standards, of course, Shakespeare was admirably well educated.

Fire at Will

A great deal was demanded from students in Shakespeare's day. Grammar school began at dawn and continued for most of the day, six days a week. If any boy was inattentive or lazy, he was whipped—sometimes savagely—by the school-master. Notice I said *boys*: Only in the highest reaches of the aristocracy was any money spent on educating girls.

They Do!

It soon became apparent that William was interested in more than books. On November 28, 1582, the Bishop of Worcester issued the marriage bond for "William Shagspere" and "Ann Hathwey of Stratford," Renaissance spelling being a causal affair, as you've already learned. The bride was Anne Hathaway, daughter of Richard Hathaway of Shottery, near Stratford.

Anne's daddy was a substantial Warwickshire farmer with a spacious house and fields. William was 18; Anne, 26. As a minor, William required his father's permission to get married. It was granted.

The *banns* were asked only once in church, rather than the customary three times. The couple's rush to the altar became plain on May 26, six months after their marriage, when Susanna Shakespeare was christened. Before we snicker at Shakespeare, however, know that during the Renaissance, a promise to marry was considered just as valid and binding as the actual marriage ceremony. Once intentions had been declared, the couple was free to act as if they were married. The practice was widely accepted; it's been estimated that one in every three Elizabethan brides was pregnant on her wedding day.

Forsooth!

Banns are the notice of an intended marriage. They are normally announced or posted three times in the parish church of each side of the betrothed.

Two years later, Anne gave birth to twins they named Hamnet and Judith.

Was Shakespeare speaking for himself in *A Midsummer Night's Dream* when he wrote:

Lysander:	The course of true love never did run smooth; But either it was different in blood… Or else misgraffed in respect of years—
Hermia:	O spite! too old to be engage'd to young.

Next to the marriage certificate, the only other mention of Shakespeare's wife appears in his will with his famous bequest of his "second-best bed" to her. Whether it is a fond remembrance or a bitter slight is not known.

Lost in Space

There is no documentary record of Shakespeare's activities from the birth of the twins until Robert Greene's complaint about him as an "upstart crow" in 1592. (I explain the complaint later.) However, this lack of detail has not stopped people from inventing tales to explain how the unknown Stratford lad ended up in London as a famous entertainment mogul.

According to the most commonly told story, Shakespeare was forced to flee Stratford to escape prosecution for poaching deer on the lands of Sir Thomas Lucy. The story was started by Richard Davies, a clergyman, who wrote around 1616 that "Shakespeare was much given to all unluckiness in stealing venison and rabbits, particularly from Sir Lucy who oft had him whipped and sometimes imprisoned and at last mad[e] him fly his native country to his great advancement." Like a bad case of poison ivy, the story has spread.

The eighteenth century Shakespearean scholar Edmond Malone speculated that our hero "was employed while he yet remained at Stratford, in the office of some country attorney." According to another tale, Shakespeare spent time as a teacher in the countryside. Even less believable theories have Shakespeare holding horses outside theaters in London and becoming a Franciscan monk. At various times, scholars, writers, and cranks have claimed that during the so-called "Lost Years" Shakespeare was a:

➤ Moneylender

➤ Sailor

➤ Soldier

➤ Gardener

➤ Coachman

➤ Printer

Fire at Will

Wandering the countryside was not wise or safe during Shakespeare's day. Even though the penalty for highway robbery was death, bandits continued to rob the well to do.

Will of the People

In 1592, we get the first documentary evidence of Shakespeare's rise to prominence in the London theater. Fate being what it is, the reference is an insult:

> …for there is an upstart Crow, beautified with our feathers, that with his Tygers hart wrapt in a Players hyde, supposes he is as well able to bombast out a blanke verse as the best of you: and beeing an absolute Johannes fac totum, is in his owne conceit the onely Shake-scene in a countrey.

"Shake-scene" is our Shakespeare, and the jealous writer was one Robert Greene, a minor Elizabethan playwright. Six years older than Shakespeare, Greene wrote the attack when he was a bitter, dying man. Greene accuses Shakespeare of stealing other playwright's techniques and using them to further his own career.

This passage is important because it verifies several facts about Shakespeare's career as it had developed by 1592:

➤ He had become successful enough to rankle Greene's jealousy.

➤ He had become a part of the professional theater world in London.

➤ He was known as a man of various abilities ("Johannes fac totem" or Jack-of-all-trades, as we would say), an actor, playwright, and play reviser ("beautified with our feathers," the techniques used by more established writers).

➤ He was recognized as a skilled poet ("bombast out a blanke verse").

➤ His *Henry VI, Part III* had become famous enough to be recognized by one of its lines (the actual line from the play being, "O, tiger's heart wrapped in a woman's hide").

As Greene's insult reveals, Shakespeare was well established in the London theater world by the end of 1592.

Plague!

Shakespeare's fortunes abruptly changed in January, 1593, when the theaters in London were closed because of the bubonic plague (the "Black Death"). The theaters were allowed to open again briefly during the winter of 1594, but were closed again in February and remained closed until spring, 1594.

Will Power

The children's nursery song "Ring Around the Rosey" originated as a plague song. *Ring around the rosey* represents the painful, puss–filled sores that erupted all over a sufferer's body. *Pockets full of poseys* are the flowers people held over their noses to block out the stench of unburied decaying corpses. *Ashes, ashes* is the sneezing that accompanied the plague; *we all fall down* is death. Sometimes the dead were burned to prevent the plague from spreading, so the "ashes" also represent the remains of the dead after they were burned. And you worry about the influence of video games on your impressionable kiddies.

This period of theater closures played havoc with the professional acting companies, which were forced into a hand-to-mouth existence of touring with much reduced companies. During this time, Shakespeare turned to writing lyric poetry, sonnets, and plays for the private entertainment of his aristocratic friends. He established himself as a playwright once and for all when the theaters reopened in 1594.

The Top Bard

The years 1594 to 1599 were momentous for Shakespeare. He produced a steady stream of plays of the highest quality. He continued as a principal actor and manager of an acting company called the Lord Chamberlain's Men, so he was blessed with a stable work environment in the all-too-unstable world of the theater. As a result, he prospered financially and created a comfortable life and a solid estate. In 1599, he became part owner in the most prestigious public theater in London, the Globe.

Apparently Anne and the kids remained home in Stratford while Shakespeare worked in London. Back then, the trip from London to Stratford took about four days on foot or two days on horseback. In August, 1596, Shakespeare's only son Hamnet died. It is often thought that Shakespeare's poignant lines from *King John* refer to this event:

Grief fills the room up of my absent child,
Lies in his bed, walks up and down with me,
Puts on his pretty looks, repeats his words,
Remembers me of all his gracious parts,
Stuffs out his vacant garments with his form.
Then have I reason to be fond of grief.

The same year, the College of Heralds finally granted John Shakespeare a coat of arms, the Elizabethan status symbol. The application must have been paid for by the playwright for his own as well as his father's benefit. The motto was "Non Sans Droit" —*not without right*. The crest is a falcon shaking a spear.

In May, 1597, Shakespeare purchased New Place, the second largest house in Stratford, along with barns, orchards, and gardens.

All the King's Horses and All the King's Men

In 1603, Queen Elizabeth died, and James VI of Scotland became James I of England. The Chamberlain's Men became the King's Men and received royal patronage. No acting company performed more at court over these years. From November 1, 1604, to October 31, 1605, the King's Men performed 11 times before the King. Seven of the performances were plays by Shakespeare. On average, the King's Men performed about a dozen times a year at court. Nice work if you can get it.

It's a Wonderful Life

Meanwhile, Shakespeare continued investing in Stratford real estate. The lofty artist amassed an enviable real estate portfolio. Life was good, according to one source:

> The latter Part of his Life was spent, as all Men of good Sense will wish theirs may be, in Ease, Retirement, and the Conversation of his Friends. He had the good Fortune to gather an Estate equal to his Occasion, and, in that, to his Wish; and is said to have spent some Years before his Death at his native Stratford. His pleasurable Wit, and good Nature, engag'd him in the Acquaintance, and entitled him to the Friendship of the Gentlemen of the Neighbourhood.

Shakespeare's eldest daughter Susanna had married Dr. John Hall in 1607. Shortly after, the couple settled in Stratford, where Hall established a prosperous medical practice and became one of the town's leading citizens. He became widely famous for his skill as a doctor. John and Susanna had a daughter, Elizabeth, who was the last survivor of the Shakespeare line. She died in 1670.

Shakespeare's youngest daughter, Judith, was not so lucky. In February of 1616, at age 31, she married Thomas Quiney, 27, a Stratford winemaker. Even though Quiney came from a good family, the wedding began sadly. Before marrying Judith Shakespeare, Quiney got another girl pregnant. A month after the wedding, the girl died in childbirth with her infant. The Quineys went on to have three children. The first, named Shakespeare, died in infancy. The other two sons, Richard and Thomas, died in 1639, at ages 21 and 19, respectively. The couple left no heirs.

The Man Behind the Myth

...My nature is subdued
To what it works in, like the dyer's hand.

—"Sonnet 111"

What was Shakespeare really like? Was he a lobster-tail-and-drawn-butter or a tuna-fish-on-rye kind of guy? Unfortunately, Shakespeare the monolith has overpowered Shakespeare the man.

John Aubrey, a noted gossip monger who lived during the Restoration period (1660), recorded in his book, *Lives of the Poets*, a story he heard third-hand from the actor William Beeston, the son of one of Shakespeare's fellow actors. According to Beeston, Shakespeare was "a handsome, well-shaped man: very good company, and of a very ready and pleasant smooth wit." Was Shakespeare like his Hamlet, "The glass of fashion and the mould of form, / Th' observed of all observers…"? Judge for yourself: here's a portrait of the Bard.

In the nearly 400 years since Shakespeare's death, over 250 "authentic" portraits of him have surfaced. There are only two portraits that can be authenticated within a reasonable doubt. This is one.

But then again, Aubrey also claimed that William's father was a butcher and the lad helped out in the shop. When Shakespeare "kill'd a Calfe, he would doe it in *high style* and make a speech," Aubrey claimed. Aubrey's love of gossip seemed to outweigh his love of truth. But hey, no one's perfect.

According to an anecdote from the 1700s, on his travels to and from London, Shakespeare used to stay at the Crown Inn in Oxford run by the glum John Davenant. His son, William Davenant (1606–1668), who became a famous poet and dramatist during the Restoration, was Shakespeare's godson. It was a tradition in Oxford that the child was "so fond of Shakespeare, that whenever he heard of his arrival, he would fly home from school to see him."

The Mystery of Shakespeare's Death

Men must endure
Their going hence even as their coming hither:
Ripeness is all.

—*King Lear*

Shakespeare died on April 23, 1616, and was buried in the chancel of Holy Trinity Church on April 25. On the slab over his grave appear the words:

GOOD FRIEND FOR JESUS SAKE FORBEARE,
TO DIGG THE DUST ENCLOASED HEARE.
BLESTE BE Ye MAN Yt SPARES THES STONES,
AND CURST BE HE Yt MOVES MY BONES.

Shakespeare had a practical reason for this request. During the Renaissance, when a burial ground became overcrowded, gravediggers would empty all the old graves and dump the remains to make way for new corpses. It would appear that Shakespeare wanted to arrive in the next world with all his body parts in one place.

So far, his wishes have been honored. A painted funerary bust was erected in the church early in the seventeenth century that has lasted to the present.

Elvis Has Left the Building

No one knows how Shakespeare died; the nature of his illness is unknown. The Shakespeare Data Bank, an ongoing project to computerize all information about Shakespeare's life, currently lists more than 20 causes of death, including Bright's disease, shock over his daughter Judith's marriage, "intolerable entrails," and writer's cramp.

A legend has grown around a diary entry made by John Ward, a Stratford vicar. Ward wrote that "Shakspear Drayton and Ben Jhonson had a merry meeting and it seems drank too hard for Shakespear died of a feavour there contracted."

Last Will and Testament

They say he parted well and paid his score:
And so God be with him!

—*Macbeth*

Shakespeare left £100 to his daughter Judith for her marriage and another £50 if she renounced any claim to the Chapel Lane cottage near New Place. He left her £150 more if she lived another three years. If Judith died within that time, the £150 was to have gone to Shakespeare's granddaughter, Elizabeth Hall.

Shakespeare left £30 to his sister, Joan Hart. He also allowed her to stay on for a token rent in one of the two houses on Henley Street, which Shakespeare had inherited from his father in 1601. He left each of Joan's three sons £5.

He left £10 to the poor of Stratford, a large amount considering similar bequeaths of the time. Shakespeare singled out "my fellowes John Hemynges, Richard Burbage, and Henry Cundell," leaving them a generous amount of money to "buy them Ringes." Heminges and Condell were, seven years later, to become the editors of Shakespeare's *First Folio*. More on this in Chapters 4, "The Play's the Thing," and 7, "Shakespeare's Literary Reputation."

Shakespeare's will doesn't mention his wife Anne (though it would have been her right through English common law to one-third of his estate, as well as residence for life at New Place), except to leave her his "second-best bed."

"All the Rest of my goodes Chattels Leases plate Jewels and household stuffe whatso-ever after my dettes and Legasies paied and my funerall expences dischared" he left to his son-in-law John Hall and his daughter Susanna.

Are you wondering why there weren't any books or play scripts mentioned in the will? Shakespeare wouldn't have owned any play scripts, since they were the property of the King's Men. Any books would not have been itemized in the will but would have been part of his "goodes."

> Now cracks a noble heart. Good night, sweet prince,
> And flights of angels sing thee to thy rest!
>
> —*Hamlet*

The Least You Need to Know

➤ Shakespeare's life is well documented for his time, although the materials are dry deeds and papers.

➤ Shakespeare was born in April, 1564, in Stratford; the day is generally accepted as April 23. He died in Stratford 52 years later on April 23, 1616.

➤ Shakespeare came from solid, middle-class stock and likely attended the local grammar school.

➤ On November 28, 1582, Shakespeare married Anne Hathaway. They had three children: Susanna and twins Hamnet and Judith.

➤ There is no record of Shakespeare's activities from 1584 to 1592, the so-called "Lost Years." It is not known how he established himself as a well-known actor and playwright.

➤ In 1599, Shakespeare became part owner in the most prestigious public theater in London, the Globe. Highly successful, he invested in real estate and was able to retire a rich man.

Chapter 2

The Renaissance 101

In This Chapter

➤ Terms for the era

➤ Economic realities of the age

➤ Fun and games in the 1600s

➤ Renaissance politics and religion

➤ The Great Chain of Being

➤ The marriage mart

➤ Family life in the fifteenth and sixteenth centuries

This royal throne of kings, this sceptered isle,
This earth of majesty, this seat of Mars,
This other Eden, demi-paradise,
This fortress built by Nature for herself
Against infection and the hand of war,
This happy breed of men, this little world,
This precious stone set in the silver sea,
Which serves it in the office of a wall,
Or as a moat defensive to a house,
Against the envy of less happier lands,
This blessed plot, this earth, this realm, this England.

So Shakespeare described the England of his day. With the founding of the Tudor
dynasty (1485), England became a force to be reckoned with. In 1588, under Queen

Elizabeth I, England blew the Spanish Armada out of the water. England was swiftly transforming herself from an island off the coast of Europe into a dominant sea power and an emerging colonial empire.

As England increased in importance, so her literature, art, and music began to flourish. In this chapter, find out what life was like in Shakespeare's merrye olde England.

What's in a Name?

What's in a name? That which we call a rose
By any other name would smell as sweet...

Romeo and Juliet were onto something when it came to the name game. What name has been given to the exhilarating era from 1485 to 1625? Check the term you think is correct:

_____ 1. Renaissance

_____ 2. Reformation

_____ 3. Age of Exploration

_____ 4. Age of Discovery

_____ 5. Elizabethan era

Stop! You're all correct! Each of these terms describes the late 1400s–early 1600s. Here are the definitions:

1. *Renaissance* (meaning "rebirth") is a term used to describe the incredible flowering of art, scholarship, and literature that took place during the fifteenth and sixteenth centuries in Europe. The movement began in Italy in the fourteenth century and jumped the Channel into England in the final two decades of the fifteenth century.

2. *Reformation* is the term used to describe the landmark movement that began when King Henry VIII (Daddy-o of Queen Elizabeth I) split from the Pope and the Catholic Church of Rome and founded the Protestant Church of England.

3. *Age of Exploration* is often used to describe the scores of geographical findings and the expansion of trade and commerce during the era. England's participation in the Age of Exploration began in 1497 when the Italian-born explorer John Cabot, sailing for an English company, reached Newfoundland and perhaps the mainland. Cabot thus laid the basis for future English claims in North America (even though it took them a while to make any).

4. *Age of Discovery* is used to describe the many scientific discoveries of the time, from Harvey's discovery of circulation of blood to the invention of the telescope. In between, decimal fractions, valves in veins, and the laws of planetary motion were discovered.

5. *Elizabethan era* has come to signify the English Renaissance at its height, under the leadership of Queen Elizabeth (likely the most able English ruler since William the Conqueror). A great patron of the arts, Queen Elizabeth gathered around her a flock of courtiers that included most of the most talented writers of the day. Many of the era's greatest literary works are dedicated to her. (Their mommas didn't raise no stupid kids.)

Of course, the inhabitants of England at that time weren't aware that they were living in a tidy historical period. They should have bought this book.

Star Quality

Because the Renaissance began in Italy, many of the leading Renaissance figures were Italian. Among them were the poet Dante Alighieri (1265–1321), who wrote *The Divine Comedy*; Francesco Petrarca (1304–1374), who wrote lyric poetry in a new form called the "sonnet"; and the painter, scientist, and engineer Leonardo da Vinci (1452–1519).

Life on the Edge

> Now is the winter of our discontent…
>
> —*Richard III*

Imagine that you're living in England in the late 1500s. Like everyone you know, you live with your family in the countryside, scraping by as best you can. If you're really lucky, your father is a yeoman farmer who owns enough land to support his family or a "husband-man" who has less land but adds to his income by wage-earning. The gap between the rich and poor is wide: Wealth and power are concentrated in the firm grasp of a lucky few. Most people can't even find jobs.

Disease and disasters are a given; nary a day goes by without a catastrophe. Last week, for instance, your neighbor's landlord decided to "enclose" the land—to stop using it for farming and turn it into pasture—and so your neighbor is now homeless.

Your stomach never stops growling; everyone you know is sick and malnourished. Heavy rains have ruined the harvest, the population is growing far faster than the crops, and famine has begun to cast its grim shadow across your region. The Carriers in Shakespeare's *Henry IV, Part I* remember a friend who "never joyed since the price of oats rose. It was the death of him." To make matters worse, there's an economic recession across the entire continent. What to do? The only solution is to hit the road.

Fire at Will

If you got sick during the Renaissance, you'd be smarter to consult a faith healer or a witch than a doctor. Doctors believed that illness resulted from an imbalance in the four **humors** (fluids) of the human body: bile, phlegm, choler, and blood. To restore the balance, doctors removed blood by having yucky leeches suck it out. X-rays and stethoscopes hadn't yet been invented. The most common operation was amputation, performed *without* anesthesia, of course.

Will Power

The invention of the printing press, together with improved methods of manufacturing paper, made possible the rapid spread of knowledge. In 1476, during the War of the Roses, William Caxton had set up England's first printing press. By 1640, that press and others like it had printed more than 26,000 different books. It is estimated that by 1530, more than half of England's population was literate.

Bright Lights, Big City

> The quality of mercy is not strained,
> It droppeth as the gentle rain from heaven
> Upon the place beneath: it is twice blessed;
> It blesseth him that gives and him that takes...

—*The Merchant of Venice*

You're astonished at the number of people traveling to London, given the hardships of travel. Important-looking government officials doing the Queen's business and well-heeled teenage boys heading off to university at Oxford and Cambridge clatter past on horseback, kicking up dust in your face. There's an unwed servant girl fired from her job and kicked out of town when her condition became obvious. Sick old people wander aimlessly because there's no system of hospitals or shelters. But most of the travelers are just like you: poor and desperate young men off to seek their fortunes in the big city.

A few days later, you reach London. The noisy, bustling metropolis is the largest city in Europe. In 1563, there had been only 93,000 people in London; by 1605, the figure had more than doubled to 224,000 people. Disease is even more prevalent here than it was in the wretched countryside. Bubonic plague is the number one killer, followed closely by smallpox and tuberculosis. No one bathes often; the toothbrush won't be invented for nearly a century. Ditches function as public toilets; butchers throw the carcasses of dead animals into the street to rot. Even so-called healthy people have bad breath, rotting teeth, constant stomach pains, and running sores all over their bodies.

Fun and Games

Need something to divert you from your growling belly and sore feet as you roam through London looking for food and shelter? How about the Renaissance version of "fun"? Here are the leading amusements of the day:

➤ Theater (including plays by that talented Shakespeare fellow)

➤ Bear- or bull-baiting (several dogs attack a bear or bull tied to a stake)

➤ Cockfighting (lots of feathers and chicken blood)

➤ Brawling and rioting (fueled by endless warm brewskis)

➤ Witch burnings (a fan favorite)

➤ Public executions (don't forget to check out the severed head; it's always displayed)

Which Way Is Up?

Maybe you're better off in London than you would be in the countryside; maybe you're worse off. But no matter where you went in England in the late 1500s and early 1600s, the social underpinnings were giving way. The world as you knew it was dissolving because everything seemed to be changing at breakneck speed. On the high seas, explorers were discovering worlds where everyone had thought nothing existed. As new horizons opened and old assumptions melted away, it seemed like the sky above and the Earth below were crumbling.

European astronomers were challenging age-old beliefs about the universe. One of them, some fellow named Copernicus, claimed that the Sun, not the Earth, was the center of the universe. He went so far as to suggest that the Earth moved! (Everyone knew it was fixed in the heavens.)

Church = State

Even though people were still deeply religious, the Church had been seesawing from Catholic (Henry VII) to Protestant (Henry VIII) to Catholic (Queen Mary) back to Protestant (Queen Elizabeth I). Politics and religion had long been familiar bedfellows in England. But since we can't follow the movers and shakers without a scorecard, let's start with one:

Will Power

The Polish astronomer Nicolaus Copernicus (1473–1543) is best known for his theory that the Sun is at rest near the center of the universe and that the Earth, spinning on its axis once daily, revolves around the Sun. After the trial of Galileo in 1633, Copernicus' theory was suppressed. It was not until Sir Isaac Newton that most major thinkers in England, France, and the Netherlands adopted Copernicus' theory. The rest of Europe held out for another century. Spoil sports.

Will Power

As the Church of England became established during Elizabeth's long reign, two main groups of nonconformists emerged. They were the radical reformers who thought that Henry VIII hadn't gone far enough to "purify" the church. These *Puritans* detested anything that smacked of Roman Catholicism. The second group, the English Roman Catholics, thought that Henry had gone *way* too far.

House of Tudor	Reign
Henry VII	1485–1509
Henry VIII	1509–1547
Edward VI (son of Henry VIII)	1547–1553
Mary I (daughter of Henry VIII)	1553–1558
Elizabeth I (daughter of Henry VIII)	1558–1603
House of Stuart	
James I (James VI of Scotland)	1603–1625
Charles I (son of James I)	1625–1649 [executed]

Politics and religion grew even closer in 1534 when Henry VIII decreed that the ruler of the nation (himself) would also be the formal head of the new Protestant church.

Following his death in 1547, there was a decade of turmoil and uncertainty as each of Henry VIII's successive heirs instituted a different religious policy. His eldest child, Mary, returned the country to Catholicism during her five-year reign, sparking violent social upheaval (hence her nickname "Bloody Mary").

When Elizabeth came to the throne in 1558, she decided to settle the matter once and for all by returning to her father's (second) religion. To this end, she made the Protestant faith England's official religion, instituted the Book of Common Prayer, and made Sunday service mandatory. A no-nonsense monarch, Lizzie warned all her subjects not to "attempt the breach, alteration, or change of any order of usage presently established within this realm." Anyone who professed atheism or criticized the church would be marched off to the nearest gallows to avail themselves of the services offered there.

Heir Today, Gone Tomorrow

And then we have the instability at the top of the heap. Boys just wanna have some fun...and have a son to take over the family business. Henry VIII became a marrying kind of guy in his quest for a legitimate male heir. All told, he had six wives. Here's the run down:

Wife	Fate	Child
Catherine of Aragon	Divorced	Mary
Anne Boleyn	Executed	Elizabeth
Jane Seymour	Died	Edward
Anne of Cleves	Divorced	none
Catherine Howard	Executed	none
Catherine Parr	Survived	none

Order in the Land

How did the Elizabethans cope with this great social upheaval? Many people clung tenaciously to the traditional ways of interpreting the world and making sense of their place in it. The more the world seemed to be plunging into chaos, the more some Elizabethans embraced the old concepts of order. The sound bite was "hierarchy."

According to this view, the world was an ordered, rational place. Each person occupied a specific rung on the social ladder. With each rank came responsibilities to those above and below in the chain. Everyone understood and accepted this hierarchy, and it was constantly reinforced in daily life.

During compulsory Sunday services at the Established Church of England, for example, ministers explained that "Every degree of people…hath appointed to them, their duty and order. Some are in high degree, some are in low, some kings and princes, some inferiors and subjects. Almighty God hath created and appointed all things…in the most excellent and perfect order."

This ranking extended to everyone and everything in the universe: Each element, creature, and spiritual being occupied a fixed place in the universe.

The rigid hierarchy even extended to clothing. Laws decreed who was allowed to wear what. Clothing Acts were passed to halt the "intolerable abuse and unmeasured disorder" caused by the poorer people dressing as their betters. No one under the rank of Knight, for example, could wear silk stockings and velvet cloaks; only people ranked as Countesses or higher were allowed to wear purple silk. Gold and silver were reserved for nobles. To the dismay of lawmakers but the delight of dressmakers, most people openly flouted the laws.

Sweets to the Sweet

How can you remember the fate of the six wives of Henry VIII? Try this rhyme, a favorite of British school kids: "Divorced, beheaded, died; divorced, beheaded, survived."

Fire at Will

To an Elizabethan, anything out of the ordinary—floods, storms, unexpected deaths—signaled a violation of order. In Shakespeare's *Julius Caesar*, terrible things happen as the conspirators hatch their plot against their king: "A lioness hath whelped in the streets, And graves have yawned and yielded up their dead…Horses did neigh, and dying men did groan, And ghosts did shriek and squeal about the streets."

Heavenly Bodies

> The heavens themselves, the planets, and this center
> Observe degree, priority and place.

As Shakespeare noted in *Troilus and Cressida*, this divinely directed order began with the heavens themselves. To the Elizabethans, the entire universe was enclosed by a sphere called the *primum mobile*. Beneath it lay the fixed stars. Next came the planets, whose motion was directed by the *primum mobile*. While no one was sure just how many planets made up the universe—was it nine? Ten? Eleven?—it was as plain as the nose on your face that these spheres revolved around a fixed Earth.

Even the angels obeyed a strict hierarchy, ranging from the highest (the Seraphs) to the lowest (the angels). This, too, made sense. After all, hadn't Satan been thrown out of heaven for offending the principles of order and trying to make himself equal with God?

This view of the universe came from Ptolemy, a Roman astronomer born in Egypt during the second century A.D. Here's how Shakespeare's contemporaries imagined the universe looked.

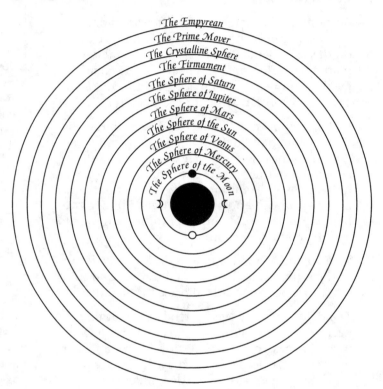

The Empyrean
The Prime Mover
The Crystalline Sphere
The Firmament
The Sphere of Saturn
The Sphere of Jupiter
The Sphere of Mars
The Sphere of the Sun
The Sphere of Venus
The Sphere of Mercury
The Sphere of the Moon

The Great Chain of Being

Heaven and its inhabitants were joined to the rest of the universe through a concept called The Great Chain of Being. It stretched from the most lowly thing in the universe all the way up to God. Of course, humans were on the top of the chain over all the other creatures.

The order of each world was reflected in all others. England's rulers, for instance, were ranked in an order that corresponded to the order of the rest of creation. The sovereign was analogous to fire, the chief element; the sun, the chief planet; and the eagle, the chief bird. Shakespeare threads The Great Chain of Being through his plays. In *The Tempest*, for example, Prospero, through his natural magic, is served by the angel-like Ariel from on high and by the bestial Caliban from not-so-high.

All is well with societies, families, and individuals when they know their duties and keep their places. But as Macbeth in Shakespeare's tragedy *Macbeth* discovered, the consequences of disregarding the hierarchy of the universe were disastrous. His violations plunged Scotland into fierce civil war.

Gilt Trip

> Tell me where is fancy bred,
> Or in the heart or the head?
> How begot, how nourished?
>   Reply, reply
> It is engenderd in the eyes,
> With gazing fed; and fancy dies.
> In the cradle where it lies.
> Let us all ring fancy's knell:
> I'll begin it — Ding, dong, bell.
> Ding, dong, bell.

This Shakespearean song is sung in *The Merchant of Venice*, when Bassanio is trying to choose among the caskets of gold, silver, and lead, knowing that only by making the correct choice will he be able to win Portia as his wife. It's an apt metaphor for the Elizabethan marriage mart, where money talked and nobody walked.

For many matchmaking parents (and their hot-to-trot kids), wealth and property were the only considerations. In Shakespeare's *The Merry Wives of Windsor*, Sir Hugh Evans notes that Anne Page is well endowed where it counts: "Seven hundred pounds and possibilities," he says, "is goot gifts."

Equality of status, religion, and age were important, too. In *Hamlet*, Polonius warns Hamlet's stepfather Claudius and Hamlet's mother Gertrude that he has warned his daughter Ophelia that "Lord Hamlet is a price out of thy star; This must not be." Couples of different ages, races, religions, or even social standings were not encouraged, and even rejected in some families. In Shakespeare's tragedy *Othello*, Desdemona's interracial marriage to the Moor (black) Othello shocks and angers her father.

Power Play

An Elizabethan father had absolute right to dispose of his daughters in marriage. Old Capulet in *Romeo and Juliet* would be considered an extremely considerate father to the Elizabethans. After all, when the question of Juliet's marriage to Paris is first discussed, he is willing to let Juliet refuse the marriage. It is not until she defies him that he gives commands.

Marriage and affairs of the heart were much less rigid among the lower classes, however. Since great property deals and clever political alliances weren't being made, parental consent was rarely a problem.

The Dream Team

Was this the face that launched a thousand ships,
And burnt the topless towers of Ilium?

—Christopher Marlowe, *The Tragical History of Dr. Faustus*

The marriage age was surprisingly late—for girls, 25 or 26; for boys, 28 or 29. Baby brides like Juliet, who "hath not seen the change of 14 years," or 15-year-old Miranda of *The Tempest* were the exceptions, even for the upper classes.

There were good reasons for delaying nuptials. First, later marriages resulted in smaller families, since big families meant big problems. Further, the later a couple married, the better the odds they would be financially stable.

The average wedding feast was a blow-out of epic proportions. Elizabethans called it the "bride-ale"; Puritans referred to it as "public incendiaries of all filthy lusts." Among the upper classes, exuberant feasting and drinking drew spectators from far and wide. But even the poorer folks had food and drink, dancing, bawdy singing, and gifts for the guests.

Fire at Will

Pregnant brides were tolerated; pregnant nonbrides weren't. Unwed mothers faced dire consequences: They were often fired from their jobs and kicked out of the parish. If unwed laboring women refused to name their partner-in-sin, many midwives refused to help them. It's not surprising that infanticide by poison or suffocation was common.

Family Matters

How sharper than a serpent's tooth it is
To have a thankless child!

—*King Lear*

As the King (or Queen, as it was for most of the Renaissance) ruled over the kingdom, so the man of the family ruled over his wife and children. A woman in *The Comedy of Errors* points this out while instructing her sister:

The beasts, the fishes, and the winged fowl,
Are their males' subjects and at their controls.
Man, more divine, the master of all these,
Lord of the wide world and wilde watery seas,
Endued with intellectual sense and souls,
Of more preeminence than fish and fowls,
Are masters of their females, and their lords;
    Then let your will attend on their accords.

Husbands were expected to provide for their families and be patient with their wives' frailties and shortcomings. Wives were expected to be meek, patient, and quiet, willing to put up with whatever their husbands dished out. Marriage was far more a partnership than this suggests—it had to be if families were to survive.

Even among the upper classes, everyone had to do their share. Upper-class women may have seemed more ornamental than essential, considering the huge staff of servants they employed, but many of these women ran major estates, especially if their husbands traveled on business. She might also be called on to deliver babies, mix herbal remedies, and make repairs.

Will Power

Children were brought up to fear and respect their parents. They called their father "Sir" and stood in his presence. The father's power and authority was part of the social order.

Ironically, of course, this elaborate structure and rigid hierarchy could not prevent the transformations that were taking place in society. All the sermons and lessons insisting on rigid obedience to a fixed system were, in the end, simply last-ditch efforts to fend off a tsunami of change that threatened to overwhelm the social order.

The Least You Need to Know

➤ The Renaissance ("rebirth") was the cultural flowering that took place in Europe during the fifteenth and sixteenth centuries.

➤ The Renaissance was a time of swift and disconcerting change. Many people clung tenaciously to traditional hierarchy.

➤ Politics and religion were intimately intertwined.

➤ In 1558, Queen Elizabeth I made the Protestant faith England's official religion.

➤ Heaven and its inhabitants were joined to the rest of the universe through a concept called The Great Chain of Being.

➤ Marriages were based on economic factors.

➤ A husband ruled over his wife and children.

Chapter 3

All the World's a Stage: Shakespeare's Theater

In This Chapter

➤ The first permanent theater

➤ Renaissance actors' *really* bad press

➤ The Globe Theater

➤ The repertory system

➤ The new Globe

All the world's a stage,
And all the men and women are merely players.
They have their exits and their entrances,
And one man in his time plays many parts...

—*As You Like It*

English drama came of age during the reign of Elizabeth I, developing into a sophisticated and very popular art form. In this chapter, you'll learn all about the Elizabethan theater and Shakespeare's role in it.

You'll learn all about the first permanent theater, built by carpenter-turned-actor James Burbage. Then you'll get the inside skinny on actors and the theater during Shakespeare's day—how were they *really* regarded? Next comes a discussion of Shakespeare's Globe Theater, including a survey of the Elizabethan repertory system. The chapter concludes with a section on the exciting new Globe Theater.

Stage #1: The First "Permanent" Theater

When I was at home, I was in a better place, but travelers must be content.

—*As You Like It*

Before Elizabethan players had a permanent home, they gave performances any place they could erect a stage and gather a crowd. As a result, they staged public shows in village halls, inn yards, and bear-baiting arenas. They put on private shows in the great halls of noblemen's houses or in one of the Queen's palaces.

At this time, the stage was simply a platform of boards resting on trestles or barrels with a curtained booth in the back where the actors could change their costumes and wait for their cue. There weren't many props or much scenery, and the limited cast meant that everyone played at least two roles—and often many more.

In 1576, when Shakespeare was 12 years old, a carpenter-turned-actor named James Burbage built England's first "real" theater. With an admirable nod toward simplicity, it was called simply The Theater. There are no existing sketches or descriptions of The Theater. Scholars believe that the stage was a rectangular platform, probably 25 by 45 feet. Instead of resting on barrels, it was supported on sturdy posts and extended well out into the yard. At the back of the stage was a wall with a few doors for entrances and exists. There was even a real dressing room!

Forsooth!

The dressing room was called the **tiring-house**. The word "tiring" came from the word "attire."

We're not really sure of this description because there's only one contemporary picture of any Elizabethan stage at all. It is a sketch made from memory by a Dutch traveler named Johannes de Witt, who visited London in 1596. In addition to making notes about the plays he saw, de Witt made a sketch of the interior of the Swan Theater. His notes, translated from Latin, include the following description:

Of all the theaters, however, the largest and most magnificent is that one of which the sign is a swan, called in the vernacular the Swan Theater; for it accommodates in its seats three thousand persons, and is built of a mass of flint stones (of which there is a prodigious supply in London), and supported by wooden columns painted in such excellent imitation of marble that it is able to deceive even the most cunning.

The Chamberlain's Men, the troupe to which Shakespeare belonged, performed publicly primarily at The Theater. From 1594 to 1599, the Chamberlain's Men had become the most popular acting company in London. It appears that Shakespeare did a great deal of acting as well as playwriting during this time.

Dens of Sin

In part, it took so long for a permanent theater to be built because of the anomalous place actors occupied in London society. On one hand, actors were frowned upon by the titled and well-to-do folk as rogues and scoundrels. On the other hand, actors were wildly popular with the common people, who clamored to see them perform. Although considered no better than vagabonds, the actors were nonetheless called on frequently to perform at court. More on that later.

Actors and other public performers were also subjected to official control. To practice their trade, they first had to find a "master," that is, a sponsor with a peerage. Shakespeare's company, for example, was sponsored in the years 1596 to 1603 by George Carey, Baron Hunsdon, who became Elizabeth's Lord Chamberlain. Thus the acting company was known as "the Lord Chamberlain's Men." (After 1603, King James adopted the company as his own, and they thus became "the King's Men.")

Star Quality

"Drama," as we accept the term, originated in ancient Greece around the sixth century B.C. as a pagan festival. Famous playwrights/poets included Aeschylus (524?–456 B.C.), Sophocles (496–406 B.C.), Euripides (480–406 B.C.), and Aristophanes (450?–385 B.C.).

Local government officials weren't the only ones who objected to the actors and the theater. The Puritan clergy viewed plays as sinful, a perilous diversion from prayer. They claimed that theater stimulated "whorish lust" (and you thought rock 'n' roll and television were responsible for the downfall of western civilization). One Puritan leader, Philip Stubbes, went so far as to claim that all acting troupes were "secret conclaves" of sodomy.

In his anti-theatrical tract *The Anatomie of Abuses* (1583), Stubbes wrote:

> You say there are good Examples to be learned in [plays]. Truly, so there are: if you will learn falsehood; if you will learn cozenage; if you will learn to deceive; if you will learn to play the hypocrite, to cog, lie, and falsify; if you will learn to jest, laugh, and leer, to grin, to nod, and mow; if you will learn to play the vice, to swear, tear, and blaspheme both Heaven and Earth; if you will learn to become a bawd, unclean, and to devirginate maids, to deflower honest wives; if you will learn to murder, flay, kill, pick, steal, rob, and row; if you will learn to rebel

against princes, to commit treasons, to consume treasures, to practice idleness, to sing and talk of bawdy love and venery; if you will learn to deride, scoff, mock, and flout, to flatter and smooth; if you will learn to play the whoremaster, the glutton, drunkard, or incestuous person; if you will learn to become proud, haughty, and arrogant; and, finally, if you will learn to contemn God and all his laws, to care neither for heaven nor hell, and to commit all kind of sin and mischief, you need to go to no other school, for all these good examples may you see painted before your eyes in interludes and plays.

And you thought TV, rock 'n' roll, and comic books corrupted youth. They can't hold a candle to the deadly effects of the theater.

Truth or Dare

Good my lord, will you see the players well bestowed? Do you hear, let them be well used for they are the abstract and brief chronicles of the time; after your death you would better have a bad epitaph than their ill report while you live.

—*Hamlet*

Nonetheless, the London Theater was the only place where the common man could hear direct and honest comments on life. That's what Shakespeare meant when he said that players are the "abstract and brief chronicles of the time."

Shakespeare's contemporary Ben Jonson was in trouble at least four times for taking liberties on stage. Shakespeare himself flirted with arrest. When Essex's followers were plotting their rebellion in February, 1601, they bribed Shakespeare's company to play *Richard II* as part of their propaganda, for the play showed how a Sovereign, who was surrounded by favorites, was overthrown and deposed by one whom he had wronged. Shakespeare must have done some nail-biting over *that* decision!

One Hand Washes the Other

You may be wondering at this point why the government didn't simply shut down the theaters and save everyone a lot of trouble. The answer? The monarch and her courtiers found the public theaters useful. Drama's ability to make action look real could serve the government's interests as much as anyone else's. Many Elizabethan plays celebrated pious and patriotic

Will Power

In the Middle Ages, drama was largely based on religion; there was little emphasis on everyday life and war. The so-called "Miracle" and "Mystery" plays of the Middle Ages were based on Catholic doctrine. The "Morality" plays, also religious, describe the "proper" life for a devoted Christian. The characters were named after abstract concepts such as "Death," "Kindness," "Strength," and "Judgment." The human figures represent "Everyman."

values; the Crown may have regarded the favor as cheaply purchased, if the price was only a little titillation.

Besides, both Queen Elizabeth I and her successor, King James I, were connoisseurs of the theater, and they would hardly have deprived themselves of crack performers by allowing the theaters to be closed. And while acting companies were paid handsomely for their courtly appearances, they had largely to support themselves. So playing to the public both kept them in practice and kept them in business. And if the Queen or any of her cohorts ever objected to what they saw, we don't know about it.

Not in My Back Yard!

But theatrical freedom was not to last. In 1594, bowing to Puritan pressure, the London aldermen banned all playhouses within the city limits. The Lord Mayor of London asked the Queen Elizabeth's Privy Council to tear down all the theaters, for they were "places of meeting for all vagrant persons and masterless men that hang about the City, thieves, horse-stealers, whoremongers, cozeners [cheaters], cony-catching persons [con men], practicers of treason, and other such like." And you thought their only crime was selling over-priced candy and soda.

Theatrical impresarios ended up locating their playhouses beyond the reach of the aldermen, setting up shop in seedy nearby suburbs ("liberties"), side by side with ale houses, bordellos, and bear-baiting arenas. Nine different theaters were located in a suburban area called "Southwark."

Where There's a Will, There's a Way: The Globe Theater

Meanwhile, three years later, Burbage and his landlords failed to see eye-to-eye, and The Theater was forced to seek a new home. Burbage bought the old Blackfriars monastery but the neighbors did a "not in my backyard" number and the project ground to a halt.

Burbage died soon after, an event the landlord seized as the perfect chance to dismantle The Theater. One step ahead of the law, Burbage's sons

Sweets to the Sweet

In 1642, anti-theatrical Puritan parliamentarians, having overthrown King Charles I, got their way when they successfully shut down all the theaters for 20 years.

Forsooth!

Southwark is pronounced *Sutherk.*

Forsooth!

Thames has a silent *H* and a few other peculiar English twists. As a result, it's pronounced *Temz.* Located in south England, the Thames flows east through London to the North Sea, a bit over 200 miles.

dismantled The Theater themselves and hauled the pieces across the Thames River to a site in Southwark. It took them six months to rebuild The Theater, and when they did, they renamed it "The Globe." It opened in 1599.

By 1600, London had more theaters than any other European capital. Its theaters includes The Rose, The Swan, The Red Bull, and The Globe.

"This Wooden O"

Can this cockpit hold
The vasty fields of France? Or may we cram
Within this wooden O the very casques
That did affright the air at Agincourt?

—*Henry V*

Scholars disagree about what The Globe actually looked like since there are no surviving drawings or any detailed written descriptions. Since Shakespeare refers to The Globe as "this wooden O," it appears it was round or octagonal. Like the bear-baiting arenas, it was open to the sky.

The building had to be small enough to ensure that the actors could be heard, but large enough to accommodate at least 2,500 to 3,000 people. Talk about a packed house!

Here's what The Globe Theater probably looked like from the outside.

From surviving bills of sale, we know that The Globe was small—the external dimensions were only 80 feet by 80 feet. The interior measured 55 feet by 55 feet.

"Play out the play"
—Henry IV, Part I

This engraving shows The Globe Theater as reconstructed by Shakespearean scholar John Cranford Adams.

As the engraving shows, there were three tiers to the stage, corresponding to Earth, heaven, and hell. A canopy, representing the heavens, extended across the stage to the back wall. The canopy was painted gold with starry spangles in the shape of the zodiac. Villains fell through a trapdoor, called the "hell mouth," into the pits of damnation. The dressing rooms were located behind the stage.

Variety Is the Spice of Life

The theater in Shakespeare's day acted on the repertory system. The company kept a considerable range of plays available and played a different one each afternoon.

How busy were the actors? We get a glimpse of their hectic schedule from this quote from Quince in Shakespeare's *A Midsummer's Night's Dream*: "But, masters, here are your parts. And I am to entreat you, request you, and desire you to con [learn] them by tomorrow night; and meet me in the palace wood a mile from the town, by moonlight, There will we rehearse." Actors learned their parts in about a week; a leading man might have to memorize 800 lines a day.

The average life of a new play was about 10 performances, but popular plays were, of course, performed more often. Continuous runs were unknown.

Will Power

The Globe was owned by a syndicate, a fact that gave it unique power and flexibility among the London playhouses. Shakespeare's share was 10 percent of the total profits. It's not possible to determine exactly how much Shakespeare earned, but it was somewhere near £200 to £250 per year, a very substantial sum by Elizabethan standards.

31

Several of the Globe's actors became nationally famous. Richard Burbage, for example, became widely admired for his ability to express emotion realistically. Shakespeare probably wrote some of his great tragic heroes—including Hamlet, King Lear, and Othello—with Burbage in mind. Will Kemp was the company's best-loved comedian.

The repertory system also gave Shakespeare another advantage, besides continuous work in a precarious career: constant "types." Shakespeare often made use of the peculiar character traits of his actors. These traits reappear when they proved to be popular. The "tall man with the hatchet face" appears in a variety of guises, including the Shadow in *Henry IV, Part II*; Sir Andrew Aguecheek in *Twelfth Night*; and Slender in *The Merry Wives of Windsor*, among others.

Forsooth!

In theater, **blocking** refers to breaking up the scenes of a play into small chunks in order to work out the details of where the actors should stand, how they should communicate, and so forth. **Mise en scene** is the play's setting; **spine** is the play's main idea or point.

As you've already learned, Shakespeare's acting company was "the Chamberlain's Men," later renamed "the King's Men." The leading acting company in London, they seem to have been very close-knit and many of the members stayed friends for life. When Shakespeare died—more than 20 years after the company was formed—he left memorial rings to his fellow actors. Seven months later, one of them, Richard Burbage, named his newborn son William. Most important of all, seven years later, Shakespeare's fellow actors John Heminges and Henry Condell printed Shakespeare's *First Folio*, giving the world its first look at printed copies of Shakespeare's plays.

From Page to Stage: Theater in Shakespeare's Day

Today, the New York theater district is as squeaky-clean as Mickey Mouse. (Maybe that's because Disney owns a chunk of the theater action, but that's another story.) Only a few years ago, however, Times Square was seedy and run-down. Shakespeare would have felt right at home in the old Times Square, for The Globe was surrounded by brothels, pubs, and taverns. Pimps and prostitutes plied their trade outside the box office; thieves and swindlers did an equally booming business.

In addition to some urban renewal, there were many significant differences between Shakespeare's theater and our own. For example, during Shakespeare's day, performances were given every day but Sunday. (Today, many New York theaters are open on Sunday but closed on Monday.) Since there were no lights, matinees were the name of the game. Shows ran from 2:00 to 5:00 in the afternoon.

Further, there were no intermissions, so the action was continuous. People didn't sit still for the entire three hours, however. They were a lively (read "rambunctious" and "rowdy") bunch. The atmosphere at an Elizabethan play was like the atmosphere at a modern baseball game—when the home team is losing.

Neither were there any curtains or sets, although the Elizabethans loved elaborate stage effects, such as the trapdoors mentioned earlier. Lack of scenery was compensated by abundant noise. The texts of the plays of the time are filled with directions for various trumpet sounds. Battle scenes were especially noisy. No king ever entered or left the stage without a trumpet flourish.

Star Quality

Other famous Elizabethan playwrights include Robert Greene, John Lyly, and a whole pack of Thomases: Thomas Kyd, Thomas Preston, Thomas Sackville, and Thomas Norton.

Pressing the Flesh

Here are some more differences you could expect if I could take you back to Shakespeare's day to take in a matinee or two:

➤ Bowing to the pressure of the Puritans, theater advertising was forbidden. Theater owners got around the ban by raising a flag and blasting a trumpet as 2:00 approached. The color of the flag indicated the day's feature: White stood for comedy; black for tragedy; and red for history.

➤ Ticket prices depended on the location of the seat—or lack thereof. Patrons could sit on cushions with the movers and shakers or stand cheek-by-jowl with the hoi poloi in the back. The real power brokers sat on the stage itself.

➤ Enterprising capitalists hawked beer, water, oranges, gingerbread, apples, and nuts. It was considered acceptable to heave any and all of the above at the actors if their performance didn't make the grade.

➤ There were no rest rooms. Think about all that beer.

➤ Scenery and props were minimal, but costumes were extravagant affairs of gold, lace, silk, and jewels. Often, they were the hand-me-downs from wealthy patrons of the arts. Actors also wore makeup, another nail in their coffins, according to the spoilsport Puritans.

Forsooth!

As people entered The Globe Theater, they would drop their admission into a box. From this practice came our term **box office**.

➤ Shakespeare and his fellow actors and playwrights were keenly aware of stage-craft, as this quote shows:

> And if the boy have not a woman's gift
> To rain a shower of commanded tears,
> An onion will do well for such a shift.

—*The Taming of the Shrew*

➤ There were no producers or directors; the actors had total control of the production.

➤ Then we have the issue of the actors...

What a Drag: Transvestite Theater and Boy Actors

Since women were forbidden to act in public in England, female roles were assumed by pre-adolescent lads. (Now you know the main reason why there's so little hanky-panky touchy-feely in Shakespeare's plays.) With his usual ingenuity, Shakespeare transformed the gender restriction into an advantage by evoking passion through language.

But what's a boffo play without a little nooky? Walking that fine line between class and trash, Shakespeare peppered his plays with bawdy puns and sexual allusions. More on this in Chapter 5, "Brush Up on Your Shakespeare."

The boy actors lived with the adult actors and received intensive training in dancing, music, elocution, weaponry, and memorization. There were far fewer boys than men in the company, which may have been one reason why there were so few female roles. (Or maybe it was the other way around—since Shakespeare didn't have the actors to play the roles, he didn't write female roles.)

The practice of boy actors ended in 1660, when females were allowed on the London stage. Some old-timers were incensed: How could any woman play Juliet as well as a boy had?

Global Meltdown

The Globe met its demise in 1613 when a canon was fired as part of a performance of *King Henry VIII* and the flaming wadding landed on the theater's thatched roof. Fortunately, everyone escaped unharmed; unfortunately, The Globe burned to the ground. (One man's pants were set afire, but the flames were doused with beer.) The Globe was immediately rebuilt and continued in operation until it was closed in 1642.

Shakespeare's Globe was pulled down two years later, when all the theaters closed. Forgotten, the land became the site of a brewery until 1984, when the brewery was pulled down and the land became a parking lot. The Globe's form and layout became an enigma. Only a few relevant documents existed and none of these provided a complete and accurate picture of its design.

In 1989, archaeologists found remains of The Globe. They believe they unearthed both the original Globe and the rebuilt version. They also found a few interesting artifacts, including a scabbard, a sword, shoes, a bear's skull—and a human skull.

Today, 200 yards from its original site, after almost 400 years, Shakespeare's Globe has been opened to the public again; it was officially inaugurated on June 12, 1997. Ironically, the force behind the project was an American actor, Sam Wanamaker.

> Our revels now are ended. These our actors,
> As I foretold you, were all spirits and
> Are melted into air, into thin air;
> And, like the baseless fabric of this vision,
> The cloud-capped towers, the gorgeous palaces,
> The solemn temples, the great globe itself,
> Yea, all which it inherit, shall dissolve,
> And, like this insubstantial pageant faded,
> Leave not a rack behind. We are such stuff
> As dreams are made on, and our little life
> Is rounded with a sleep.
>
> —*The Tempest*

Near the end of his life, Shakespeare, in this magnificent passage, identified the role of the theater and imagination with the dreamlike nature of life itself.

Star Quality

The Royal Shakespeare Company, headquartered in Stratford-upon-Avon, is the foremost Shakespearean theater group in the world. Unlike many other international theater companies, the RSC operates on a repertoire system under which actors take on several roles in a range of plays. The RSC has three different theaters in Stratford. The largest, the world famous Royal Shakespeare Theatre, built in 1932, was recently completely refurbished. The Swan Theatre is a galleried playhouse, while The Other Place provides a modern and intimate theater experience.

The Least You Need to Know

➤ In 1576, James Burbage built England's first permanent theater.

➤ Although wildly popular with the common folks, actors were considered rogues and scoundrels by those in power.

➤ Shakespeare's Globe Theater opened in 1599. His acting company, the Chamberlain's Men (later the King's Men), was London's premier acting troupe.

➤ The theater in Shakespeare's day acted on the repertory system.

➤ Destroyed by fire in 1613, The Globe was immediately rebuilt. It closed in 1642, and this time wasn't rebuilt until 1997.

Romeo and....?

Chapter 4

The Play's the Thing

In This Chapter

➤ The chronology of Shakespeare's canon

➤ Types of evidence used to date the plays

➤ Basic dramatic terms

➤ Shakespeare's plots

In America, it's hard to find an inn in the 13 original states that doesn't claim that "Washington slept here." In England, a similar situation exists when it comes to Shakespeare. And whether we're talking about where General Washington laid his head or William Shakespeare laid his pen, no one is losing too much sleep when it comes to the truth.

For example, in 1877, the head of the Stratford grammar school proudly displayed Shakespeare's desk to visitors. "William was a studious lad and selected that corner of the room so that he might not be disturbed by the other boys," he said with no proof whatsoever to support this claim.

In this chapter, you'll get the whole truth and nothing but the truth about Shakespeare's plays. First, I'll help you get a handle on *what* he wrote *when*. You'll survey the "Shakespearean canon" by learning the evidence used to figure out when Shakespeare wrote each play. Then you'll learn some terms that will make it easier for you to read and appreciate the plays. Finally, we'll examine Shakespeare's plots to see how he "borrowed" from a variety of different sources but crafted the commonplace raw material into something of rare brilliance.

The Dating Game

The time is of joint. O cursed spite
That ever I was born to set it right!

—*Hamlet*

Things aren't quite as bad as that when it comes to Shakespeare's plays, but there *is* some disagreement about when Shakespeare wrote what. Elizabethan plays such as Shakespeare's can seldom be dated with complete accuracy since records are spotty. One precise theater owner, Philip Henslowe, recorded the dates when plays were performed in his theater—even including details about payment to dramatists—but only a few of Shakespeare's plays were staged at this particular theater, and few other theater owners were so anal-retentive.

Will Power

According to Henslowe's diary, in a typical month (March, 1592) Shakespeare's *Henry VI* plays were performed five times in rotation with 13 other plays. Shakespeare's play was apparently the most popular at the time (it was new to Henslowe on March 3), since the next most performed plays during the month was Thomas Kyd's *Spanish Tragedy* and Marlowe's *Jew of Malta*.

It's important to know when Shakespeare wrote each play so you can trace the development of his topics, themes, and artistry. The plays are usually dated by three criteria:

1. *External evidence*: Clear reference to the play in a diary, letter, account book, journal, bill, or other outside document.

2. *Internal evidence*: An unmistakable reference to an identifiable event within the play itself. Unfortunately, Shakespeare rarely mentions current events within a play.

3. *The play's style*: Similar word choice, subject, or mood among a specific series of plays. This evidence, along with both external and internal evidence, helps scholars deduce when Shakespeare wrote specific plays.

Forsooth!

The time *after* which a play could not have been written is called **terminus ad quem**.

Hidden in Plain Sight: External Evidence

A diary entry made by a Swiss traveler named Thomas Platter who visited London in 1599 serves as good external evidence that Shakespeare's *Julius Caesar* was being performed in 1599:

After dinner on the 21st of September, at about two o'clock, I went with my companions over the water, and in the strewn roof-house [i.e., a playhouse with a thatched roof] saw the tragedy of the first Emperor Julius with at least 15 characters very well acted.

Dig We Must: Internal Evidence

We can date *Henry V* because it contains internal evidence: the triumphant departure of the Earl of Essex for Ireland on May 27, 1599. Since Essex failed and returned to London secretly on September 28, we can conclude that this part of *Henry V* was written within a six-month period in 1599. Here's the proof, straight from the play:

> But now behold,
> In the quick forge and working-house of thought,
> How London doth pour out her citizens,
> The Mayor and all his brethren in best sort,
> Like to the Senators of th'antique Rome,
> With the plebeians swarming at their heels,
> Go forth and fetch their conquering Caesar in;
> As by a lower, but by loving likelihood,
> Were now the General of our gracious Empress,
> As in good time he may, from Ireland coming,
> Bringing rebellion broached on his sword;
> How many would the peaceful City quit,
> To welcome him?

The Medium Is the Message: Analyzing Style

Scholars generally divide Shakespeare's career into four phases based on the similarities among the works he wrote during each time. It's a nice, neat division. Here's how it shakes out:

Category	Time	Achievements
Apprenticeship	1588–1593	Wrote comedies and early history plays
Second Phase	1593–1600	Mastered comedy and tragedy
Tragic Period	1600–1609	Produced greatest plays
Last Phase	1609–1611	Created the tender and magical romances

Each style has its unique features that can be used as one method to help date the plays. In Shakespeare's early plays, for instance, he is often more interested in fine writing than fine drama. In addition, these early plays are characterized by:

➤ Regular rhythms

➤ Rhyming, often in couplets

➤ Sonnets occasionally included in the text

➤ Witty word play (especially in the comedies)

➤ Imagery often used for its own sake rather than to clarify the characters, one of the hallmarks of a novice writer

➤ Heroic speeches (especially in tragedies)

The stylistic similarities between *Romeo and Juliet* and *A Midsummer Night's Dream*, for example, suggest that Shakespeare wrote them at the same time. There is other external evidence to bolster this conclusion.

Scholars use a combination of all three types of evidence—external, internal, and stylistic—to date the plays. That hasn't prevented a great deal of controversy over dates of composition, however.

Can I Take Your Order?

O Time, thou must untangle this, not I;
It is too hard a knot for me t'untie.

—*Twelfth Night*

Given the problems with establishing the chronology of the plays, it's no wonder that different sources list different dates. In most cases, there's plenty of room for argument.

For example, according to the august *Riverside Shakespeare*, second edition (Houghton Mifflin, 1997), the chronology of Shakespeare's plays looks like this:

Work	Probable Date of Composition
King Henry VI, Part I	1589–1590
King Henry VI, Part II	1590–1591
King Henry VI, Part III	1590–1591
King Richard III	1592–1593
"Venus and Adonis" (poem)	1592–1593
Comedy of Errors	1592–1594
Sonnets	1593–1609
"The Rape of Lucrece" (poem)	1593–1594
Titus Andronicus	1593–1594
The Taming of the Shrew	1593–1594
Two Gentlemen of Verona	1594
Love's Labor's Lost	1594–1595, revised 1597
King John	1594–1596
King Richard II	1595
Romeo and Juliet	1595–1596
A Midsummer Night's Dream	1595–1596
The Merchant of Venice	1596–1597
King Henry IV, Part I	1596–1597
The Merry Wives of Windsor	1597, revised 1600–1601
King Henry IV, Part II	1598
Much Ado About Nothing	1598–1599
King Henry V	1599
Julius Caesar	1599
As You Like It	1599
Hamlet	1600–1601
"The Phoenix and the Turtle" (poem)	1601
Twelfth Night	1601–1602
Troilus and Cressida	1601–1602
"A Lover's Complaint" (poem)	1602–1608
All's Well That Ends Well	1602–1603
Measure for Measure	1604
Othello	1604
King Lear	1605
Macbeth	1606
Antony and Cleopatra	1606–1607
Coriolanus	1607–1608

continues

continued

Work	Probable Date of Composition
Timon of Athens	1607–1608
Pericles	1607–1608
Cymbeline	1609–1610
The Winter's Tale	1610–1611
The Tempest	1611
King Henry VIII	1612–1613

Not so fast! According to the respected scholar Sylvan Barnet in the *Signet Classic Shakespeare* series, Shakespeare composed his works in the following order. As you'll see, there are wild discrepancies between this chronology and the previous one.

Work	Probable Date of Composition
Comedy of Errors	1588–1593
Love's Labor's Lost	1588–1594
King Henry VI, Part II	1590–1591
King Henry VI, Part III	1590–1591
King Henry VI, Part I	1591–1592
"Venus and Adonis" (poem)	1592
King Richard III	1592–1593
Titus Andronicus	1592–1594
Sonnets	1593–1600
The Taming of the Shrew	1593–1594
"The Rape of Lucrece" (poem)	1593–1594
Two Gentlemen of Verona	1593–1595
Romeo and Juliet	1594–1596
King Richard II	1595
A Midsummer Night's Dream	1594–1596
King John	1596–1597
The Merchant of Venice	1596–1597
King Henry IV, Part I	1597
King Henry IV, Part II	1597–1598
Much Ado About Nothing	1598–1600
King Henry V	1598–1599
Julius Caesar	1599–1600
As You Like It	1599–1600
Twelfth Night	1599–1600
Hamlet	1600–1601

Work	Probable Date of Composition
The Merry Wives of Windsor	1597–1601
"The Phoenix and the Turtle" (poem)	1600–1601
Troilus and Cressida	1601–1602
All's Well That Ends Well	1602–1604
Othello	1603–1604
Measure for Measure	1604–1605
King Lear	1605–1606
Macbeth	1605–1606
Antony and Cleopatra	1606–1607
Timon of Athens	1605–1608
Coriolanus	1607–1609
Pericles	1608–1609
Cymbeline	1609–1610
The Winter's Tale	1610–1611
The Tempest	1611–1612
King Henry VIII	1612–1613

As these lists show, there's more than a little wiggle room when it comes to determining when Shakespeare wrote his plays and poems.

In 1623, seven years after Shakespeare's death, two actor friends of the Bard's (John Heminges and Henry Condell) collected 36 of his plays in what has come to be known as the *First Folio*. *Pericles* is the only play in Shakespeare's official canon missing from the *First Folio*. About 240 of the 1,000 copies printed still exist.

Some of the plays in the *First Folio* are the same as those in the previously published quarto editions, but others are not. This considerably complicates the dating issue since it raises the possibility that some topical allusions may have been inserted while the plays were revised some years previously. Of course, there is also the probability of garbled text, missing text, and other errors.

As a result, it's important to read carefully prepared copies of Shakespeare's plays and poems, such as the *Riverside Shakespeare*, the Signet editions, and the Norton Critical editions. You can be sure that these editions were carefully prepared to include all the verified corrections and changes (even if no one can agree on the dating!).

Fire at Will

Eighteen of Shakespeare's plays were published within his lifetime in small pamphlets. Some pamphlets have the plays in finished forms; others, in contrast, are very rough texts, perhaps based on the actors' memories or shorthand notes rather than written scripts. This further complicates the issue of dating each play's composition.

43

Words to the Wise

Before you start reading Shakespeare's plays, it's helpful to become familiar with some basic vocabulary so we're all reading from the same page, so to speak. (Stay tuned; in the next chapter, we'll delve into Shakespeare's English.)

Let's start with some terms that describe the structure and content of the plays. Here are a half dozen handy terms that will help you understand what's happening when you watch or read the plays:

➤ *Aside*: A speech in which the actor turns away from the other performers and reveals his feelings to the audience.

➤ *Bed trick*: The surreptitious substitution of a virgin wife for another woman who is sinfully desired. It occurs in *Measure for Measure* and *All's Well that Ends Well*.

➤ *Foil*: A minor character used as a contrast to a main character. Banquo, for example, serves as a foil to Macbeth.

➤ *Setpiece*: An elaborate poetic passage that follows the rules of dramatic oratory. Setpieces do not move the action forward and are often filled with quotations that become memorable. Hamlet's famous soliloquy "To be, or not to be" is a setpiece.

➤ *Soliloquy*: A speech in which a character is alone with his private thoughts; it tells the audience what the character is thinking.

➤ *Stock character*: A standard character who appeared in many plays and thus would be instantly recognizable to members of Shakespeare's audience. *The Braggart Soldier* or *Miles Gloriosis* is an example of a stock character. A comic figure drawn from ancient Roman comedy, he appears in Shakespeare's plays most famously as the wildly entertaining buffoon Falstaff in *Henry IV, Part I* and *Part II*.

Forsooth!

A **concordance** is a reference book that lists every word that an author used. *The Harvard Concordance* is the authoritative Shakespeare concordance; it is especially useful for authenticating Shakespeare's works.

Below are eight terms used to describe Shakespeare's works, as printed and published in his day. Most have to do with the actual printing process and are very important when it comes to determining authoritative texts of each play. Knowing these terms can help you understand where each edition belongs in the pecking order.

➤ *Sheet*: A page. In Shakespeare's day, the size of a sheet varied a great deal, from 20 by 15 inches to 16 by 12 inches.

➤ *Folio*: A book format in which each individual sheet has been folded once, across the middle of the longer side, creating two leaves for each sheet. The folded sheets vary from 15 by 10 inches to 12 by 8 inches—with many sizes in between.

➤ *Quarto*: A book format in which the individual sheets have been folded twice, creating four sheets. Shakespeare's quartos were about the size of a modern magazine.

➤ *Octavo*: A book format in which the individual sheets have been folded three times, creating eight sheets. The measurements of an octavo are a fourth that of a folio.

➤ *Broadside*: A single folio sheet (half the size of a regular sheet), printed on one side only. Broadsides were used to publish ballads, proclamations, and other announcements.

➤ *Recto:* The front of a leaf, always the right-hand page.

➤ *Verso:* The back of a leaf, always the left-hand page.

➤ *Edition*: All copies of a book printed from the same setting of type (allowing for differences between copies resulting from press-corrections).

Forsooth!

In case you decide to ply the publisher's trade, many of these same terms are used in printing today.

And while we're on the topic, some Shakespearean experts insist that you see the plays before you read them; others insist that you read the plays before you see them. One camp claims you must read the plays aloud to understand their real meaning; another camp cheers for Shakespeare on tape. I'm sure there's even a scholar somewhere who insists you read Shakespeare in the shower.

Is your head spinning yet? Here's my practical advice for getting the most gain with the least pain.

➤ Start with a goods edition of the plays. You want all the words in the right places. You can't go wrong with the Riverside edition, Penguin editions, or the Norton's critical editions. Technobunnies, try the MIT Shakespeare site on the Internet.

➤ Read one entire scene at a time. This will help you grasp the sweep of the action.

➤ Don't sweat the footnotes. You don't have to understand every single word to understand Shakespeare.

➤ If there's a production of a Shakespearean play near by, go see it. If it's lousy, leave. (But don't blame Shakespeare. He's been murdered more often than the English language itself.)

The Plot Thickens

A university creative writing class was asked to write a concise essay containing these four elements:

➤ Religion

➤ Royalty

➤ Sex

➤ Mystery

The prize-winning essay read:

"My God," said the Queen. "I'm pregnant. I wonder who did it?"

Someone once said that there are only a handful of plots; if so, Shakespeare managed to steal them all. "What!" you scream in protest, shocked to your shoes. Before you start e-mailing me letters of stunned protest, let me assure you that "borrowing" from another writer's work was perfectly acceptable in Shakespeare's day. So widespread and accepted was the practice that many seventeenth century artists didn't even bother to sign their paintings; many poems were published anonymously. Art wasn't a personal expression of emotion; rather, it was a public display of an era.

It's only recently that we've come to regard literary share-and-share-alike as plagiarism. Nonetheless, there's still a little note-passing and looking-over-the-shoulder among writers. As the twentieth century poet T. S. Eliot said, "Bad poets borrow, good poets steal."

Here's a brief run-down of some of the sources Shakespeare drew on as he created his plots:

Shakespeare's Play	Source
Julius Caesar	Plutarch's *Lives*
Antony and Cleopatra	Plutarch's *Lives*
Coriolanus	Plutarch's *Lives*
Othello	Cinthio's *Gli Hecatommithi*
As You Like It	Thomas Lodge's *Rosalynde*, a popular romance of the day

If that's all there was to it, few people would bother to read Shakespeare. After all, no one remembers Thomas Lodge, the author of *Rosalynde*, or Cinthio, the author of *Gli Hecatommithi*. Nope; there's clearly more at work here. And it's genius, pure and simple.

For the story itself doesn't matter. What *does* matter is how Shakespeare transformed a plot into art. And how did he do it? He added keen observations about the human condition, shrewd psychological drama, and exquisite poetry. As fellow writer John Dryden concluded in 1668, "He was the man who of all modern, and perhaps all ancient poets, had the largest and most comprehensive soul."

Judge for yourself. Here is a translation of Plutarch's *Lives* that Shakespeare used as the basis for a section of *Antony and Cleopatra*:

> [Cleopatra would] take her barge in the river Cydnus, the poop whereof was of gold, the sails of purple, the oars of silver, which kept stroke in rowing after the sound of the music in flutes, hautboys, citherns, viols, and other such instruments as they played upon the barge. And now for the person of herself: she was laid under a pavilion of cloth of gold tissue, appareled and attired like the goddess Venus, commonly drawn in picture; and hard by her, on either hand of her, pretty fair boys appareled as painters do set forth god Cupide, with little fans in their hands, with the which they fanned wind upon her. Her ladies and gentlewomen also, the fairest of them were appareled like the nymphs.

Star Quality

Taking a tip from Shakespeare's modus operandi, Leonard Bernstein created the brilliant *West Side Story* from *Romeo and Juliet*. Similarly, Cole Porter created his musical *Kiss Me Kate* from *The Taming of the Shrew*; Tom Stoppard's drama *Rosencrantz and Guildenstern are Dead* sprang from *Hamlet*. And not only Broadway borrowed from the Bard: The sci-fi cult classic *Forbidden Planet* was based on *The Tempest*.

And here's what Shakespeare did with the raw story:

> The barge she sat in, like a burnished throne,
> Burned on the water. The poop was beaten gold;
> Purple the sails, and so perfumed that
> The winds were lovesick with them. The oars were silver,
> Which to the tune of flutes kept stroke and made
> The water which they beat to follow faster,
> As amorous as their strokes. For her own person,
> Is beggared all description. She did lie
> In her pavilion, cloth-of-gold tissue,
> O'erpicturing that Venus where we see

The Fancy outwork nature. On each side her
Stood pretty dimpled boys, like smiling cupids,
With divers colored fans, whose wind did seem
To glow their delicate cheeks which they did cool,
And what they undid did.

Plot becomes art.

The Least You Need to Know

➤ Knowing the chronology of Shakespeare's plays helps you trace the development of his topics, themes, and artistry.

➤ Scholars analyze external evidence, internal evidence, and style to determine when Shakespeare wrote each play.

➤ Knowing basic terms about the conventions of Elizabethan theater and printing can help you understand the plays.

➤ Shakespeare transformed already existing stories into art.

Chapter 5

Brush Up on Your Shakespeare

In This Chapter

➤ Old English, Middle English, Modern English

➤ "Translate" Shakespeare's English

➤ Shakespeare's grammar and vocabulary

➤ Elizabethan swearing

As imagination bodies forth
The forms of things unknown, the poet's pen
Turns them into shapes, and gives to airy nothing
A local habitation and a name.

—*A Midsummer Night's Dream*

In Shakespeare's hands, words are the stuff of magic. Like an alchemist who changed lead into gold, Shakespeare transmuted base words into shimmering poetry. In this chapter, you're going to explore the magic of Shakespeare's language.

You'll start by surveying Old English, Middle English, and Modern English to understand how they are similar and different. Then you'll try your hand at a little "translating" to see how Shakespeare's English compares to our own. Next we'll explore what makes Shakespeare's English seem difficult to read and understand. And just because I like saving the most fun for last, the chapter ends with a primer on Elizabethan swearing.

Walk the Walk and Talk the Talk

Before you start reading Shakespeare's plays, it's helpful to become familiar with Shakespeare's language—not because it's difficult, but rather because it scares some readers needlessly. (Save your fear for something *really* important like cellulite.)

Forsooth!

Assail (verb) and **assault** (noun) referred to laying siege to a lady's chastity. "Front her, board her, woo her, assail her," Sir Toby urges in *Twelfth Night*. Praising the chaste Imogen as "goddess-like," Pisanio notes that she resists "such assaults / As would take in [conquer] some virtue" (*Cymbeline*).

My students swear that Shakespeare wrote *Old English*. (They also swear that Pez and pop make a nutritious breakfast, but I love them anyway.) Here's the truth: Shakespeare wrote Modern English. I kid you not.

There are three main stages in the development of the English language: *Old English, Middle English,* and *Modern English.* Here's how it shakes out:

➤ *Old English*: A.D. 449–1066

➤ *Middle English*: 1066–1450

➤ *Modern English*: 1450–present

Since Shakespeare lived from 1564–1616, he falls smack into the category of Modern English. (And no, he wasn't deliberately writing Old English to make you crazy.) Let's look at this language thing a little more closely.

Old English (Anglo-Saxon)

Old English, a variation of West Germanic, was spoken by the Angles, Saxons, and Jutes who lived in what we now call southern Denmark and northern Germany. Around A.D. 449, the Jutes invaded Britain and drove the Celtic-speaking people, notably the Britons, to the north and west. As time passed, Old English developed and mellowed into different dialects, all equally impossible to read or understand without dropping a bundle at Berlitz.

Try your hand reading this passage from *An Ecclesiastical History of the English People, The Story of Caedmon* (c. 673–735). Because we've grown rather close in the short time we've known each other, I've included a translation:

This is Old English. You'll need your Magic Decoder Ring.

weorc Wuldor-Fæder
the work of the Glory-Father,

ece Drihten
eternal Lord,

He ærest sceop
He first created

heofon to hrofe
heaven as a roof,

swa he wundra gehwæs
when he of wonders of every one,

or onstealde
the beginning established.

ielda bearnum
for men's sons

halig Scyppend
holy Creator;

∂**a** *middangeard*	*moncynnes* Weard
then middle-earth	manking's Guardian,
ece Drihten	*æfter* teode
eternal Lord,	afterwards made—
firum foldan	Frea ælmihtig
for men earth,	Master almighty.

Beowulf, the oldest of the great long poems written in English, dates from this era.

Middle English

Middle English dates from the Norman Conquest of 1066 to around 1450. The big change was in the structure of the language. Old English was inflectional: The form of a word changes to show its function in a sentence. By the end of the period, the relationship between the elements of the sentence depended on word order rather than word form. We are also grateful for what has come to be called The Great Vowel Shift, a major change in pronunciation of vowels that took place between 1350 and 1500. It was a biggie; 18 out of 20 vowels were pronounced differently.

Middle English masterpieces of literature include *Sir Gawain and the Green Knight*, *Piers Plowman*, and Geoffrey Chaucer's *The Canterbury Tales*. Here's an excerpt from *The Canterbury Tales*, so you can read a little Middle English.

From *The Canterbury Tales*

The General Prologue

This is Middle English. No translation here; you're on your own.

 Whan that April with his showres soote
The droughte of March hath perced to the roote,
And bathed every veine in swich licour,
Of which vertu engendred is the flowr;
Whan Zephyrus eek with his sweete breeth
Inspired hath in every holt and heeth
The tendre croppes, and the yonge sonne
Hath in the Ram his halve cours yronne,
And smale fowles maken melodye
That sleepen al the night with open yë—
So priketh hem Nature in hir corages—
Thanne longen folk to goon on pilgrimages,
And palmeres for to seeken straunge strondes
To ferne halwes, couthe in sondry londes;
And specially from every shires ende
Of Engelond to Canterbury they wende,
The holy blisful martyr for to seeke

continues

continued

That hem hath holpen whan that they were seke.
 Bifel that in that seson on a day,
In Southwerk at the Tabard as I lay,
Redy to wenden on my pilgrimage
To Canterbury with ful devout corage,
At night was come into that hostelrye
Wel nine and twenty in a compaignye
Of sondry folk, by aventure yfalle
In felawshipe, and pilgrimes were they alle
That toward Canterbury wolden ride.
The chambres and the stables weren wide,
And wel we wern esed at the beste.
And shortly, whan the sonne was to reste,

Modern English

Modern English is subdivided into two categories: Early Modern English (1500–1660) and Later Modern English (1660–today). Grammar as we know it was established in the late seventeenth century. By the nineteenth century, vocabulary had increased at a dazzling pace, as new words streamed into the language from around the world.

Will Power

As you learned in Chapter 2, "The Renaissance 101," the Elizabethans had a very socially stratified society. Unlike modern-day America, Elizabethans were highly aware of their social standing, as compared to the social standing of the person they were addressing. While it's not uncommon to address someone as "Sir" or "Madame" today, most people don't use such honorifics in casual conversation. The Elizabethans did. Fortunately for the snobs, Elizabethans wore clothing in accordance with their social standing, making it easy to judge status.

What Did He Say?

"Sir, You speak a language that I understand not."

—*The Winter's Tale*

You've accepted reality: Shakespeare wrote Modern English, albeit the Early version. So why does his language sometimes seem so hard to understand? Here are three top reasons:

➤ His vocabulary is sometimes incomprehensible.

➤ His word order can be inverted and seem perverted.

➤ His grammar is unfamiliar and often seems incorrect.

See what I mean with the following examples.

Below are five quotations from Shakespeare's plays. Each quotation contains what we today consider a grammatical error. Match the error to the sentence. One error will be used twice.

Incorrect preposition use	Adjective placement
Subject/verb agreement	Double negative

1. "I pray you, bear with me; I cannot go no further." (*As You Like It*)

   _____

   _____

2. "The posture of your blows are yet unknown." (*Julius Caesar*)

   _____

   _____

3. "Is there not wars?" (*Henry IV, Part II*)

   _____

   _____

4. "...whether the body public be / A horse whereon the governor doth ride" (*Measure for Measure*)

   _____

   _____

5. "Methoughts I saw a thousand fearful wracks; Ten thousand men that fishes gnawed upon." (*Richard III*)

   _____

   _____

Answers:

1. The phrase "can*not* go *no*" is a double negative. That's a no-no today.

2. The error is in subject/verb agreement. Since *posture* is singular, the verb *are* should be *is*. The sentence should read: "The posture of your blows *is* yet unknown." (Ignore the intervening prepositional phrase *of your blows*. Intervening prepositional phrases don't affect agreement.)

3. Same as #2: This sentence has an error in subject/verb agreement. Since *wars* is plural, the sentence should read: "Are there not wars?"

4. In this quotation, the adjective follows the noun instead of coming before it, the usage in favor today. We would write the phrase *body public* as *public body*.

5. This quotation ends in a preposition (*upon*), a fearful error to a grammar purist. Rephrasing the sentence as: "fishes gnawed upon ten thousand men" would correct the error. Okay, so it's lousy poetry; you want everything?

But before the grammar police arrest Shakespeare, it's important to recognize that grammar was a much more casual affair in the seventeenth century than it is today. Back then, language was pretty much a free-for-all. Prefixes, suffixes, and compound words were often created at will. Hence we get such Shakespearean creations as *heady-rash, rocky-hard, mumble-news, beef-witted, childish-foolish.* Since Shakespeare's verbal virtuosity knew no bounds, it's fortunate that the language was flexible enough to accommodate him.

Fire at Will

Although Shakespeare's plays contain archaic words that are hard to decipher, these words aren't as tricky as they seem. That's because it's simple to check a footnote or dictionary for a definition. The wily words are those that *seem* familiar but really mean something different now than they did in Shakespeare's day. For example, Shakespeare's **humor** means "tone," not our "amusement."

From Good to Verse

When a man's verses cannot be understood…it strikes a man more dead than a great reckoning in a little room.

—*As You Like It*

I'll bet my good copy of Shakespeare's works that his audience didn't understand every word they heard issued from the stage. And I'm sure they didn't worry too much about it, either. That's because they were too busy enjoying the spectacle. If they got the gist of the language, they were fine.

That's how you should approach Shakespeare, too. Whether you're reading one of his plays or watching it come alive in the theater, enjoy the experience. Don't sweat the small stuff, like a word here or there. Let the majesty of the language sweep over you and sink in.

Try it now with the following passage from *Romeo and Juliet* (II, ii, 33–51). "Translate" the passage by rewriting it in your own words. Don't worry about rhyme; go for a paraphrase that captures the essential meaning.

Juliet: O Romeo, Romeo, wherefore art thou Romeo?
Deny thy father and refuse thy name;
Or, if thou wilt not, be but sworn my love,
And I'll no longer be a Capulet.

Romeo [*aside*]:   Shall I hear more, or shall I speak at this?

Juliet: 'Tis but thy name that is my enemy;
Thou art thyself, though not a Montague.
What's Montague? It is not hand nor foot,
Nor arm nor face [nor any other part]
Belonging to a man. O, be some other name!
What's in a name? That which we call a rose
By any other name would smell as sweet;

So Romeo would, were he not Romeo call'd,
Retain that dear perfection which he owes
Without that title. Romeo, doff thy name,
And for thy name, which is no part of thee,
Take all myself.

Romeo: I take thee at thy word.
Call me but love, and I'll be new baptiz's;
Henceforth I never will be Romeo.

Juliet:

_____

_____

_____

Romeo:

_____

_____

_____

Juliet:

_____

_____

_____

Romeo:

_____

_____

_____

Here's one possible version:

Juliet: O Romeo, Romeo, why are you called Romeo?
Deny your heritage and refuse your name;
Or, if you won't, tell me you love me and I'll give
up my name.

Romeo [*aside*]:   Shall I listen, or shall I speak now?

Juliet: It's only your name that is our enemy.
You are yourself, even if you don't have the
same last name [Montague]. What's Montague?
It is not hand, foot, arm, face or any other

part of a man's body! O, take a different
name! What's in a name? The flower we call a
rose would smell just as sweet if we called
it something else. You would be just as
perfect if you had a different name.
Romeo, get rid of your name, and take me instead.

Romeo: I believe you. Just call me your lover, and
I'll take a new name.

Now that wasn't so bad, was it?

Groove to the Beat

No, I was not born under a rhyming planet.

—*Much Ado About Nothing*

Now that we've dealt with the fear factor, we can turn our attention to the *form* of
Shakespeare's language. Shakespeare wrote all his plays (as well as his poems) in poetry.
Not only was it common in Shakespeare's time to write plays in poetry, but the strong
rhythm of the verse also made it much easier for the actors to memorize their lines.

Shakespeare used a verse form called *blank verse*. It's unrhymed *iambic pentameter*. Huh?
Piece of cake! Look at the words themselves for clues to the meaning of the term:

Iamb: A poetic foot or unit with one unstressed syllable followed by
one stressed syllable, as in the word "a/fraid."

Pentameter: Ten syllables or beats in each line.

Therefore, blank verse has five feet, or beats, per line and
every other syllable is stressed.

Poetry is poetry because it has a rhythmical pattern,
called its *meter*. This pattern is determined by the
number and type of beats in each line. To describe the
meter of a poem, you must *scan* its lines. Scanning
involves marking the stressed and unstressed syllables.

Each stressed syllable is marked with a slanted line (´)
and each unstressed syllable is marked with a horseshoe
symbol (˘). The stresses are then divided by vertical lines
into groups called *feet*. Here's an example from *Macbeth*:

Forsooth!

Language that has a deliberate
meter (rhythm) is called poetry.
Poems can rhyme, but they don't
have to. All other types of writing
are called **prose**.

ˇ ´ ˇ ´ ˇ ˇ ´ ˇ ´ ˇ ´

Your face / my thane, / is as / a book / where men /

ˇ ´ ˇ ´ ˇ ´ ˇ ˇ ´ ˇ ´

May read / strange man / ners. To / beguile / the time,

Blank verse, which was introduced into English by the Earl of Surrey, can be smooth and dignified, but it can also mimic the pattern of natural speech more effectively than any other metrical pattern. As result, it is one of the most versatile and flexible verse forms, a favorite not only of the Renaissance poets but also of many later poets.

Don't assume that Shakespeare was wedded to blank verse; rather, he used it to his advantage. When the occasion suited, Shakespeare shifted gears into prose. King Lear goes mad in prose; the Nurse in *Romeo and Juliet* patters in prose. *As You Like It* is written almost entirely in prose.

A Pox on Your House!

Few people insult with Shakespeare's skill. Yes, you have that traditional Greek slam, "May red goats eat out your stomach lining and the white mice, too." Yiddish has some juicy curses as well. Here are my two favorites: "May all your teeth fall out—but one remain for a headache" and "May your sex life be as good as your credit."

These are admirable and effective curses, but for a really good whammy, you have to turn to ol' William. Shakespearean insults come in two versions: long and satisfying and short and satisfying. Here's an example of the former variety from *Timon of Athens*:

> Live loathed and long,
> Most smiling, smooth, detested parasites,
> Courteous destroyers, affable wolves, meek bears,
> You fools of fortune, trencher-friends, time's flies

And the latter type from *Richard III*. It's brief and bitter:

> Thou toad, thou toad.

Forsooth!

An **iamb** is not the only poetic foot in English. Among the most common poetic feet are the **trochee** (one stressed syllable followed by one unstressed syllable), **anapest** (two unstressed syllables followed by one stressed syllable), **dactyl** (one stressed syllable followed by two unstressed syllables), and **spondee** (two stressed syllables).

Take That...and That!

Here are my favorite 15 Shakespearean insults. Feel free to memorize the ones you can use in your dealings with cement-heads, banana-brains, and all-purpose jerks.

1. I do desire that we may be better strangers. (*As You Like It*)

2. This Triton of the minnows? (*Coriolanus*)

3. So much for him. (*Hamlet*)

4. Thou wretched, rash, intruding fool, farewell! (*Hamlet*)

5. There's neither honesty, manhood, nor good fellowship in thee. (*Henry IV, Part I*)

6. This bed-presser, the horseback-breaker, this huge hill of flesh... (*Henry IV, Part I*)

7. ...you starveling, you eel-skin, you dried neat's tongue, you bull's pizzle, you stockfish... (*Henry IV, Part I*)

8. You blocks, you stones, you worse than senseless things! (*Julius Caesar*)

9. I had rather be a dog, and bay at the moon, Then such a Roman. (*Julius Caesar*)

10. I have seen better faces in my time. (*King Lear*)

11. Egregiously an ass. (*Othello*)

12. A lunatic, lean-witted fool. (*Richard II*)

13. When he is best he is a little worse than a man, and when he is worst he is a little better than a beast. (*The Merchant of Venice*)

14. Thou deboshed fish thou. ("Deboshed" means "drunk.") (*The Tempest*)

15. Ajax, who wears his wit in his belly and his guts in his head. (*Troilus and Cressida*)

Forsooth!

In Shakespeare's day, **cock** had a curious double meaning. It's hard to miss the vulgarity of "Pistol's cock is up" (*Henry V*). Outside such double entendres, cock was also a substitute for the even more shocking word "God," as in "By Cock" (*Hamlet*) and "Cock's passion" (*Taming of the Shrew*).

Bonus insult: You Banbury cheese! (*The Merry Wives of Windsor*)

Do-It-Yourself Insults

Unfortunately, since Shakespeare has shuffled off this mortal coil, you probably think that once you've memorized all the curses he penned, you're out of luck. Not so fast! We're a resourceful bunch, able to repair everything from a leaky faucet to a leaky roof. (Okay, some of us can do the repair thing, while others of us should never be allowed to handle anything more complex than a pencil.) But everyone can create his or her own Shakespearean curses, thanks to the easy do-it-yourself system below. Here's how to curse like the Bard:

1. Memorize some choice terms from the list below.

2. Combine one word from each of the three columns, prefaced with "Thou."

3. Scowl.

For example: "Out of my path, thou Spongy Rat-Faced Foot Licker!"

Column 1	Column 2	Column 3
artless	base-court	apple-john
bawdy	bat-fowling	baggage
beslubbering	beef-witted	barnacle
bootless	beetle-headed	bladder
churlish	boil-brained	boar-pig
cockered	clapper-clawed	bugbear
clouted	clay-brained	bum-bailey
craven	common-kissing	canker-blossom
currish	crook-pated	clack-dish
dankish	dismal-dreaming	clotpole
dissembling	dizzy-eyed	coxcomb
droning	doghearted	codpiece
errant	dread-bolted	death-token
fawning	earth-vexing	dewberry
fobbing	elf-skinned	flap-dragon
forward	fat-kidneyed	flax-wench
frothy	fen-sucked	flirt-gill
gleeking	flap-mouthed	foot-licker
goatish	fly-bitten	fustilarian
gorbellied	folly-fallen	giglet
impertinent	fool-born	gudgeon
infectious	full-gorged	haggard
jarring	guts-griping	harpy
loggerheaded	half-faced	hedge-pig
lumpish	hasty-witted	horn-beast
mammering	hedge-born	hugger-mugger
mangled	hell-hated	jolthead
mewling	idle-headed	lewdster
paunchy	ill-breeding	lout
pribbling	ill-nurtured	maggot-pie
puking	knotty-pated	malt-worm
puny	milk-livered	mammet
quailing	motley-minded	measle
rank	onion-eyed	minnow
reeky	plume-plucked	miscreant
roguish	pottle-deep	moldwarp
ruttish	pox-marked	mumble-news
saucy	reeling-ripe	nut-hook
spleeny	rough-hewn	pigeon-egg

continues

continued

Column 1	Column 2	Column 3
spongy	rude-growing	pignut
surly	rump-fed	puttock
tottering	shard-borne	pumpion
unmuzzled	sheep-biting	ratsbane
vain	spur-galled	scut
venomed	swag-bellied	skainsmate
villainous	tardy-gaited	strumpet
warped	tickle-brained	varlet
wayward	toad-spotted	vassal
weedy	urchin-snouted	whey-face
yeasty	weather-bitten	wagtail

Sweets to the Sweet

Elizabethan English had a different *R* sound, drawn out into a pirate-sounding *ARRRRRRRRR*.

Forsooth!

Bum or **bogs** referred to the buttocks. "Troth," Escalus tells Pompey, "and your bum is the greatest thing about you, so that in the beastliest sense you are Pompey the Great" (*Measure for Measure*).

The Bard was a professional, so he had a handle on what would fly and what wouldn't. Verbal extravagance, violence, bile, and bawdy were hallmarks of literature high and low in the seventeenth century. Passion, corruption, disease, and death were handled boldly and frankly. Scenes of anguish, terror, and lust were played to audiences of both sexes and all classes. Shakespeare usually sidestepped the censor, but he managed to keep his plays emotionally provocative.

Talk Dirty to Me

Remember the three topics that well-mannered ladies and gentlemen never discuss in public: politics, religion, and sex? Polite but oh! so *dull*. Shakespeare knew that a little bawdy speech (okay, so a lot of lewd banter) went a long way to keeping the box office receipts healthy. For a complete list of Shakespeare's sexual slang, check out *A Dictionary of Shakespeare's Sexual Puns and Their Significance* (Frankie Rubinstein) or *Shakespeare's Bawdy* (Eric Partridge). See? Scholarship doesn't have to be boring.

In the meantime, here's a list of the most common sexual slang you're likely to encounter as you see and read the plays. After all, I wouldn't want you to miss the naughty bits.

Elizabethan Word	Double Meanings
Arise	Stand up/to have an erection
Beef	Meat/prostitute
Cod	Fish/male organ
Count	Numbers/pun on female genitalia
Die	Pass away/sexual intercourse or orgasm
Green	Color/virility
Hell	Hades/female genitalia
Jade	Gem/prostitute
Thing	Object/male genitalia
Will	Shakespeare's name/sexual desire

The Least You Need to Know

➤ There are three stages in the development of English: Old English (A.D. 449–1066), Middle English (1066–1450), and Modern English (1450–present).

➤ Shakespeare wrote Modern English.

➤ Shakespeare can be hard to understand because of his vocabulary, grammar, and word order—but don't let it scare you off.

➤ Shakespeare used a verse form called blank verse, unrhymed iambic pentameter.

➤ Elizabethan English contains enough curses and sexual references to make anyone's ears burn.

Chapter 6

Something Fishy About the Man from Stratford: The Authorship Question

In This Chapter

➤ The thrill of the hunt

➤ The case for Edward de Vere, Earl of Oxford

➤ The case for Sir Francis Bacon

➤ The case for Christopher Marlowe

➤ The case for William Shakespeare

In 1903, the famous novelist Henry James wrote, "I am 'sort of' haunted by the conviction that the divine William is the biggest and most successful fraud ever practiced on a patient world." Henry wasn't alone in his suspicion that Shakespeare didn't write the plays and poems attributed to him.

Other famous doubters span an astonishing array of writers, statesmen, performers, and philosophers. These include Mark Twain, Walt Whitman, John Galsworthy, Charles Dickens, Otto von Bismarck, Benjamin Disraeli, Charles de Gaulle, Charlie Chaplin, and Sigmund Freud. There are also a surprising number of lawyers who question Shakespeare's authorship, including the late editor of the *American Bar Association Journal* and the authors of publications requiring hundreds of pages to list. (There's a lot of cranks, eccentrics, and oddballs, too, but we don't have to pay attention to *them*.)

New doubters come forth every day. In 1998, one of England's most famous politicians and classical scholars, Enoch Powell, stood contemplating the Shakespeare monument in the Stratford church, muttering, "Isn't it disgusting? It's a lie. I can't look at it." And he wasn't referring to the artwork.

Fortunately for all these doubters, there's no shortage of pretenders to the throne of the True Author. Nearly 60 claimants to that title have been put forward. The front-runners are Edward de Vere, the seventeenth Earl of Oxford; Sir Francis Bacon; and Christopher Marlowe. Let's look behind the scenes at the reasons for the great Shakespeare hunt.

Suspicion Dominates My Heart

Something is rotten in the state of Denmark.

—Hamlet

No one proposes that Christopher Marlowe's plays weren't written by Christopher Marlowe or Ben Jonson's by Ben Jonson. So why is Shakespeare singled out for doubt? The answer lies mainly in Shakespeare's greatness; he is the best, and so he is the target of intense scrutiny and speculation. Think of the famous pizza slogan, "You've tried the rest, so why not try the best?" The question of Shakespearean authorship sometimes seems like the variation, "You've attacked the rest, so why not attack the best?"

Furthermore, Shakespeare represents the Establishment in British literature, the greatest of the Dead White Guys we were force-fed in school. We live in an age that salivates to find flaws in our heroes, whether they be politicians, titans of industry, or sports figures. As the *ne plus ultra* of the Old Guard, Shakespeare is automatically suspect. In effect, he is the god of English Letters. And to some people, gods are meant to be toppled.

Star Quality

PBS's 1989 *Frontline* broadcast of *The Shakespeare Mystery* further increased awareness and interest in this authorship debate.

What's more, solving mysteries is exciting, whether it be the Loch Ness monster, the Kennedy assassination, or the Shakespeare authorship question. Detective work of this kind appeals to educated professionals, such as lawyers and businesspeople who like to pursue Shakespeare as a hobby. Of course, it's a natural for Shakespearean scholars and wannabe academicians eager to make their bones.

Imagine being the one to prove that all of Western culture has been bamboozled for centuries by a hoax, and that Shakespeare is really someone else. Gosh and golly. It's like winning the lottery—only you don't have to pay income tax on your winnings because they're all psychological.

I Coulda Been a Contenda: Edward de Vere, Seventeenth Earl of Oxford

Who wrote the plays and poems we know as William Shakespeare's? Was Shakespeare the man you learned about in Chapter 1, "Whose Life Is It Anyway?"—or was he someone quite different? Did he hide behind a pen name, just as Stephen King called himself *Richard Bachman* or Marian Evans called herself *George Eliot*? (This also raises the issue of Shakespeare's gender, but let's not go there.)

Well, then, who was the man we know as Shakespeare?

The father of psychoanalysic theory, Sigmund Freud, answered the question for some when he wrote in 1937, "I am almost convinced that the assumed name [William Shakespeare] conceals the personality of Edward de Vere, Earl of Oxford. The man of Stratford…seems to have nothing at all to justify his claim, whereas Oxford has almost everything." Freud hit the mark with the Oedipal theory and penis envy. Was he correct when it came to the Bard? Now vee may perhaps to begin? Yes?

Forsooth!

Oxfordians are those who support the theory that Shakespeare's plays were written by Edward de Vere, the Earl of Oxford.

Always a Bridesmaid, Never a Bride

Whether he was in fact Shakespeare or not, Edward de Vere, the Seventeenth Earl of Oxford, had such an outrageous life that he could have been one of Shakespeare's characters come to life. Born in 1550, Edward de Vere was a descendant of a family that had served at the right hand of the English monarchy, beginning with the Norman Invasion in 1066.

He was a recognized poet in his own day, and Oxfordians make the most of this fact in their attempts to prove that he actually wrote Shakespeare's works. Oxford was praised in print as a poet and playwright when he was alive, a fact that Oxfordians understandably use to their advantage. In doing so, though, they quote this praise selectively and present it out of context, leading unwary readers to a greatly inflated view of Oxford's reputation as a poet. While Oxford's work had its admirers, nobody seems to have considered him a great poet or playwright.

Oxfordians from the unfortunately named J. Thomas Looney to the present have noted that some of the verse forms Oxford used were also used by Shakespeare, and they have seized upon this coincidence as support for their theories. In *The Verse Forms of Shakespeare and Oxford*, scholar Terry Ross looks at this issue in detail and shows how badly Oxfordians have distorted the facts in an attempt to exaggerate Oxford's similarity to Shakespeare and his role in the history of English poetry.

Star Quality

At more than 800 pages, Charlton Ogburn's *The Mysterious William Shakespeare: The Myth and the Reality* is the single most important attempt to make the case for Oxford as Shakespeare. The "classic" work is J. Thomas Looney's "*Shakespeare*" *Identified in Edward de Vere, Seventeenth Earl of Oxford, and the Poems of Edward de Vere*. The only full-length biography of Oxford is *The Seventeenth Earl of Oxford, 1550–1604*, by B. M. Ward.

The X-Files

Oxfordians find it suspicious that the original manuscripts of Shakespeare's plays have not survived. They darkly hint that this is evidence of a cover-up and have gone so far as to x-ray the Shakespeare monument in Stratford to prove it contained manuscripts. (It doesn't.) Unfortunately for the Oxfordians, there is nothing the slightest bit suspicious about the absence of Shakespeare's manuscripts since virtually no playhouse manuscripts from that era have survived.

Sweets to the Sweet

Dave Kathman's article, "Why I'm Not an Oxfordian," explains why academic Shakespeareans do not take Ogburn and his Oxfordian chums seriously.

Furthermore, indifference to the preservation of manuscripts was not peculiar to Shakespeare and his fellow dramatists. In his *English Literary Hands from Chaucer to Dryden*, Anthony G. Petti concluded:

Even literary figures preoccupied with posthumous fame did not apparently place value on preserving their holograph manuscripts after publication, much less their earlier drafts, and neither, generally speaking, did anyone else, other than close friends, for the cult of collecting literary autographs did not begin in earnest until the end of the eighteenth century.

Besides, the manuscript of a play was the property not of the playwright but of the company that produced it; unless an unauthorized printer got hold of it first, a play could not be published without the consent of the theater shareholders. Oxfordians dismiss this contention, but the publication history of the Chamberlain's Men and the King's Men plays reveal that the companies did indeed control publication.

Publish and Perish

If Oxford did write the works of Shakespeare, why did he never acknowledge them? Oxfordians claim that the plays and poems contain dangerous political allegories, and that Oxford could not safely allow them to appear under his own name. Hence, he used the name "Shakespeare." To support this claim, Oxfordians cite George Puttenham's 1589 book, *The Arte of English Poesie*. However, a close examination of Puttenham's work shows that Oxfordians have relied on doctored evidence, and that Puttenham's actual words contradict the Oxfordian claim. Hey, nothing's perfect.

Some Oxfordians further claim that Edward de Vere could not have used his own name because doing so would have violated the Elizabethan social code, which prohibited aristocrats from having works published under their own names. The scenario goes something like this: Unable to control his compulsion to write plays of unparalleled genius, the Earl of Oxford recognized the disgrace this would bring to his ancient title and honorable name and agreed to suppress his authorship. Thus he fobbed off the authorship of his works to an actor. But the alleged code, handy and time-honored as it had become, did not square with the evidence, since a great many Tudor aristocrats published early and often.

Ergo, the stigma of print is a myth. During Elizabeth's reign, anyone, of whatever exalted standing in society, might issue a sonnet or play without fear of losing status.

Fire at Will

Using computer analysis, the Shakespeare Clinic at Claremont College compared Shakespeare's poetry with the work of other contemporary poets by means of various objective tests. The goal was to see if any of the claimants' poetry matched the Bard's, and none did. Furthermore, the Earl of Oxford was one of the poorest matches for Shakespeare out of all the poets tested.

Perish and Publish

The greatest difficulty with the case for Oxford is the candidate died in 1604. In general, dead men usually stop writing. No scholars doubt that many of the greatest plays were produced subsequent to this date, including *King Lear, Macbeth, Antony and Cleopatra, Coriolanus, Cymbeline, The Winter's Tale, The Tempest,* and *Henry VIII.*

How does the Oxford camp get around this? Don't worry; be happy. They argue that Oxford wrote these plays *before* he died, and that they were brought out as needed for performance, sometimes with added contemporary references to events after 1604 in order to make them look timely.

The argument propounds a conspiracy of staggering proportions. According to this script, Shakespeare agreed to serve as a front man for Oxford because writing plays was below the dignity of a great man. Here are just a few problems this theory presents:

➤ Shakespeare's fellow actors had to agree to dish out the plays after Oxford's death and publicize them as Shakespeare's.

➤ Shakespeare's friends, such as Ben Jonson, had to go along with the fiction.

➤ The *First Folio* had to be a sham.

➤ The writers who praised Shakespeare as England's great national poet and playwright had to be deceived by the presumed cover-up or play part of the hoax.

Of course, this line of reasoning discounts considerable evidence that Shakespeare's plays are a cohesive whole, showing stylistic development that can be traced into the late years.

Ultimately the case for Oxford as the author of Shakespeare's plays and poems collapses on lack of motive as well as lack of evidence. And let us not overlook lack of logic. But no problem: There are more candidates waiting in the wing.

Sweets to the Sweet

The Shakespeare Oxford Society sends forth a steady stream of books, newsletters, and journals to make the case for Edward de Vere's authorship of the Shakespeare canon. Noted writers: Charlton and Dorothy Ogburn, Charlton Ogburn, Jr., Charles Wisner Barrell, Louis Benezet, Gelett Burgess, Ruth Loyd Miller, and A. Bronson Feldman.

Shake-n-Bacon

Ever notice that you never see a picture of Francis Bacon, Queen Elizabeth, and William Shakespeare in the same room together? Ah ha—there's a conspiracy afoot! Even in our highly suspicious times, it's *really* hard to make a case for Sir Francis Bacon as William Shakespeare—not that many haven't tried.

Star Quality

The Advancement of Learning (1605) is the best of Bacon's philosophical works; for literature, check out his *Essays* (1597–1625). His writings on the law include *Maxims of the Law* (1630) and *Reading on the Statue of Uses* (1642).

The philosopher and statesman was born in 1581 and died in 1626. A pioneer of modern scientific thought, Sir Francis Bacon held a variety of governmental positions, including that of attorney general, privy councilor, and lord chancellor. His writings fall into three categories: philosophical, literary, and professional.

Until the 1920s, Francis Bacon was the favorite candidate of those who doubted that Shakespeare wrote the plays and poems that have been attributed to him. The Oxford faction is today more numerous, but the Baconians still have some sizzle in them. A small but tenacious band of zealots, they come up with some pretty silly evidence. One Baconian, Penn Leary, claims he found cryptographical proof that Bacon wrote Shakespeare's works. *Please!*

Francis Bacon, that brilliant rationalist, was simply too busy as a statesman and essayist to moonlight as Shakespeare. Besides, his literary style doesn't match the style of Shakespeare's plays and poems. The best refutation of the Baconian case was made by scholar J. M. Robertson in *The Baconian Heresy*.

Will Power

Encouraged by the American writer and philosopher Ralph Waldo Emerson, an American woman named Delia Bacon (no relation) wrote a passionate book arguing that Sir Francis Bacon and Sir Walter Raleigh, whose poetry was much admired by Elizabethans, collaborated on the works. The unfortunate woman fueled the prejudices of Stratfordians by once spending the night beside Shakespeare's tomb in Holy Trinity Church armed with a shovel. She later was committed to an institution.

Marvelous Marlowe

"Lord, what fools these mortals be."

—*A Midsummer Night's Dream*

Then we come to the case of Christopher Marlowe, a wild and crazy kind of guy. Claiming that Marlowe wrote Shakespeare's works is really a stretch—but that hasn't stopped his fans from sticking their necks out.

Christopher Marlowe was born on February 6, 1564, the eldest son of a shoemaker. It seems he never wanted to follow in his father's footsteps (okay, it's a bad pun—but I couldn't resist), for at age 23 he scooted off to London and became a dramatist. Writing for the theater gets old fast, but Marlowe had several absorbing hobbies—like schmoozing with his buddy Sir Walter Raleigh, practicing atheism, and getting arrested on a regular basis.

While on parole, Marlowe produced some great stuff, including *The Famous Tragedy of the Rich Jew of Malta, Edward the Second*, and *Dr. Faustus*. His most ambitious work was the heroic epic *Tamburlaine the Great*, a play in two parts of five acts each that has the added distinction of being the first play written in blank verse. Marlowe's pioneering use of blank verse likely encouraged Shakespeare to try it. Marlowe was the first to write a genuine tragedy in English, again paving the way for Shakespeare.

In the spring of 1593, a friend of Marlowe's was captured and tortured by the Queen's Privy Council. Based on this "evidence," the Council was preparing to arrest Marlowe. Before the police could clap on the cuffs, however, Marlowe was killed in a brawl at a rooming-house.

He was staying there with three of his friends: a con artist, a fence (a fellow who sells stolen goods), and a spy for Her Majesty's Secret Service. Apparently Marlowe and his sterling companions started arguing over the dinner check ("No, you take it; I insist."). A dagger appeared and Marlowe checked out for good.

Both the timing of Marlowe's death and the lack of any retribution against his murderer have led some scholars to theorize that Marlowe faked his death to escape the Privy Council. The new identity? William Shakespeare, of course. Then Marlowe began a second career as the Bard.

We all know there are no second acts in literature or life. Besides, Marlowe's writing style was nothing like Shakespeare's, especially when it comes to comedy. And we have it on good authority that he was seriously dead early on.

The Incumbent: The Man from Stratford

Aside from real estate and other worldly goods, Shakespeare left 37 plays, 154 sonnets, and several longer poems. The exact numbers are in dispute. Shakespeare wrote only some parts of some of the plays, so different scholars have come up with different totals. Some credit him with *Two Noble Kinsmen* (written with John Fletcher), which would increase the number of plays to 38.

The most obvious evidence that William Shakespeare wrote the works attributed to him is that everyone at the time said he did: He was often praised in writing as a poet and playwright. Further, he was named as the author of many of the works while he was alive. Finally, seven years after his death, the *First Folio* explicitly attributed the rest of the works to him.

Will Power

As the Shakespearean actor Ian McKellen puts it today, "Some people, intellectual snobs perhaps, like to think that the philosopher Francis Bacon wrote the plays. Then there are social snobs who like to think that the Earl of Oxford wrote the plays. And no doubt somewhere there's a keen viewer of Masterpiece Theatre who thinks that Alistair Cooke wrote the plays."

Oxfordians try to account for this evidence by claiming that the man from Stratford was actually "William Shaksper" (or "Shakspere"), a man whose name was spelled and pronounced differently from that of the great poet "William Shakespeare," and that nobody at the time would have thought to confuse the two. As you've already learned, such claims bear little resemblance to reality.

Some doubters hold Shakespeare's origins against him. England's top poet couldn't have come from such a backwater town as Stratford, they tell us, and a bumpkin like Shakespeare couldn't have had access to the materials that the author of the play drew upon. Yet Shakespeare wasn't the only shining star to make his way from Stratford to London. Richard Field, who grew up a few hundred yards down the road from Shakespeare and in very similar circumstances, became one of the leading publishers and booksellers in London during the seventeenth century.

Besides, the sheer number of candidates put forward as having had the qualifications to be the "real author" is evidence that these qualifications were not unique in Shakespeare's time. After all, there's little in Shakespeare's plays that required knowledge beyond materials that were publicly available at the time.

Nonetheless, the authorship question still sparks intense controversy. With its centuries of debate, scholarship, sublimation, and conjecture, the Shakespeare war is not likely to abate in the foreseeable future.

The Least You Need to Know

➤ Edward de Vere, Earl of Oxford, did *not* write Shakespeare's plays and poems.

➤ Sir Francis Bacon did *not* write Shakespeare's plays and poems.

➤ Christopher Marlowe did *not* write Shakespeare's plays and poems.

➤ Bingo! William Shakespeare wrote the plays and poems attributed to him.

Chapter 7

The BIG CHEESE

Shakespeare's Literary Reputation

In This Chapter

➤ Shakespeare's reputation during his life

➤ Good press and bad press

➤ Shakespeare becomes a classic

➤ Like cleanliness, Shakespeare gets next to godliness

➤ Twentieth century criticism

In 1756, nearly a century and a half after Shakespeare died, the Reverend Francis Gastrell moved to Shakespeare's house in Stratford. The Reverend was furious to find his property overrun by tourists. They congregated around a huge mulberry tree, scraping off souvenir shards of bark. Why this specific tree? According to legend, Shakespeare had planted the mulberry tree with his very own hands and enjoyed sitting under it on sultry days.

Desperate to drive away the fans, Gastrell had the tree cut down. Sacrilege! According to one eyewitness, "Excited by the discovery of his profanation, [there was a] general furor against the perpetrator, and the enraged populace surrounded the premises and vowed vengeance." Things haven't changed much over the centuries: The locals got their revenge by smashing the windows in the Reverend's house.

But one neighbor had a better idea. The aptly named Thomas Sharp bought the wood from the tree and made it into a steady stream of trinkets—toothpick holders, goblets, chairs, salt shakers, boxes, and canes—that tourists eagerly snatched up. The trash proved to be treasure. As the years passed, just one of these trinkets would sell for more than an Old Master's painting. How did Shakespeare transform from a well-respected playwright to the number one writer in English? That's what you'll find out in this chapter. We'll go 'round and 'round the mulberry bush so you can see how Shakespeare's reputation grew to its current epic status.

The Big Cheese in His Day

Good name in man and woman, dear my lord,
Is the immediate jewel of their souls.
Who steals my purse steals trash; 'tis something, nothing;
'Twas mine, 'tis his, and has been slave to thousands;
But he that filches from me my good name
Robs me of that which not enriches him
And makes me poor indeed.

—*Othello*

Today, no home is complete without the premier icons of religion and culture prominently displayed on a bookshelf: a copy of the Bible and a complete set of the works of William Shakespeare. Shakespeare was not always a symbol of art and attainment, however. Although Shakespeare is now the undisputed king of English letters, in his own day it was far from obvious that his writing would prove of lasting value. The very idea would have made his contemporaries laugh—and it's a pretty safe bet that Shakespeare would have laughed with them.

Forsooth!

Shakespeare's works are so revered that there's even a name for Shakespearean worship—**Bardolatry**.

As far as Shakespeare was concerned, he was an entertainer, not a genius for the ages. He was focused on the dual goals of entertaining his audience and making piles of money. And in the eyes of many Elizabethans, his chosen medium, the theater, was as far from "uplifting" as you could get. Rather than temples of moral improvement, the theaters were viewed as "bawdy houses" (brothels).

"He did not in his own day inspire the mysterious veneration that afterward came to surround his works," writes celebrated Shakespearean biographer Sam Schoenbaum in his seminal study, *Shakespeare's Lives*. "No playwright in that day did, and certainly no actor."

Sweets to the Sweet

Well into the eighteenth century, fellow writers Ben Jonson and John Fletcher were esteemed as Shakespeare's equals.

Second, Shakespeare's chief rival among early Elizabethan playwrights (then as now) was Christopher Marlowe, who produced his Tamburlain plays, *Dr. Faustus* and *The Jew of Malta*. Had Shakespeare died in the same year as Marlowe, his accomplishment would have been thought remarkable, but Marlowe would undoubtedly have been given the precedence as the better of the playwrights by subsequent critics. Fortunately for us, Shakespeare lived long enough to write a great deal more.

Everyone's a Critic

Exhibit A:

> Soul of the age!
> The applause, delight, the wonder of our stage!
> Mr. Shakespeare rise.
>
> —Ben Jonson, *To the Memory of My Beloved, the Author, Mr. William Shakespeare* (1632)

Exhibit B:

> The players have often mentioned it as an honor to Shakespeare that in his writing (whatsoever he penned) he never blotted out a line. My answer hath been, "Would he had blotted a thousand."
>
> —Ben Jonson, *Timber; or Discoveries Made Upon Men and Matter* (1640)

You just can't please some people, and fans of the Bard are no exception. Shakespeare's first public notice was definitely a slam. In the fall of 1592, fellow author Robert Greene clobbered Shakespeare with his now famous remark about "an upstart Crow, …with his Tygers hart wrapt in a Players hyde." (See Chapter 1, "Whose Life Is It Anyway?" for the complete insult.)

Shakespeare's reputation picked up six years later, in 1598, when a student named Francis Meres praised the Bard as the top English author. How sweet it was…

As Plautus and Seneca are accounted the best for comedy and tragedy among the Latins, so Shakespeare among the English is the most excellent in both kinds for the stage. For comedy, witness his *The Gentlemen of Verona, Comedy of Errors, Love's Labor's Lost, A Midsummer Night's Dream*, and *The Merchant of Venice*; for tragedy, his *Richard the II, Richard the III, Henry the IV, Titus Andronicus*, and *Romeo and Juliet*.

Will Power

If golf and Shakespeare do it for you, why not enjoy a round at Club Shakespeare? Located in Atlanta, Georgia, the 640-acre golf course features holes named for Shakespeare's plays. And as we all know, golf features all the elements of tragedy, comedy, and romance. Shakespeare and golf are a match made in heaven.

The Fickle Finger of Fate

In 1612, four years before his death, Shakespeare had slipped a bit in the polls. The Bard had made the Hit Parade, but not the top of the charts.

When John Webster published his play *The White Devil* that year, he wrote an introduction in which he accorded his fellow dramatist a dab of praise:

> ...the full and heightened style of Master Chapman, the laboured and understanding works of Master Jonson, the no less worthy composures of the both worthily excellent Master Beaumont and Master Fletcher, and lastly (without wrong last to be named) the right happy and copious industry of M. Shakespeare, M. Dekker, and M. Heywood.

Movin' Uptown

In 1668, about half a century after Shakespeare had shuffled off this mortal coil, fellow writer John Dryden published *The Essay of Dramatic Poesy*, a biggie in the world of the *glitterati literati*. At this time, Shakespeare was no longer a contemporary, yet not quite a classic—think "Classic Lite." Dryden's assessment is important because it started Shakespeare on the road to assuming his rightful place at the head of the class:

> To begin then with Shakespeare; He was the man who of all Modern, and perhaps Ancient Poets, had the largest and most comprehensive soul. All the Images of Nature were still present to him, and he drew them not laboriously, but luckily: when he describes any thing, you more than see it, you feel it too. Those who accuse him to have wanted learning, give him the greater commendation: he was naturally learn'd; he needed not the spectacles of Books to read Nature; he look'd inwards, and found her there.

Sweets to the Sweet

In England, the Restoration occurred in 1660 when Charles II was restored to the throne of England after the fall of the Commonwealth and Protectorate. In France, the first Restoration refers to the accession of King Louis XVIII in 1814 after the abdication of Napoleon; the second Restoration refers to Louis's reinstatement in 1815.

Though John Dryden was an admirer of Shakespeare's, he confessed that Francis Beaumont and John Fletcher "had with the advantage of Shakespeare's wit, which was their precedent, great natural gifts, improv'd by study." For this reason, "their Plays are now the most pleasant and frequent entertainments of the Stage; two of theirs being acted through the year for one of Shakespeare's or Jonson's."

Whether or not Dryden's estimate is reliable, the Restoration audiences of Jonson, Beaumont, and Fletcher saw the plays as they had been written. But Shakespeare offended this refined age, violating its idea of dramatic form and good taste. Not many of his plays escaped thorough adaptation. The *Macbeth* that Restoration audiences saw owed more to Sir William Davenant than to Shakespeare; *Antony and Cleopatra* was newly made by Dryden to become *All for Love*. And so on.

Shakespeare was derided "for neglecting the unities, for ignoring the ancients, for violating decorum by resorting to tragicomedy and supernatural characters, and for using puns and blank verse."

In 1709, Shakespeare's greatest interpreter in Restoration theater, the tragedian Thomas Betterton, looked down loftily upon the man who "liv'd under a kind of mere Light of Nature...in a state of almost universal License and Ignorance."

A Classic Is Born

> Make but my name thy love, and love that still,
> And then thou lovest me, for my name is *Will*.
>
> —"Sonnet 136"

It took nearly another half century for Shakespeare to become established as a classic. The elevation occurred when Nicholas Rowe, a Restoration dramatist, issued the first edited collection of Shakespeare's plays, called *The Collected Plays of William Shakespeare*. Rowe included a short biography of Shakespeare and praise for passages he especially admired. Most important, however, he considerably revised the text, adding place headings to the scenes and new stage directions. As a result, Rowe gets the credit for the form in which Shakespeare's plays are usually printed.

The dam was breached: After Rowe, the editions of Shakespeare's works followed fast and furious. Between 1709 and 1799, over 50 editions of the plays appeared. Here's a rundown of the major editions:

➤ 1723–1725: Alexander Pope's edition

➤ 1733: Theobald's edition

➤ 1743–1744: Hammer's edition

➤ 1765: Dr. Johnson's edition

➤ 1790: Edmund Malone's edition

Shakespeare's reputation continued to swell, and Alexander Pope heaped his share of accolades on the growing pile. "If ever any Author deserved the name of an Original," Pope wrote, "it was Shakespeare." Pope continued:

> Homer himself drew not his art so immediately from the fountains of Nature... The poetry of Shakespeare was Inspiration indeed: he is not so much an Imitator, as an Instrument, of Nature; and 'tis not so just to say that he speaks from her, as that she speaks through him...

The Power over our Passions was never possessed in a more eminent degree, or displayed in so different instances. Yet all along, there is seen no labour, nor pains to raise them; no preparation to guide our guess to the effect, or be perceived to lead toward it; But the heart swells, and the tears burst out, just at the proper places; We are surprised, the moment we weep; and yet upon reflection find the passion so just, that we should be surprised if we had not wept, and wept at that very moment.

Star Quality

Poet and writer Alexander Pope (1688–1744) dominated his era not only because of his great powers of invention but also because of his technical mastery of the forms he used. The first writer to support himself solely on his writing, Pope is best known for *The Rape of the Lock*, *Essays on Criticism*, *An Essay on Man*, and *Moral Essays*.

In 1765, Dr. Samuel Johnson chimed in with his famous *Preface*. By now, Shakespeare had unquestionably been enshrined as a classic. Johnson wrote:

> The Poet, of whose works I have undertaken the revision, may now begin to assume the dignity of an ancient and claim the privilege of established fame and prescriptive veneration. He has long outlived the century, the term commonly fixed as the test of literary merit.

> Shakespeare is above all writers, at least above all modern writers, the poet of nature: the poet that holds up to his readers a faithful mirror of manners and of life. His characters are not modified by the customs of particular places, unpracticed by the rest of the world…they are the genuine progeny of common humanity, such as the world will always supply, and observation will always find.

Party Hearty

With the three-day Shakespeare Jubilee in 1769, Shakespeare became a full-fledged cultural icon. Although the actual event was a disaster from beginning to end, it marked the unofficial beginning of the Shakespeare industry.

Actor David Garrick, in charge of the event, was not a detail-oriented kind of guy. As a result, the amphitheater was barely completed on time, props and furnishings were a disaster, and the local Stratford residents refused to cooperate. The firecrackers fizzled and the cannons thudded. Nonetheless, the event commenced. So what if the attendees were deluged by days of torrential rains? So what if benches collapsed and hundreds of spectators tumbled to the ground? So what if Garrick was £2,000 in the hole? After all, it's the thought that counts.

Star Quality

The British actor, theatrical manager, and playwright David Garrick (1717–1779) is regarded as one of the greatest actors of the British theater. A sensational triumph in the title role of *Richard III* (1746), Garrick became the greatest actor of his day. As a theatrical manager, Garrick worked to make Shakespeare's plays popular in eighteenth century England, eventually producing 24 of them.

Kiss the Ring

"Our myriad-minded Shakespeare."

—Samuel Taylor Coleridge, *Biographia Literia*, 1817

Around the turn of the century, Shakespeare was no longer merely a great English dramatist; now he was a god-like figure. Think "peasant-who-became-prophet."

Samuel Taylor Coleridge was principally responsible for Shakespeare's deification at this point: "In the successive courses of lectures delivered by me," Coleridge wrote, "since my first attempt at the Royal Institution, it has been, and it still remains, my object to prove that in all points from the most important to the most minute, the judgment of Shakespeare is commensurate with his genius."

For at least a hundred years after Coleridge's pronouncement, it was still common for people to speak Shakespeare's name in the solemn tones usually reserved for religious occasions.

The Man and Myth

By 1875, Shakespeare's reputation had dipped a little. Although still the greatest thing since sliced bread, he was now once again human. By focusing on Shakespeare's life rather than mythology, Sidney Lee's 1898 biography, *Life of William Shakespeare*, furthered this realistic approach.

E. K. Chambers' 1930 two-volume set, *William Shakespeare: A Study of Facts and Problems*, was an impressive collection of every fact, legend, and document on Shakespeare. This provided scholars and students with a nifty reference tool.

Twentieth Century Shakespeare Criticism

> With the single exception of Homer, there is no eminent writer, not even Sir Walter Scott, whom I can despise as entirely as I despise Shakespeare when I measure my mind against his.

—George Bernard Shaw, *Saturday Review*, September 26, 1896

The twentieth century marked the explosive growth of many things, including the suburbs and the American waistline, but these pale beside the stupendous growth of the Shakespeare industry. Many graduate students struggling to find academic jobs and college teachers struggling to attain tenure have tithed their contribution to Bardoltry—and they have been generous indeed. Below is a summary of Shakespeare criticism in the twentieth century.

1. **A. C. Bradley: Plot and Character**

   "The centre of tragedy…may be said with equal truth to lie in action issuing from character, or in character evolving from action."
   —Bradley

   His insightful studies of character and plot have made the British scholar A. C. Bradley one of the most influential Shakespearean critics of the first half of the twentieth century. His analyses were issued in two collections: *Shakespearean Tragedy: Lectures on Hamlet, Othello, King Lear, and Macbeth* (1904) and *Oxford Lectures on Poetry* (1909).

2. **Harley Granville-Barker: Stagecraft**

   Granville-Barker drew on his experience as a playwright, director, and actor in his analysis of the Bard. In *On Dramatic Method* (1931) and his six-volume *Prefaces to Shakespeare* (1927–1974), Granville-Barker dispensed practical advice on performing Shakespeare, including suggestions for costumes and sets—even intermission!

3. **Hardin Craig and Theodore Spencer: Historical Approach**

   In *The Enchanted Glass: The Elizabethan Mind in Literature* (1935), Craig focused on the Elizabethans themselves, scrutinizing their attitudes toward education, religion, politics, science, and so on. Spencer's *Shakespeare and the Nature of Man* (1942) also took a historical approach to the Bard, analyzing Elizabethan attitudes toward the cosmos, nature, and the state.

4. **Ernest Jones: Psychoanalytic Approach**

   Jones, a disciple of Sigmund Freud, applied the tools of Freudian analysis to Shakespeare. The result was *Hamlet and Oedipus* (1949). The impact of Jones' criticism can be seen in many subsequent Shakespearean analyses, and even in the movies. For example, the famous 1948 screen version of *Hamlet*, starring Laurence Olivier, draws from Jones' emphasis on sexuality as motivation.

5. **G. Wilson Knight: Image and Theme**

   Although many Shakespearean critics of the 1930s through the 1950s scrutinized image and theme, Knight's seven books on the topic proved unusually influential. Among the most famous of his works are *The Wheel of Fire: Interpretations of Shakespearean Tragedy* (1930, 1949) and *The Imperial Theme: Further Interpretations of Shakespeare's Tragedies including the Roman Plays* (1931, 1951).

Fire at Will

In 1965 alone, *Shakespeare Quarterly* recorded that nearly 2,000 books and articles had been published on the Bard. You don't want to know the 1990s numbers: Trust me.

6. **Cleanth Brooks: New Criticism**

   New Criticism shunned the historical, biographical, or psychoanalytical approaches. Instead, it advocated studying the literary text as an object and so zeroed in on language. One of the leaders of the band, Brooks set the tone with his book, *The Well Wrought Urn: Studies in the Structure of Poetry* (1947).

7. **Structuralism, Deconstructionism, and Other -Isms**

   Rampant in the 1970s and 1980s, Structuralists and Deconstructionists, such as Patricia Parker and Geoffrey Hartman, obsess over repeated structural patterns, seeing them as shattering the text and its meaning.

8. **New Historicism and Cultural Studies**

   These approaches mark a return to grounding the text in history. Some critics look at the role of the monarch in Shakespeare's works; others look at the influence of power in the plays.

9. **Marxism**

   The Marxist approach to Shakespeare became influential after 1970. In addition to the expected concern with class system and economic determinism, the Marxists argue that a stable self is a myth, so discussion of character has been banished in some circles.

10. **Feminism**

    Since the 1970s, some Shakespeare critics have moved into the hot realm of feminism (sometimes called "Gender Studies"), an approach that has sparked vociferous attack from the non–Gender Study crowd. While feminists such as Coppelia Kahn focus on Shakespeare's female characters, opponents such as Richard Levin fire off salvos in literary journals.

11. **Gay and Lesbian Theory, Queer Theory**

    This approach to Shakespeare has become a significant force in literary studies in the 1990s. Eve Kosofsky Sedgwick's book *Between Men: English Literature and Male Homosocial Desire* (1985) is seen by some as the standard-bearer. The same-sex friendships common in Shakespeare's plays and the frequent cross-dressing have come under scrutiny and reevaluation by these critics.

12. **Summer Reruns: Psychoanalytic Approach**

    Although condemned by feminists as patriarchal, psychoanalytic Shakespeare criticism has made a comeback lately. C. L. Barber and Marjorie Garber are two of the heavy hitters in this field.

This brief summary merely highlights the major movements in Shakespearean criticism: You could build a stairway to heaven with all the books that have been written on the Bard in the last 100 years. Not to worry, though: You don't have to read a zillion works of scholarship and criticism to understand Shakespeare. You don't even have to read one. Read the plays. Then you can turn to a critic if you want further enlightenment.

The Least You Need to Know

➤ In his own day, Shakespeare was considered a successful playwright and actor, not The Great Man of English Letters.

➤ By the early 1700s, Shakespeare had become a force to be reckoned with. By 1765, Shakespeare had unquestionably been enshrined as a classic.

➤ With the Shakespeare Jubilee in 1769, Shakespeare became a full-fledged cultural icon.

➤ Twentieth century Shakespeare criticism takes many different forms, an industry that keeps a lot of scholars off the streets and out of trouble.

Part 2

The Comedies (or "Love Makes the World Go 'Round")

Receive what cheer you may.
The night is long that never finds the day.

—Macbeth

Looking for some cheer? How about a little song, a little dance, a little seltzer down your pants? If so, look no further than Shakespeare's comedies.

But don't forget that during the Renaissance, a play didn't have to be a barrel of laughs to be considered a comedy. Any drama with a generally optimistic viewpoint fit the bill. Throw in a little hanky-panky, and you've got a romantic comedy. Shakespeare cornered the market from 1595–1600 with his three so-called "joyous" comedies: Much Ado About Nothing, As You Like It, *and* Twelfth Night. *Not to worry: The rest of his comedies are pretty funny, too.*

To get the most from these delightful sweets, you have to enter the world Shakespeare has created—no matter how improbable it seems. So what if the solution is contrived? With Shakespearean comedy, the rules of logic are temporarily suspended: girls become boys, servants become their masters, enemies become best friends. Go with the flow and enjoy the elves, fairies, and extraordinary coincidences.

Chapter 8

The Comedy of Errors and Two Gentlemen of Verona

Let me not to the marriage of true minds
Admit impediments; love is not love
Which alters when it alteration finds,
Or bends with the remover to remove.
O, no, it is an ever-fixed mark...

—"Sonnet 116"

Shakespeare's romantic comedies revolve around love: its trials, torments, and transports. And since love and marriage go together like coffee and donuts, you can guess that the characters in Shakespeare's comedies end up in wedded bliss—or at least legally married!

Let's start with two early comedies, *The Comedy of Errors* and *Two Gentlemen of Verona*. First I'll teach you about Shakespeare's humor so you can get all the jokes. Then we'll explore Shakespeare's sources for *The Comedy of Errors*. Next comes a character list and a complete summary of the story.

In the second half of the chapter, we'll look into Shakespeare's sources for *Two Gentlemen of Verona*. This is followed by a character list for *Two Gentlemen of Verona* so you'll know who's who. The chapter concludes with a plot summary of *Two Gentlemen of Verona*. Along the way, there are plenty of quotes from each play to help you get the flavor of these two early comedies.

Laugh-In

> A jest's prosperity lies in the ear
> Of him that hears it, never in the tongue
> Of him that makes it.
>
> —*Love's Labor's Lost*

Shakespeare's humor takes three primary forms: word play, running jokes, and topical allusions. Let's survey each type of humor so you can catch all the yuks—'cause there are quite a few!

Word Play

> How every fool can play upon the word!
>
> —*The Merchant of Venice*

The Elizabethans loved word plays, especially *puns*. A pun may involve:

➤ Using a word or phrase that has two different meanings. For example, in *Romeo and Juliet*, as Mercutio dies, he says, "Ask for me tomorrow, and you shall find me a *grave* man." The pun is on the two meanings of *grave*, "serious" and "dead."

➤ A word or phrase with the same sound (as in *son* and *sun*).

Forsooth!

A **pun** is a play on words.

According to one scholar, there are more than a hundred puns in *Macbeth* alone—and that's a tragedy! Imagine how many puns the comedies contain.

Running Jokes

> It would be argument for a week, laughter for a month, and a good jest forever.
>
> —*Henry IV, Part I*

Every generation has its series of running gags. Mothers-in-law are a perennial favorite, right up there with lawyers. The Elizabethans were no different. Their most popular running gag concerned cuckolds, men married to unfaithful wives. Since cuckolds were associated with horns, even an offhand reference to cheating, horns, or related subjects sparked gales of laughter. Here's an example from Shakespeare's *Love's Labor's Lost*:

Sweets to the Sweet

Notice the pun on "deer" and "dear" in this passage. Shakespeare often combined two or more forms of humor to get an even bigger laugh.

Boyet:	My lady goes to kill horns, but, if thou marry, Hang me by the neck if that year miscarry. Finely put on!
Rosaline:	Well then, I am the shooter.
Boyet:	And who is your deer?
Rosaline:	If we choose by the horns, yourself...

Topical Allusions

Ever feel like you're the only one not getting the joke? It can happen anywhere, but it's a special problem with Shakespeare when the joke is based on current events—seventeenth century current events, that is.

Some of the jokes Shakespeare uses depend on references to celebrities long forgotten, but there are also jokes that depend on a word's various meanings. Since the meanings have changed over 400 years, the joke can be rather hard to get. Here's an example:

> Get thee away, and take
> Thy beagles with thee.
>
> —*Timon of Athens*

Now, this jab may be directed at anyone who has one pooch too many, and that's probably the way we would take it today. But during the seventeenth century, "beagles" also to referred to women of easy virtue. We need to know that meaning to get the full sly humor of the jab.

Now that you know something about Shakespeare's humor, you're ready to appreciate his comedies. So let the curtain rise on Shakespeare's first comedy, *The Comedy of Errors*.

The Comedy of Errors

As with most of Shakespeare's comedies, *The Comedy of Errors* begins in sorrow and ends in joy. There's a grand finale in which all the characters are paired off. At the same time, however, Shakespeare manages to introduce a deeper note into the comedy because of the near tragedy of Egeon (more on that later).

To get the joke upon which the play is based, you have to accept the initial assumption that twins can be mistaken for one another by everyone in the play. From there, it's just a hop, skip, and jump to grant the second assumption, that these twins should have equally identical servants. Then all the incidents follow with perfect—although absurd—logic.

Fire at Will

There's a long-standing debate over whether *The Comedy of Errors* is a farce or a true comedy. **Farce** is much broader than a comedy, relying on a single ridiculous situation that becomes faster and more confusing as the play progresses until the tangle is unraveled in the last scene. **Comedy**, in contrast, relies more on character development or clever language. Why not read the play and then decide the issue for yourself?

Go to the Source

Shakespeare based *The Comedy of Errors* on three sources.

1. The story of twins who can't be told apart comes from *The Menaechmi* (*The Two Men Called Menaechmus*) by the Roman playwright Plautus. Shakespeare, however, created a subplot and added to the confusion by giving the twins equally indistinguishable servants.

Star Quality

Titus Maccius Plautus (254?–184 B.C.), a Roman comic dramatist, was enormously popular in his day. He is supposed to have written more than 100 comedies, but only 20 have survived. His plays were usually based on love affairs, with complications arising from deception or mistaken identity. His plays ranged from mythological parody to romance, from burlesque to farce.

2. In addition, Shakespeare used another play, the *Amphitruo*, by Plautus, as a source for the situation of a husband locked out of his own house while his wife entertains another man.

3. The frame narrative of the Egeon–Emilia plot comes from a third possible source, *Appolonius of Tyre*. Shakespeare lessened the part of the Courtesan in his play and gave Adriana, the wife of Antipholus of Ephesus, a sister, Luciana, possibly to add further doubling. This change also adds romantic interest to the character of Antipholus of Syracuse. The character of Adriana, the shrew, is also contrasted with that of Emilia, the Abbess, who delivers a speech on wifely behavior.

They Talk Alike, They Walk Alike—You Could Lose Your Mind

The action of *The Comedy of Errors* is based largely upon one dramatic device, mistaken identity. The two sets of twins are constantly confused.

The final reconciliation and recognition is accomplished by means of coincidence and also confrontation. Both of the twins are wearing jewels, which help to establish their identities. The appearance of the Abbess and her identification as the long-lost wife of Egeon is pure coincidence, while the happy ending with the reprieve of Egeon is a conventional requirement for such a farce.

Who's Who in *The Comedy of Errors*

Can't tell the players without a scorecard? Here's the scorecard:

➤ Solinus, *Duke of Ephesus*

➤ Egeon, *merchant of Syracuse*

➤ Antipholus of Ephesus, *twin brother of Antipholus of Syracuse*

➤ Antipholus of Syracuse, *twin brother of Antipholus of Ephesus*

➤ Dromio of Ephesus, *twin brother of Dromio of Syracuse*

➤ Dromio of Syracuse, *twin brother of Dromio of Ephesus*

➤ Balthazar, *a merchant*

➤ Angelo, *a goldsmith*

➤ First merchant of Ephesus, *friend of Antipholus of Syracuse*

➤ Second merchant of Ephesus, *to whom Angelo is a debtor*

➤ Doctor Pinch, *a conjuring schoolmaster*

➤ Emilia, *wife to Egeon, an abbess at Ephesus*

➤ Adriana, *wife to Antipholus of Ephesus*

➤ Luciana, *her sister*

Forsooth!

An **abbess** is a woman who runs an abby—the head nun.

➤ Luce, *servant to Adriana (also known as "Nell")*

➤ Courtesan

➤ Jailer, Headman, Messenger, Officers, and other Attendants

Sweets to the Sweet

The Comedy of Errors is one of the few Shakespearean plays that deals almost entirely with middle–class characters.

Sweets to the Sweet

Because they exist to further the story, the minor characters are not developed. That's because *The Comedy of Errors* is a play of events, not of character development.

On the whole, *The Comedy of Errors* is peopled with the stock characters of classic comedy. We have the old man (Egeon), the witty slaves (the two Dromios), and the slightly immoral men-about-town (the two Antipholi). Today, we can recognize the slave and his master in a host of situations, among them the comedy acts of Laurel and Hardy, Abott and Costello, and the myriad of action "buddy" movies.

The female characters, however, are slightly more fleshed out. Of them, Adriana is the only one who shows any character development in the course of the play. She is a shrew, yet we have sympathy for her because she is treated badly. She wants equality with men and objects to the strictures that society places upon wives. By the end of the play, her shrewish attitude and sharp tongue are both softened by her experience so that she seems altogether a different person. She has learned some of the rules of matrimonial behavior in the seventeenth century.

Both the Abbess and Luciana exceed the usual one-dimensional characters in a comedy. The Abbess, Emilia, exists mainly to deliver a speech in favor of matrimonial fidelity and behavior. She urges submission on Adriana. When her own identity is revealed, she also takes on aspects of the stereotypical mother-in-law.

Who's on First? What's on Second?

So what's *The Comedy of Errors* all about? Here's a summary:

Egeon, a merchant from Syracuse, has been arrested in Ephesus and condemned to death because he cannot pay the fine levied on all Syracuse residents found in Ephesus. About 20 years before, Egeon's wife, Emilia, had given birth in Epidamnum to twin sons. At the same time, a poor woman also gave birth to twin sons, whom Egeon bought to be servants to his own sons. When Egeon's business in Epidamnum was done, he and his wife sailed for Syracuse, but their ship was wrecked and they were separated. Emilia, with one of her own sons and one of the poor boys, was picked up by a different ship from the one Egeon took. Unable to find the rest of the party, Egeon reared the remaining twin and his servant, giving them the names of their respective brothers.

Five years earlier, when he was 18 years old, Egeon's son set off to search for his brother. Egeon has received no word of his son, so he has set out to look for him. Touched, the Duke gives Egeon an extra day to raise the money for his fine.

Meanwhile, Antipholus of Syracuse and his servant Dromio have arrived in Ephesus. To avoid the fine, Antipholus of Syracuse claimed to be from Epidamnum and sends Dromio of Syracuse away on an errand. Then Dromio of Ephesus arrives and tells Antipholus of Syracuse to come home to dinner. Antipholus of Syracuse is angered and beats Dromio of Ephesus, thinking that he is chastising his own servant.

Adriana, the wife of Antipholus of Ephesus, is angry that her husband has not yet arrived for dinner. Dromio of Ephesus arrives with the message that his master must be mad.

Antipholus of Syracuse meets his servant again and complains about his brother. Antipholus of Ephesus and his Dromio are locked out while the servant, Dromio of Syracuse, claims they are already dining inside.

Antipholus of Ephesus is so furious that he decides to give a courtesan the gold chain he had promised to his wife. Luciana enters with Antipholus of Syracuse and asks him to be kind to her sister Adriana. Antipholus of Syracuse responds that he is interested in Luciana herself, much to that young lady's horror, because she thinks that her own brother-in-law is making love to her. The goldsmith Angelo gives Antipholus of Syracuse a gold chain. Antipholus tries to pay him, but Angelo says that the matter can wait. The Syracusan sends Dromio to fetch a ship so they can leave Ephesus.

Pressed for payment of a debt, Angelo promises to get the money from Antipholus of Ephesus to whom, he thinks, he gave the gold chain. At this moment, Antipholus of Ephesus enters with his Dromio, whom he sends to fetch a rope to use to beat Adriana. Much to Angelo's rage, Antipholus of Ephesus disclaims all knowledge of the chain; therefore, Angelo has him arrested.

Will Power

The Comedy of Errors contains an unexpectedly long introduction or frame narrative in which Egeon recounts the events that preceded the opening of the play. The first scene, therefore, serves as dramatic exposition. At the same time, the sad tale of the old man gives depth to the comedy. It also indicates qualities that Shakespeare later added to comedy—sympathy and humanity.

Will Power

Ephesus is one of the 12 cities of Iona (an ancient Greek district on the western coast of Asia Minor), located near modern Turkey. A port city, Ephesus was a major departure point for trade routes into Asia Minor. Known in ancient times for its fabulous shrines, especially a famous temple (one of the Seven Wonders of the Ancient World), the city was also an important center of Christianity. Excavations at Ephesus, begun in 1863, have uncovered astonishing temples, public buildings, and sculpture.

91

Star Quality

Here are three well-known quotes from *The Comedy of Errors*: "Small cheer and great welcome makes a merry feast," "Let's go hand in hand, not one before another," and "Home-keeping youth have ever homely wits."

Fire at Will

In Shakespeare's day, considerable debate had taken place in England concerning the right of a husband to beat his wife. Legally, the practice was permitted, but matrimonial experts advised against it because such corporal punishment could cause enmity between husband and wife. Now, *that's* a surprise.

Dromio of Syracuse discusses the ship he has obtained for his master. Enraged, Antipholus of Ephesus sends this Dromio to Adriana to get money as payment for the debt he is supposed to have contracted. Adriana sends the required money by Dromio of Syracuse. On the way back, Dromio of Syracuse meets his master and hands him the money he has received from Adriana. While Antipholus of Syracuse is recovering from this shock, the courtesan arrives and demands the ring she had given him at dinner. When he's mystified, the courtesan assumes he's mad and goes to inform Adriana.

By now, Antipholus of Ephesus is under arrest. The scene reaches its high point of confusion when Adriana, Luciana, the courtesan, and a doctor arrive to take Antipholus away as a madman. Instead, Antipholus and Dromio of Ephesus are put under house arrest. Antipholus and Dromio of Syracuse arrive and are mistaken for their "mad" brothers. The two decide to leave Ephesus as quickly as possible.

Star Quality

Stuck for cocktail chatter? Here are two famous quotes from *The Comedy of Errors*: "The pleasing punishment that women bear" and "Every why hath a wherefore."

The final act begins with the merchant and Angelo discussing that Antipholus of Ephesus has not yet paid his debt; the Syracusan pair enter and Angelo asks for his money. Antipholus's honesty is questioned and he draws his sword to satisfy his honor. Adriana, Luciana, and the courtesan arrive and the Syracusans take refuge in a nearby convent. Emilia, the Abbess, comes out to see what the altercation is about and Adriana tells her that she is looking for her husband, who has gone mad. The Abbess delivers a sermon on wifely conduct and refuses to give Antipholus up to Adriana.

The Duke passes on his way to observe Egeon's execution. Antipholus and Dromio of Ephesus enter and Antipholus tells his side of the story. The Duke is mystified, but Egeon thinks he has found his Syracusan son. The two pairs of twins confront each other and the confusion is cleared up. The Abbess reveals herself as Egeon's long-lost wife, Emilia. Overwhelmed by these revelations, the Duke pardons Egeon. Rejoicing is universal, and Antipholus of Syracuse hints at marriage to Luciana. Everyone leaves the stage for a feast, at which they will discuss the events of the past 23 years.

Two Gentlemen of Verona

This early play has many of the elements that Shakespeare would use in his later comedies, including the two contrasting pairs of lovers, the girl disguised as a page, the rope ladder, and clowns.

Shakespeare likely drew the plot outlines from three sources:

➤ The pastoral romance *Diana Enamorada.* The courtship of Felismena and Don Felix in *Diana Enamorada* is almost identical to the courtship of Julia and Proteus in *Two Gentlemen of Verona.*

➤ In addition, the play *Felix and Philiomena* (now lost but not forgotten) may have influenced Shakespeare as well.

➤ The conflict between friendship and love may also be related to the novel *Euphues,* by the Elizabethan writer John Lyly.

Will Power

The Comedy of Errors is strikingly like Shakespeare's last plays—*Pericles, Cymbeline, The Winter's Tale,* and *The Tempest.* Both the early and late plays deal with reunions of lost children and parents, husbands and wives, and adventures and wanderings. Shakespeare's odyssey through the human soul in tragedy and comedy brought him back to his beginnings with a sharper sense of yearning, poignancy, and the feeling of loss.

Fire at Will

Shakespeare's grasp of Italian geography is shaky: Verona, Padua, Mantua, and Milan are jumbled together, and people seem to take a ship to go from Verona to Milan. Big deal. So he never earned the Boy Scout Orienteering merit badge; wanna make something of it?

Who's Who in *Two Gentlemen of Verona*

You know I take good care of you, bunky. So here's a list of the characters in *Two Gentlemen of Verona*; it will help you keep them untangled.

➤ Duke of Milan, *Silvia's father*

➤ Valentine, *one of the two Gentlemen of Verona*

➤ Proteus, *the other Gentleman of Verona*

➤ Antonio, *Proteus' father*

➤ Thurio, *Valentine's foolish rival*

➤ Eglamour, *agent for Silvia in her escape*

➤ Host, *where Julia lodges*

➤ Outlaws, *with Valentine*

➤ Speed, *Valentine's page*

➤ Launce, *Proteus' clownish servant*

➤ Panthino, *Antonio's servant*

➤ Julia, *Proteus' beloved*

➤ Silvia, *Valentine's beloved*

➤ Lucetta, *Julia's waiting-woman*

➤ Assorted attendants and musicians

Will Power

It was a common sixteenth century custom, both in England and in Italy, to send young people to a noble's court to learn good manners and seek suitable marriages. This custom of service to a noble was an important part of education. It also got your own hormonally charged adolescents out of *your* house. (Besides, we all know that kids are better behaved in someone else's house.)

The Plot Thickens

When the play opens, Valentine leaves his friend Proteus in Verona to go to Milan to continue his education at the Duke's court. Proteus, smitten by the lovely Julia, decides to stay home. After Valentine's departure, Proteus' father Antonio decides to send his son to Milan. After bidding Julia a tender farewell and exchanging rings with her, Valentine leaves.

In Milan, Proteus finds that Valentine has fallen in love with Silvia. However, the instant Proteus lays eyes on Silvia, he also falls madly in love with her and plots to gain her for himself.

Valentine and Silvia decide to elope. Proteus thwarts his friend by telling the Duke of their plans. Banished, Valentine flees to the forest where he meets a band of outlaws who elect him their leader.

Valentine and Proteus run through their paces at Stratford-upon-Avon.

Meanwhile, Proteus tries unsuccessfully to win Silvia for himself. His plan? He pretends to be helping Sir Thurio, the foolish knight who is Valentine's rival. Julia disguises herself as a page to be with her beloved—who no longer cares for her. Proteus takes Julia into his service and sends her to woo Silvia for him. Heartbroken, Julia does as she is told, only to be amazed at Silvia's loyalty. When Silvia hears that the Duke is going to force her to marry Thurio, she arranges to escape to the forest with Sir Eglamour, a knight sworn to love's service.

Proteus, Thurio, Julia, and the Duke end up in the forest. When Proteus gets Silvia in his power, he attempts to force the unwilling maiden to yield to his will. Valentine chides his disloyal friend, who immediately repents. As a sign of forgiveness, Valentine offers Silvia to Proteus. Julia faints and is identified by her ring. Thurio gives up all claims to Silvia and the Duke consents to Valentine and Silvia's marriage. Valentine suggests a double wedding and asks the Duke's pardon for the outlaw band.

The wrongs are righted, love and friendship are restored, and everyone lives happily ever after.

Sweets to the Sweet

A good sixteenth century father always thought about his daughter's financial security. The concept of love before marriage was distrusted because love might cool, especially if the couple were poor.

Star Quality

Two Gentlemen of Verona has also contributed its share of famous sayings. Here are two: "Is she not passing fair?" and "O heaven! were man / But constant, he were perfect."

The Least You Need to Know

➤ Shakespeare's humor takes three main forms: word play, running jokes, and topical allusions.

➤ Word play was extremely popular in Elizabethan theater—in both drama and comedy.

➤ *The Comedy of Errors* revolves around mistaken identity: Two sets of twins are constantly confused.

➤ *Two Gentlemen of Verona* concerns love and marriage.

Chapter 9

The Taming of the Shrew and Love's Labor's Lost

In This Chapter

➤ Elizabethan marriage customs

➤ Who's who in *The Taming of the Shrew*

➤ The plot of *The Taming of the Shrew*

➤ Who's who in *Love's Labor's Lost*

➤ The plot of *Love's Labor's Lost*

God looks over the millions of people and says, "Welcome to Heaven. I want the women to go with Saint Peter, and the men to form two lines. Make one line of the men that dominated their women on earth, and the other of men who were dominated by their women."

There's much movement and eventually the women are gone and there are two lines. The line of the men who were dominated is 100 miles long. The line of men who dominated women has only one man.

God says, "You men should be ashamed of yourselves. I created you in my image, and you were all dominated by your mates. Look at the man who stood up and made me proud. Learn from him!"

He turns to the man and says, "Tell them, my son. How did you manage to be the only one on that line?"

The man says, "I don't know; my wife told me to stand here."

This attitude definitely wouldn't fly in Shakespeare's day! Nonetheless, Shakespeare would get the basics.

The battle of the sexes was fought just as vigorously in the seventeenth century as it is being fought today. And nobody does it better than Shakespeare. So sit back and see how one uh, *loving*, couple resolve their different attitudes toward the "proper" role of men and women in *The Taming of the Shrew*. Then get a different take on the subject in *Love's Labor's Lost*. Since both plays revolve around love and marriage, let's start with a look at the state of holy matrimony in the seventeenth century.

Fire at Will

Although *The Taming of the Shrew* is set in Italy, Shakespeare was using the attitudes and customs of his own native England rather than those of Italy.

Sweets to the Sweet

Although secret marriages without church ceremonies were legal, getting married according to Hoyle helped ensure that the right of primogeniture (inheritance) would be strictly observed.

I Do, I Do

In Shakespeare's day, marriage fell under the jurisdiction of the Church of England. As a result, church law and civil law were one and the same. Church law governed the method of engagement and the wedding ceremony. *The Taming of the Shrew* shows a legal engagement to marry. Kate and Petruchio join hands before Baptista, Kate's father. The bridegroom expresses his wish to be married on the following Sunday, the father gives his consent, and two buddies act as witnesses. This is a perfectly legal engagement in seventeenth century England. Kate doesn't actually agree to the deal, but silence was taken as consent. It was almost impossible to break an engagement, except in certain cases of adultery before the actual church ceremony.

The actual wedding ceremony follows the ritual of the Church of England as laid down in the Book of Common Prayer. All marriages were supposed to take place in church, usually the bride's parish church. The church ceremony began with the priest asking if there was any known impediment to the match. The couple then exchanged vows and rings, and the groom could kiss his bride. To close the ceremony, the couple drank a glass of wine in which pieces of cake had been soaked. Then came a feast marked by bawdy merrymaking at the newlyweds' expense.

Like a Virgin

Today we have Dear Abby and Miss Manners to give us advice; the Elizabethans had marriage manuals. According to these guidebooks, a lady seeking to enter the state of wedded bliss must be:

➤ Virtuous
➤ Silent
➤ Obedient to her parents
➤ Modest

A lady never showed that she wanted to get married since that indicated willfulness—as well as immodesty in wishing to lose her virginity. Also, she was not to offer an opinion in the choice of a husband, but instead was to entrust the choice to her parents, with the notion that they knew much better than she what was good for her.

A young man, however, was to look carefully at his proposed bride, picking her for compatibility and domestic virtues, as well as for her equality with him in age, rank, and wealth. A rich heiress was a great prize; a wealthy widow the same as a winning lottery ticket. When it was all said and done, marriages often took place for money, money, and more money. In *The Taming of the Shrew*, we see this in Baptista, who first considers the economic advantages of a match.

Fire at Will

Although church law insisted on the free consent of the married, there were many instances of forced marriage. The ideal was a marriage of mutual respect; love would come later. But reality rarely collides with the ideal, and many young women were entrapped into unwanted marriages by the political and economic ambitions of their parents.

The Stepford Wives

After marriage, the wife should be just as obedient to her husband as she had been to her parents. She should mirror or sympathize with his every mood and carry out his wishes. Her duties would be primarily domestic, so she wouldn't have to worry her pretty little head about her husband's business. In turn, hubby would have complete control over his wife's money and property, and also over her person. Some writers even contended that he had the right to beat her if she proved recalcitrant.

But you can't keep 'em down on the farm once they've seen gay Paree. Some Elizabethan women were being educated and feeling their freedom. The so-called "new woman" of the Renaissance considered herself almost the equal of men and refused to be treated as the household chattel that advocates of male superiority wished her to be. We see this in the beginning of *The Taming of the Shrew* in Kate and sister Bianca. Their opposition of character represents the conflict of attitudes found in sixteenth century England.

Star Quality

Here are two famous lines that trace their birth to Shakespeare's *The Taming of the Shrew:* "I'll not budge an inch" and "There's small choice in rotten apples."

Meet the Gang

Here's a rundown of the characters and their roles:

➤ Lord, *in the Induction*

➤ Christopher Sly, *a tinker in the Induction*

➤ Hostess, Page, Players, Huntsmen, and servants, *in the Induction*

➤ Baptista, *a rich gentleman of Padua*

➤ Vincentio, *an old gentleman of Pisa*

➤ Lucentio, *Vincentio's son, in love with Bianca*

➤ Petruchio, *a gentleman of Verona, Katherina's suitor*

➤ Gremio, *Bianca's suitor*

➤ Hortensio, *Bianca's suitor*

➤ Tranio, *Lucentio's servant*

➤ Biondello, *Lucentio's servant*

➤ Grumio, *Petruchio's servant*

➤ Curtis, *Petruchio's servant*

➤ Pedant, *Petruchio's servant*

➤ Katherina, *the shrew, Baptista's daughter*

➤ Bianca, *Baptista's daughter*

➤ Widow, *Baptista's daughter*

➤ Tailor, Haberdasher, and servants

Will Power

It is generally agreed that Shakespeare drew the plot of *The Taming of* the *Shrew* from *The Taming of* a *Shrew*, published anonymously in 1594. *A Shrew* is a more formally constructed play than *The Shrew*, particularly concerning the Induction. Shakespeare drastically altered the part of Christopher Sly, and he disappears from the play after the first act.

Forsooth!

Shrew is the common name applied to small mammals from the family *Soricidae*. Somewhat mouse-like in appearance, shrews have a long, pointed snout and soft, velvety fur. In Shakespeare's day, it was believed that shrews had the power to poison cattle and young children by running over them. A shrew was the derogatory term applied to an assertive woman. Kate was as "assertive" as we get!

Plot a Lot

A lord enters with his hunting party and finds a tinker named Christopher Sly lying in a drunken stupor. To amuse his friends, the Lord dresses Sly in fine clothes and treats him as if he were a lord to see if the tinker will forget his true identity. A troop of strolling players is hired to give a show. The lord disguises a page as a woman to pretend that he is Sly's wife.

Despite the fine clothing, Sly reveals his humble roots. Sly and the page sit down to watch the play—*The Taming of the Shrew*. After these two scenes Sly has one more speech, and then disappears from the play.

Baptista, a rich gentleman from Padua, has two daughters. The elder, Katherine, is beautiful but a shrew. The younger, Bianca, is her opposite—submissive, obedient, and gentle. As a result, she is being wooed by Hortensio, a young man, and Gremio, a wealthy but foolish old man. Katherine has no suitors, but Baptista will not let Bianca marry first, and therefore wants to remove Bianca from society until Kate marries. Lucentio, a young student from Pisa, sees Bianca and falls in love at first sight. He decides that he must marry her.

The two original suitors decide to join forces temporarily to find a husband for Kate. Meanwhile, Lucentio decides to pass himself off as a literature teacher so Baptista will hire him to teach Bianca.

Will Power

Elizabethans believed that if a younger sister married before the elder, the older girl must dance barefoot at her sister's wedding in order to avoid spinsterhood. Leading apes in hell was generally considered the eternal fate of an old maid.

The shrew Katherina, as played by Elizabeth Taylor in the 1967 film version of The Taming of the Shrew.

Petruchio, Hortensio's friend, arrives in Padua to find a wealthy wife. Hortensio suggests Kate, warning his friend that she's rich but a shrew. Petruchio claims that he doesn't care at all about her temper: Money talks and nobody walks.

Star Quality

The Taming of the Shrew has been remade more often than Michael Jackson's face. In the early eighteenth century, the play became a farce, *The Cobbler of Preston*. In 1756, David Garrick created a reworking he called *Catherine and Petruchio*. In 1828, it became an opera; in 1953, a smash musical, *Kiss Me Kate*, with a book by Sam and Bella Spewack and music and lyrics by Cole Porter. My favorite is the 1967 movie version starring Richard Burton as Petruchio and Elizabeth Taylor as Kate. It's Dick and Liz making love in period costumes.

Hortensio asks Petruchio to introduce him to Baptista as a music teacher for Bianca, while Lucentio has persuaded Gremio to present him to Baptista as a literature tutor. Tranio, disguised as Lucentio, throws his hat into the ring as well.

Petruchio asks for Kate's hand flat out. Baptista offers a generous dowry, Petruchio makes his offer, and the two men agree to draw up documents. Baptista suggests that Petruchio gain Kate's consent. Baptista warns Petruchio that it won't be smooth sailing. He's right.

Fire at Will

According to Elizabethan medicine, the only way to regulate the balance of fluids was through the diet. Consequently, an angry person should avoid all foods that might cause an increase of anger, such as red meat, burnt meat, and highly seasoned foods. Instead, angry people should eat cooling foods, such as white meats, fish, poultry, and cold meats. Could a new diet fad be coming soon?

Kate enters, and Petruchio begins by praising her beauty, mildness, and virtues. Kate replies punningly and rudely. Petruchio tops her remarks and continues to praise her for all the advantages of personality that she is famous for lacking. Nothing seems to put him out of temper, and the witty remarks fly fast, furious, and bawdily. Kate is very confused and for once in her life seems unable to reply.

Petruchio and Kate are formally betrothed, and Petruchio leaves to make arrangements for their reception at his country house. He promises to return in time for the ceremony on Sunday.

Tranio outbids Gremio and so wins Bianca. Baptista shrewdly insists that "Lucentio's" father ratify the financial agreement that his son has just made. Tranio seeks a father. Bianca's other suitors also make their bids.

Katherine's wedding day arrives, but there is no sign of the bridegroom. Convinced that she's going to be left at the altar, Kate bursts into tears. In his quest to humble Kate and show that he's the boss, Petruchio arrives dressed in rags on a broken-down old nag. Horrified, Baptista suggests that Petruchio change his clothes, but Petruchio refuses. The wedding is a shambles; Petruchio swears, knocks down the parson, kisses Kate with "a clamorous smack," and throws cake at the sexton.

Kate is speechless by his behavior. After the ceremony, Petruchio announces that he and Kate must leave immediately for his country house. Kate refuses, but Petruchio asserts his authority, and Kate has no choice. She leaves without attending her own wedding feast.

And so the taming begins. Despite his cruelty, Petruchio is unfailingly charming, which Kate finds extremely frustrating. Every one of his actions is performed under the name of perfect love for her. She must not eat or drink because the food is not well prepared. She must not sleep because the bed is not properly made. How can Katherine be angry at a husband who seems to only have her welfare at heart?

Back in Padua, Lucentio's suit to Bianca is progressing well. Tranio has managed to find an elderly pedant to act as Vincentio. The agreement is ratified, and Baptista agrees to the marriage of Bianca to Lucentio (Tranio). It's clear that Bianca is not as docile as she had seemed; in fact, she's almost as independent as Kate. Hortensio decides to marry a wealthy widow. The real Lucentio and Bianca marry in secret.

In the last act, all the disguised persons confront each other and Tranio is revealed as posing as Lucentio. The real Lucentio arrives with his bride Bianca. Everyone celebrates at a great feast. Subplots involving disguises and the resulting misunderstandings help reveal Shakespeare's theme—and amuse his audience.

Will Power

The Taming of the Shrew is Shakespeare's second treatment of the comic aspects of marriage to a shrewish wife, the first being *The Comedy of Errors*. *The Taming of the Shrew*, however, hints at what Shakespeare was later to do in drawing the portraits of his superb witty women of the three great comedies: Beatrice in *Much Ado About Nothing*, Rosalind in *As You Like It*, and Viola in *Twelfth Night*.

Women Speak in Estrogen and Men Listen in Testosterone

At the end of the play, Kate lectures the other wives on their duties. We know that the roles of men and women *have* changed a great deal since the seventeenth century. As a result, *The Taming of the Shrew* presents a sticky problem to twentieth century audiences. What do we make of Kate's speech of submission?

Such duty as the subject owes the prince,
Even such a woman oweth to her husband.
And when she is forward, peevish, sullen, sour,
And not obedient to his honest will,
What is she but a foul contending rebel
And graceless traitor to her loving lord?

Does this speech show that Shakespeare lived in a world where a man, no matter how loving, is still a woman's lord and master? That's how it was played in the 1980 BBC (British Broadcasting System) production. Former Monty Python cast member John Cleese played Petruchio without the slightest hint of irony.

On the other hand, maybe this speech is sly and subversive, an ironic look at female power? In the 1990 performance of *The Taming of the Shrew* at the New York Shakespeare Festival, Kate, as played by Tracey Ullman, ended her speech by "accidentally" kicking Petruchio (actor Morgan Freeman), sending him sprawling. There was no doubt where the director stood on the issue of female submission in that version.

Or perhaps the shrew is tamed, yet she is not fully crushed and her spirit remains intact. In this reading, Kate and Petruchio are equal in wit and intellect, and therefore their happiness seems assured.

The choice is yours, dear reader. It depends all on how you read the words. You can take them at face value or see them as ironic. Let's take another look at the battle of the sexes in *Love's Labor's Lost*.

Will Power

Have you ever heard this line from Shakespeare's *The Taming of the Shrew*: "And thereby hangs a tale"? How about this one: "Who wooed in haste, and means to wed at leisure"?

Looking for Love in All the Right Places

The Song

[*Spring.*] When daisies pied, and violets blue,
    And lady-smockes all silver-white,
And cuckoo-buds of yellow hue
    Do paint the meadows with delight,
The cuckoo then on every tree
Mocks married men; for thus sings he,
        "Cuckoo;
Cuckoo, cuckoo"—O word of fear,
Unpleasing for married ear!...

Winter. When icicles hang by the wall,
    And Dick the shepherd blows his nail,

And Tom bears logs into the hall,
 And milk comes frozen in pail;
When blood is nipp'd, and ways be [foul],
Then nightly sings the staring owl,
 "Tu-whit, to-who!"—
A merry note,
While greasy Joan doth keel the pot. …

So ends *Love's Labor's Lost*, the most "Elizabethan" of all Shakespeare's plays in its use of language. It's also the most unusual of all his comedies because sorrow intrudes in the end. The couples don't pair off in wedded bliss. Nonetheless, the conclusion parallels the beginning: The world of sorrow and pain intrudes on the world of love.

Fire at Will

The play is filled with topical allusions. As a result, it's more dated than any other Shakespearean play. It's harder to get the jokes, so don't kick yourself too hard if you find this one tough sledding.

Who's Who in *Love's Labor's Lost*

The play is divided into two sections: the main plot, which deals with the difficulty of the country characters, and the subplot, which deals with the affair of Don Armado and Jacquenetta.

Keep this in mind as you skim the character list. It will help you see how each character figures in the action.

➤ Ferdinand, *King of Navarre*
➤ Biron, *lord attending the King*
➤ Longaville, *lord attending the King*
➤ Dumain, *lord attending the King*
➤ Boyet, *lord attending the Princess of France*
➤ Marcade, *lord attending the Princess of France*
➤ Don Adriano de Armado, *a fantastical Spaniard*
➤ Sir Nathaniel, *a curate*
➤ Holofernes, *a schoolmaster*
➤ Dull, *a constable*
➤ Costard, *a clown*
➤ Moth, *Armado's page*
➤ A Forester
➤ The Princess of France
➤ Rosaline, *lady attending the Princess*

Sweets to the Sweet

Here are two useful and well-known phrases from *Love's Labor's Lost*: "They have been at a great feast of languages, and stolen the scraps" and "Let me take you a button-hole lower."

➤ Maria, *lady attending the Princess*

➤ Katherine, *lady attending the Princess*

➤ Jaquenetta, *a country wench*

A Plot of Promises

When the play opens, Ferdinand, King of Navarre, and his friends Longaville, Dumain, and Biron have decided to spend three years without pleasure to pursue fame and glory. The four young men prepare to sign an oath to deny the flesh in service to the mind.

Will Power

We all want to make a big splash, but establishing a reputation that would live after one's death was a real obsession in the Renaissance. The Lords in *Love's Labor's Lost* are trying to follow the Stoic philosophy, which held that a wise man would set aside passion to concentrate on reason. To achieve their aims, the Stoics ignored both pleasure and pain.

Fire at Will

The Elizabethan ideal of beauty was based on Queen Elizabeth's appearance. As a result, women with light golden hair, gray or blue eyes, and a high, noble forehead were hot. Therefore, dark-haired, dark-eyed Rosaline wouldn't have made the cut, as dark indicated peasants or foreigners who spent time outdoors.

Biron has second thoughts, however. He protests the strictness of the oath and asks what purpose the studying will serve. Then he reminds the King that he can't swear off the company of women since the Princess of France and her ladies are on their way to his estate on a diplomatic mission from the French king. The King is willing to dispense with the oath, but Biron insists on signing.

The Constable, Anthony Dull, drags in a peasant named Costard who has been caught with the dairy maid, Jaquenetta. Dull has a letter setting out the charges against Costard from Don Adriano de Armado, a wild Spaniard. The King sends Costard to Armado.

The Princess of France arrives with her bevy of beautiful ladies: dark-haired, dark-eyed Rosaline; red-gold-haired Katherine; and Maria. Rosaline falls in love with Biron, Katherine falls in love with Dumain, and Maria falls in love with Longaville. The King arrives, and the Princess begins to carry out her diplomatic mission, the terms of a debt the King of France owes Navarre. The couples pair off.

Armado gives Costard a love letter to deliver to Jaquenetta, for Armado has fallen hopelessly in love with the illiterate wench. Biron gives Costard a letter to deliver to his beloved Rosaline.

The Princess and her attendants are hunting in the park when Costard arrives with the letter for Rosaline. Costard has switched the letters; as a result, Rosaline is treated to the overblown rhetoric of Armado while Biron's letter has gone to Jaquenetta. Since Jaquenetta can't read, she takes the letter to Holofernes and his friend Sir Nathaniel to read to her. The men discover that the letters have been switched and send the dairymaid to report who's been playing footsie with whom.

Jonathan Kent as Ferdinand, the King of Navarre, and Maureen Lipman as the Princess in the BBC's 1984 production of Love's Labor's Lost.

Meanwhile, Biron wanders through the woods moaning about his love:

> And to begin: wench—so God help me, Law!—
> My love to thee is sound, *sans* crack or flaw.

He hides himself when he sees the King approach and read a love poem to the Princess. After the King finishes and hides, Longaville enters and sings Maria's praises. You guessed it: Then Longaville hides and Dumain reads a poem to his beloved Katharine. The three men emerge from hiding and admit their love for the ladies.

Star Quality

The 1984 BBC production of *Love's Labor's Lost* is an absolute romp. Set in the eighteenth century, this production is gorgeous, as well as funny.

107

Disguised as Muscovites, the men agree to pursue their beloved. (There's no reason for the disguise; could there ever be?) The ladies get wind of the plan and disguise themselves so each man ends up pitching woo to the wrong woman. Upset, the men shed their disguises and the women joke about the way the "Muscovites" had tried to charm them. The men realize they have been duped.

Holofernes, Sir Nathaniel, Moth, Dull, and Costard perform a pageant, which Boyet and Biron mock. Marcade, a French lord, brings word that the King of France, the Princess's father, has died.

The Princess announces that she will return home at once. Realizing that it's now or never, the young men promptly declare their love to their ladies. The Princess asks the King to do a year of penance in a hermitage so he can be sure of his love. Maria and Katharine follow suit, but Rosaline tells Biron to spend a year in the hospital cheering up the patients. So the play ends with the promise of marriage, but no actual nuptials:

> Our wooing doth not end like an old play:
> Jack hath not Jill. These ladies' courtesy
> Might well have made our sport comedy.

The Least You Need to Know

➤ *The Taming of the Shrew* concerns the "proper" behavior of women, especially with regard to marriage.

➤ Women of the Elizabethan era were expected to be modest, virtuous, and obedient to their husbands.

➤ Was Kate the shrew actually tamed? The answer frequently seems to be left to the actor's and director's interpretations.

➤ *Love's Labor's Lost* explores different attitudes toward love: something to be denied, something to be tested, and something to be exalted.

Chapter 10

A Midsummer Night's Dream and *The Merchant of Venice*

How sweet the moonlight sleeps upon this bank!
Here we will sit and let the sounds of music
Creep in our ears: soft stillness and the night
Become the touches of sweet harmony.
Sit, Jessica. Look how the floor of heaven
Is thick inlaid with patines of bright gold:
There's not the smallest orb which thou behold'st
But in his motion like an angel sings,
Still quiring to the young-eyed cherubins.
Such harmony is in immortal souls;
But whilst this muddy vesture of decay
Doth grossly close it in, we cannot hear it.

—*A Midsummer Night's Dream*

Great poetry and a great story—what more could you ask? *A Midsummer Night's Dream* is a jolly holiday from reality. The same cannot be said of Shakespeare's *The Merchant of Venice*—it's a comedy with an attitude. Read on to find out how these plays are the same and different.

Things That Go Bump in the Night

Do you know why it's bad luck to break a mirror or walk under a ladder? Or why knocking on wood can help protect you against bad omens? Who knows? If you stop to think about it, you'll realize that we don't have any rational explanation for these beliefs.

Forsooth!

The "midsummer night's dream" was **midsummer madness**, the proverbial name for being sick with love.

Nevertheless, superstition still exerts a powerful influence on the way we act. Otherwise, how can you explain the fact that there are almost no office buildings or apartment houses with a floor numbered 13? And why do so many of us believe in lucky numbers, lucky charms, and just plain luck?

The Elizabethans were no different from superstitious people today: In fact, magical beliefs played an even larger role in the seventeenth century than they do today. Back then, nearly every one believed in charms, potions, fairies, elves, and spirits.

Something Wicked This Way Comes

Renaissance fairies weren't the tiny, sweet creatures we think of today. Neither were they the cute animated figures born in Disney's studio, shimmering on gossamer wings and sprinkling fairy dust in their wake.

No, Elizabethan fairies were life-sized creatures, malicious and fiendish. They could sour milk and sicken livestock. They often pinched people at night, making their victims "as blue as bilberry." Fairies loved practical jokes, too, such as spilling huge pails of milk and leading unwary travelers astray. Fairies were most feared for their practice of stealing human babies and replacing them with fairy changelings. These replacements were usually deformed, hideous, or retarded.

Unfortunately for the Elizabethans, there was quite an assortment of evil fairies. Here are a few:

➤ Hostile river fairies who lured sailors to their death

➤ Fairy aristocrats who spent their days hunting and dancing

➤ Ordinary, everyday, garden-variety goblins

➤ Giants and ogres

A wise Elizabethan family took precautions against fairies. Their preemptive strikes included charms, conjurations, obedience, and flattery. Food and drink were thought to offer great protection against bad fairies; as a result, most Elizabethan households set out a bowl of cream every night for the fairies. Elizabethans also took special pains never to speak to a fairy—even though no human had ever seen one. "They are fairies," Falstaff yells. "He that speaks to them shall die. I'll wink and couch; no man their works must eye."

So how did we get the cute little fairies we know and love today? You guessed it; Shakespeare created them.

Will Power

Fortunately, there were a few good fairies, the most well-known being Robin Goodfellow or Puck. "A shrewd and knavish sprite," in Shakespeare's words, Puck was the special guardian of the hearth and home. Puck and his cohorts re-warded a good housewife by helping with the chores and bringing luck.

A Fairy Tale

The fairies in *A Midsummer Night's Dream* are Shakespeare's invention. Shakespeare's fairies differ from Elizabethan fairies in three important ways:

➤ They are tiny.

➤ They are associated with flowers.

➤ They are benevolent, not wicked.

Further, Shakespeare's fairies are not members of a powerful kingdom with its own rulers, as people believed in the seventeenth century. Rather, these new, improved fairies serve as attendants to mortals, especially rulers.

Star Quality

In Peter Brook's celebrated production of *A Midsummer Night's Dream* at Stratford and New York in 1970, Titania and Puck swing on trapezes while watching the shenanigans of earthbound mortals. The whole play was staged within a white box.

Elizabethan fairies: the stuff of nightmares.

Who's Who in *A Midsummer Night's Dream*

Meet the cast of *A Midsummer Night's Dream*:

- ➤ Theseus, *Duke of Athens*
- ➤ Egeus, *Hermia's father*
- ➤ Lysander, *in love with Hermia*
- ➤ Demetrius, *in love with Hermia*
- ➤ Philostrate, *Master of the Revels to Theseus*
- ➤ Quince, *a carpenter, presenting the Prologue*
- ➤ Bottom, *a weaver, presenting Pyramus*
- ➤ Flute, *a bellows-member, presenting Thisby*
- ➤ Snout, *a tinker, presenting Wall*
- ➤ Snug, *a joiner, presenting Lion*
- ➤ Starveling, *a tailor, presenting Moonshine*
- ➤ Hippolyta, *Queen of the Amazons, betrothed to Theseus*
- ➤ Hermia, *Egeus's daughter, in love with Lysander*
- ➤ Helena, *in love with Demetrius*
- ➤ Oberon, *King of the Fairies*

➤ Titania, *Queen of the Fairies*

➤ Puck, or Robin Goodfellow

➤ Peaseblossom, Cobweb, Moth, Mustardseed, *fairies*

➤ Other fairies

Love Potion #9

Lord, what fools these mortals be!

—*A Midsummer Night's Dream*

The play opens in the palace of Theseus with the Duke of Athens, who is about to marry Hippolyta, Queen of the Amazons. On the mortal plane, Hermia wants to marry Lysander, but Egeus, her father, wants her to marry Demetrius. Meanwhile, Demetrius has abandoned Helena, but she still loves him. All four lovers go to the woods: Hermia and Lysander to elope; Demetrius to prevent this, having been warned by Helena; and Helena to be with Demetrius.

Quince, Bottom, Flute, Snout, Snug, and Starveling, Athenian workmen, are preparing a play, *Pyramus and Thisby,* for the Duke's wedding. Only Bottom the weaver has any play-acting ability; the rest are hopelessly inept.

The King and Queen of the Fairies quarrel because the Queen has a male changeling that the King wants, but she won't give him the boy. To get what he wants, Oberon plans to enchant the Queen's eyes with a love juice that will cause her to fall madly in love with anyone or anything she sees. While she's thus diverted, he'll swipe the change- ling. Oberon sends Puck to obtain the flower that has the magic juice. Oberon sees Helena's one-sided love for Demetrius and tells Puck to apply the juice to Demetrius so that he'll love Helena.

Forsooth!

Hobgoblin means "Robin the goblin," **Hob** being a country form of Robert or Robin.

Will Power

The story of Pyramus and Thisby is a tale of tragic love familiar to Shakespeare's public. It concerns the traditional situation of lovers whose parents are enemies. The lovers' secret meeting one moonlit night results in death for both, in a manner similar to that of Romeo and Juliet. The story is related to the situation that has begun to unfold in the first scene concerning young love and its conflict with parental authority.

By mistake, Puck anoints Lysander's eyelids. Lysander awakens, sees Helena first, and falls in love with her. Helena leaves, and Lysander follows. Hermia awakens and goes to look for Lysander. Now, Hermia loves Lysander, but Lysander loves Helena; Helena loves Demetrius, but Demetrius loves Hermia.

Star Quality

The 1935 Warner Brothers film version of *A Midsummer Night's Dream* is a mess of mismatched actors, scenery, and plots. Want proof? It stars Mickey Rooney as Puck and James Cagney as Bottom. Bonus: There's even Anita Louise (later to make a splash in *Gilligan's Island*) as Titania.

James Cagney as Puck in A Midsummer Night's Dream.

Meanwhile, Bottom and his companions are rehearsing in the woods close to Titania's sleeping place. To make mischief, Puck puts an ass's head on Bottom. The other workmen flee in fright, and Bottom sings to show his courage, even though he's quite frightened himself, not knowing why they've run away. Awakened by Bottom's song, the enchanted Titania falls in loves with him, ass's head and all.

Oberon realizes that Puck has enchanted the wrong Athenian. To remedy the situation, he decides to charm Demetrius. As a result, Lysander and Demetrius now both love Helena. Hermia discovers that Lysander no longer loves her. Helena and Hermia quarrel; Oberon has Puck cure Lysander so that he'll love Hermia again. Demetrius remains enchanted so that he'll love Helena.

The King gets his changeling and then removes the charm from Titania. Since all the partners are now correctly matched, the Duke plans a triple wedding. Bottom awakens and describes what has happened to him, which he assumes had been a dream.

Theseus and Hippolyta, Hermia and Lysander, and Helena and Demetrius are married. The workmen present their play. After the household is asleep, the fairies bless everything.

Dream on

> If we shadows have offended,
> Think but this, and all is mended,
> That you have but slumb'red here
> While these visions did appear.
> And this weak and idle theme,
> No more but a dream,
> Gentles, do not reprend.
> If you pardon, we will mend.
>
> —*A Midsummer Night's Dream*

Sweets to the Sweet

Because *A Midsummer Night's Dream* is concerned so centrally with marriages and a royal wedding, it is thought that Shakespeare wrote the play to celebrate a wedding between two noble persons.

Puck's last words suggest that the whole play may be only a dream. Indeed, the final act is concerned with the relationship between dreams and reality, art and life. In effect, Shakespeare has resolved the entire plot in Act IV, leaving time to explore these issues in the conclusion.

Like a dream, the play presents an odd mix of realistic and fantastic characters, everyday speech and sublime poetry, realistic events and wild flights of fantasy.

Fire at Will

The 1913 film version of *A Midsummer Night's Dream* is famous for having sparked one of the first censorship ratings—"Forbidden for Juveniles." The director transformed Puck and Oberon into foxy ladies, with Oberon played by a sexy Russian ballerina. Save yourself.

Love Me Tender

But something wonderful is happening under the cover of a dream. Take a close look at the pairs of human lovers: It's mix and match. Hermia and Lysander, Demetrius and Hermia, Helena and Demetrius. Don't feel bad if you can't tell them apart, especially Helena and Hermia—everyone gets confused. But it really doesn't matter; any variation would work as well, as far as the plot is concerned.

And that's Shakespeare's point: Love transforms ordinary people into rare and perfect beings. When we fall in love, we suspend reason and overlook the flaws in our beloved. Here's what Shakespeare says:

Things base and vile, holding no quantity,
Love can transpose to form and dignity.
Love looks not with the eyes, but with the mind.
After all, what's more dream-like than love?

Star Quality

Peter Hall's "mod" version of *A Midsummer Night's Dream* was hailed as groundbreaking
when it was released in 1968. Time has been cruel: There's too much 1960's realism
coupled with bad costumes. Woody Allen's *A Midsummer Night's Sex Comedy* (1982) is
more fun. Woody, Mia Farrow, Jose Ferrer, Mary Steenburgen, and Julie Hagerty wander
though the forest and pay homage to the Bard.

The Merchant of Venice

The quality of mercy is not strain'd,
It droppeth as the gentle rain from heaven
Upon the place beneath. It is twice blest:
It blesseth him that gives and him that takes.
'Tis mightiest in the mightiest: it becomes
The throned monarch better than his crown;
His sceptre shows the force of temporal power,
The attribute to awe and majesty,
Wherein doth sit the dread and fear of kings;
But mercy is above this sceptred sway,
It is enthroned in the hearts of kings,
It is an attribute to God himself;
And earthly power doth then show likest God's,
When mercy seasons justice. Therefore, Jew,
Though justice be thy plea, consider this,
That in the course of justice none of us
Should see salvation: we do pray for mercy;
And that same prayer doth teach us all to render
The deeds of mercy.

—*The Merchant of Venice*

The Merchant of Venice is a disturbing play. It's classified as a comedy, yet at times it seems more like a tragedy. As a comedy, it should be a story about love, but at times it seems like a story of hate. Learn about the characters, story, and background so you can decide for yourself how to classify this play.

Who's Who in *The Merchant of Venice*

Meet the cast:

➤ The Duke of Venice

➤ The Prince of Morocco, *Portia's suitor*

➤ The Prince of Arragon, *Portia's suitor*

➤ Antonio, *a merchant from Venice*

➤ Bassanio, *his friend and Portia's suitor*

➤ Solanio, *friend of Antonio and Bassanio*

➤ Gratiano, *friend of Antonio and Bassanio*

➤ Salerio, *friend of Antonio and Bassanio*

➤ Lorenzo, *in love with Jessica*

➤ Shylock, *a rich Jew*

➤ Tubal, *a Jew, Shylock's friend*

➤ Launcelot Gobbo, *a clown, Shylock's servant*

➤ Old Gobbo, *Launcelot's father*

➤ Leonardo, *Bassanio's servant*

➤ Balthazar, *Portia's servant*

➤ Stephano, *Portia's servant*

➤ Portia, *a rich heiress, of Belmont*

➤ Nerissa, *her waiting-gentlewoman*

➤ Jessica, *Shylock's daughter*

➤ Magnificoes of Venice, Officers of the Court of Justice, Jailer, Portia's servants, and other attendants

Fire at Will

If you ever get a chance to see *The Merchant of Venice* performed in a theater, nix on the orchestra seats. You want to sit in the back because there's a lot of spitting going on in this play. To Elizabethans, spitting was common; Queen Elizabeth once "spat on a courtier's cloak" when he displeased her.

Therein Lies a Tale

Bassanio, a young Venetian nobleman, seeks to win back his fortune and gain his beloved by marrying Portia of Belmont. He asks his friend Antonio (*the* merchant of Venice) to lend him the money he needs for the trip to Belmont. Antonio doesn't have the cash, so he borrows the money from Shylock, a Jew and a professional usurer.

Shylock is very bitter against Antonio, but since he says he wants to make friends with the Christians, he offers to lend the 3,000 ducats for three months if Antonio will promise that if the money is not repaid in time, he will forfeit a pound of flesh. Antonio, confident that his ships will return a month before the date, agrees to the terms.

Meanwhile, Portia is being wooed by numerous suitors attracted by her wealth, beauty, and virtue. Her father had stipulated before his death that she must marry whichever man correctly chooses which of three caskets contains her picture. Others have tried and failed the test.

Star Quality

A recent BBC production of *The Merchant of Venice* did a fine job of displaying the complexity of Shylock's character. Interestingly, the director (Jonathan Miller), Jessica (Leslie Udwin), and Shylock (Warren Mitchell) are all Jewish.

Back in Venice, Bassanio's friend Lorenzo elopes with Shylock's daughter Jessica, who takes a large part of her father's possessions with her. She also converts to Christianity. Furious, Shylock feels that the entire Christian community has conspired against him.

Bassanio chooses the correct casket and marries Portia. Portia's maid Nerissa and Bassanio's friend Gratiano also wed. The two women each give their husbands a ring they must never remove. Antonio's ships failed to return on time and so his bond to Shylock is forfeited. Although various friends have offered to pay what Antonio owes, Shylock insists on claiming his pound of flesh. Bassanio returns to Venice with three times the sum necessary to repay Shylock.

Sweets to the Sweet

Here are two quotes from the play that have become popular sayings: "In the twinkling of an eye" and "All that glisters is not gold." We've updated the latter to "All that glitters is not gold."

Portia tells Lorenzo that she and Nerissa will stay in a convent while their husbands are away. Actually, Portia disguises herself as a lawyer and defends Antonio in court. Shylock demands his pound of flesh, and the Duke of Venice, presiding at the trial, reluctantly agrees to his claim. Portia, however, tells Shylock that he may take one pound of flesh but not a drop of blood, for the contract says nothing about blood. Shylock then agrees to take the money, but Portia is not yet finished with him.

Walter Mitchell as Shylock and John Franklyn-Robbins as Antonio in the BBC production of The Merchant of Venice.

Portia says that Shylock is guilty of planning the murder of a Venetian citizen, for which he has incurred the death penalty. The Duke sets aside the sentence but tells Shylock that he must convert to Christianity and divide his wealth between Antonio and the state. When Shylock protests that the sentence is too harsh, Antonio agrees not to claim his full share, provided that Shylock will leave that money to his daughter when he dies. Bassanio offers the "lawyer" a large fee, but the lawyer wants only Bassanio's ring. Bassanio reluctantly agrees. As the lawyer's page, Nerissa gets Gratiano's ring.

In Belmont, Jessica and Lorenzo pass the time happily, entertained by the clownish Launcelot.

At home, Portia and Nerissa chide their husbands for no longer wearing their rings but then confess their role in the trial. The play ends with general joy on all sides.

Will Power

Launcelot Gobbo, the clown, is a type well known in Italian commedia, where he was probably played as a hunchback or dwarf. (The name Gobbo is Italian for "crook't-backed.") Renaissance audiences found unnatural and misshapen creatures amusing.

Some of My Best Friends Are...

You call me misbeliever, cut-throat dog,
And spit upon my Jewish gaberdine.

—*The Merchant of Venice*

Sweets to the Sweet

The quotations "The devil can cite Scripture for his purpose" and "It is a wise father that knows his own child" come from *The Merchant of Venice.*

Shylock is one of the most fascinating—and controversial—characters in Shakespeare. Discussions *of The Merchant of Venice* generally center around Shylock, especially how to judge him and Shakespeare's attitude toward Jewish people.

On one side, we get the critics who claim that Shakespeare intended Shylock as the stereotype of the infidel Jew and a complete villain. On the other side, we get those who argue that Shylock is a tragic figure, more sinned against than sinning. Was the Bard anti-Semitic? Let's start with a little background to put the issue in context.

Kick Me

> I am a Jew. Hath not a Jew eyes? Hath not a Jew hands, organs, dimensions, senses, affections, passions?
>
> —*The Merchant of Venice*

After the Norman Conquest in 1066, the Jewish people, fleeing from the persecutions of the French clergy, traveled to England. Restricted from owning property and keeping serfs, essential to the agrarian economy of the Middle Ages, more and more Jews became tradesmen and financiers.

Fire at Will

During the Jews' 400-year absence from England, it became common to attribute unexplained deaths, plagues, and other disasters to Jewish hatred for Christians and their desire for revenge against their persecutors. Jews were considered devils, and stories of ritual murders grew.

Henry I (1100–1135) granted the Jews a charter in exchange for a percentage of their profits. As a result, moneylenders were forced to charge higher interest rates, which increased as the King's demands grew. Thus, the Jew became the buffer for the King's extortion and the symbol of the hated usurer.

Soon after, anti-Semitism became official government policy: Massacres of Jews formed part of the celebrations at the coronation of Richard I. Richard's brother and successor replenished some of his depleted funds by imprisoning or executing Jews to seize their properties.

By 1254, conditions were so bad that the Jewish people petitioned the King to allow them to leave the country. England did not see Jews again until the latter half of the seventeenth century, when, because he needed them, the Puritan leader of Parliament Oliver Cromwell allowed them to return.

Harder and Harder

In the 1800s, the critics saw *The Merchant of Venice* extolling the Christian virtues of mercy and charity over the cruel justice of the Old Testament. According to this reading, as the stereotyped Jew, Shylock remains staunch in his cruelty, just as Antonio remains the epitome of Christian forgiveness. Thus, *The Merchant of Venice* is a romantic comedy, in which the heroic Antonio serves as a model for all good men and through whose Christian generosity Bassanio, Lorenzo, and Shylock are led to the good way of life.

Times change, and today we tend to view the play in a different light. Now, many readers see Bassanio, Gratiano, and Salerio as shallow and spoiled. Antonio gives them all chump change in exchange for making the "A" list on the party circuit. Shylock has become a Jewish King Lear, sinned against, a victim of vicious cruelty.

Sweets to the Sweet

Remember that Shylock has been spat upon, called a dog, and vilified for pursuing the only trade that the Christian world has left open to him; he has had his daughter "stolen" by a Christian, and for this he is expected to show mercy.

Patrick Stewart's 1978 portrayal of Shylock in John Barton's production of The Merchant of Venice *is especially fascinating.*

The fact that readers perceive Shylock so differently is a tribute to Shakespeare's ability to create a real, complex character. Perhaps Shylock is neither a monster nor the noble victim of persecution. Rather, he is a combination of many qualities that are themselves affected by the circumstances in which he finds himself.

The Least You Need to Know

➤ *A Midsummer Night's Dream* shows the mysterious power of love to transform ordinary people into perfect beings.

➤ *The Merchant of Venice* is a troubling play: Is it a comedy or a tragedy? A tale of love or a tale of hate?

➤ *The Merchant of Venice* has sparked more controversy than any other Shakespearean play, leading some readers to label Shakespeare anti-Semitic.

Chapter 11

As You Like It and Much Ado About Nothing

> **In This Chapter**
>
> ➤ Who's who in *As You Like It*
>
> ➤ The plot of *As You Like It*
>
> ➤ Who's who in *Much Ado About Nothing*
>
> ➤ The plot of *Much Ado About Nothing*

And so from hour to hour we ripe and ripe,
And then from hour to hour we rot and rot;
And thereby hangs a tale.

—*As You Like It*

As You Like It is a delicious comedy, one of Shakespeare's best. In this play, love letters seem to grow on trees, and an evil duke undergoes a miraculous conversion. Yet there's a message in all this fun: The play satirizes *pastoralism*, the glorification of the supposedly "pure" country over the "wicked" city or court. (But don't worry; you can still enjoy the play without worrying about the satire at all. Promise.)

Much Ado About Nothing, on the other hand, is a screwball romantic comedy in which everyone but the lovers realize the attraction underneath the banter. The brilliant Beatrice and Benedick dance around their love...until it's impossible to ignore.

While romantic comedies never go out of style, let's see why these two particular examples are as popular today as they were in Shakespeare's era.

Who's Who in *As You Like It*

Shakespeare took the plot of *As You Like It* from a pastoral romance by Thomas Lodge called *Rosalynde*, published in 1590.

Lodge's story was a serious pastoral romance; Shakespeare's play, in contrast, is a satire that pokes fun at country life. Shakespeare also added characters such as William, Audrey, Jaques, and Touchstone, who completely changed the tone of Lodge's original story.

Meet the cast. Then you'll see what knots they tie themselves into—and how they disentangle themselves!

➤ Duke Senior, *living in banishment*

➤ Duke Frederick, *his brother, and usurper of his dominions*

➤ Amiens, *lord attending the banished Duke*

➤ Jaques, *lord attending the banished Duke*

➤ Le Beau, *a courtier attending Duke Frederick*

➤ Charles, *wrestler to Duke Frederick*

➤ Oliver, *Sir Rowland de Boys' son*

➤ Jaques, *Sir Rowland de Boys' son*

➤ Orlando, *Sir Rowland de Boys' son*

➤ Adam, *Oliver's servant*

➤ Dennis, *Oliver's servant*

➤ Touchstone, *a clown*

➤ Sir Oliver Martext, *a vicar*

➤ Corin, *shepherd*

➤ Silvius, *shepherd*

➤ William, *a country fellow in love with Audrey*

➤ A person representing Hymen

➤ Rosalind, *the banished Duke's daughter*

➤ Celia, *Duke Frederick's daughter*

➤ Phebe, *a shepherdess*

➤ Audrey, *a country wench*

➤ Lords, pages, foresters, and attendants

Forsooth!

A **pastoral romance** is a long tale of love and adventure in which shepherds use witty and sophisticated language to woo shepherdesses. Think *Green Acres* with real wit.

Forsooth!

Jaques is pronounced *Jayqueeze*—Shakespeare's stab at French pretension.

A production of As You Like It.

Makin' Whoopee in the Woods

> No sooner met but they looked; no sooner looked but they loved; no sooner loved but they sighed; no sooner sighed but they asked one another the reason; no sooner knew the reason but they sought the remedy.
>
> —*As You Like It*

When the play opens, Orlando has been deprived of his inheritance by his brother Oliver. Orlando and Oliver live in the country of Duke Frederick, who has usurped the throne from his brother, Duke Senior. Duke Senior and his friends have been banished to the Forest of Arden where they live like Robin Hood and his band of merry men. Duke Senior's daughter Rosalind stays at Frederick's court with Frederick's daughter Celia, her close friend.

Oliver plots to have Orlando killed in a wrestling match, but Orlando wins the match. Frederick boots Orlando out of the court, but Rosalind and Orlando have fallen in love.

Fire at Will

Laurence Olivier made a dashing Orlando in the 1936 movie version of *As You Like It*, but the less said about the rest of the cast, the better.

Poster advertising the film version of As You Like It *starring Sir Laurence Olivier.*

Duke Frederick exiles Rosalind, too, and Celia decides to come along for the ride. Rosalind disguises herself as a man she calls "Ganymede"; always a good sport, Celia disguises herself as a servant girl and calls herself "Aliena." Touchstone, a court jester, accompanies the women as they set out to find Rosalind's father in the Forest of Arden.

Meanwhile, Orlando hotfoots it to the forest to avoid being killed by his not-so-loving brother.

Rosalind and her companions arrive in Arden, where they meet two shepherds, Corin and Silvius. Orlando shows up in the forest and is taken under Duke Senior's wing.

Duke Frederick orders Oliver to find his brother and bring the fugitives back. Back in the forest, Orlando has been expressing his love for Rosalind by hanging love poems to her on the trees. Rosalind finds the poems and figures out that Orlando loves her. Disguised as Ganymede, she offers to cure Orlando of his love by pretending to be Rosalind and rebuffing his advances. Touchstone, meanwhile, has met a country wench called Audrey, whom he wishes to marry.

Sweets to the Sweet

Both "Answer me in one word" and "Neither rhyme nor reason" came from *As You Like It.* So did the phrase "For ever and a day."

Phebe rejects Silvius' advances. When Rosalind reprimands Phebe for her cruelty to Silvius, Phebe falls in love with Rosalind (who is still disguised as Ganymede). Orlando arrives late for his first lesson on anti-love. Silvius realizes that Phebe loves him.

Oliver, sleeping in the forest, is just about to be attacked by wild animals when Orlando comes upon his brother and saves his life. As a result, the brothers reconcile. Oliver and Celia fall in love with each other.

The next day, Rosalind reveals her identity to her father and Orlando. At last, the couples are correctly paired: Rosalind and Orlando, Oliver and Celia, Touchstone and Audrey, and Phebe and Silvius. Just as the marriage ceremonies are about to begin, the couples learn that Duke Frederick has decided to become a hermit and return his brother's throne to him. Jaques decides to remain with Frederick in Arden. The rest return joyfully to the court.

The March of Time

Jaques's "The Seven Ages of Man" speech from *As You Like It* is very famous. On the surface, it seems to reveal that love is a passing fancy, and every aspect of life is but part of a much larger canvas.

According to the Elizabethan "Seven Ages" idea, each age has its appropriate activity. For example, a young man was supposed to fall in love; an old man, hoard money. In this speech, life is defined in terms of physical disintegration. Each stage in life is predicable: Nothing lasts because the pattern repeats and repeats. It's a cynical mouthful:

> All the world's a stage,
> And all the men and women merely players.
> They have their exits and their entrances;
> And one man in his time plays many parts,
> His acts being seven ages. At first the infant,
> Mewling and puking in the nurse's arms.
> And then the whining school-boy, with his satchel
> And shining morning face, creeping like snail
> Unwillingly to school. And then the lover,
> Sighing like furnace, with a woeful ballad
> Made to his mistress' eyebrow. Then a soldier,
> Full of strange oaths and bearded like the pard;
> Jealous in honour, sudden and quick in quarrel,
> Seeking the bubble reputation
> Even in the cannon's mouth. And then the justice,
> In fair round belly with good capon lined,
> With eyes severe and beard of formal cut,
> Full of wise saws and modern instances;
> And so he plays his part. The sixth age shifts
> Into the lean and slipper'd pantaloon,
> With spectacles on nose and pouch on side;

His youthful hose, well saved, a world too wide
For his shrunk shank; and his big manly voice,
Turning again toward childish treble, pipes
And whistles in his sound. Last scene of all,
That ends this strange eventful history,
Is second childishness and mere oblivion,
Sans teeth, sans eyes, sans taste, sans everything.

—*As You Like It*

Yet in the very next scene we get a reminder that individual moments do matter, and a great deal at that. Through this juxtaposition, Shakespeare suggests that life cannot be reduced to hard terms and brutal images; there is love, respect, and admiration to distinguish our days.

Star Quality

To date, the award for the oddest production of *As You Like It* would have to go to the 1967 version staged at the National Theatre. In this version, everything seemed real and unreal, fake and authentic at the same time. (Please don't call or write if you've seen a weirder version. I don't want to share your pain.)

Who's Who in *Much Ado About Nothing*

Don Pedro: She were an excellent wife for Benedick.

Leonato: O Lord, my lord! If they were but a week married, they would talk themselves mad.

—*Much Ado About Nothing*

While *Much Ado About Nothing* has always been on the top of Shakespeare's hit parade, it is notoriously difficult to perform because of the flashing wit and obscure quibbles that pass between Benedick and Beatrice. Before we explore the wit, let's meet the witty ones:

➤ Don Pedro, *Prince of Arragon*

➤ Don John, *his bastard brother*

➤ Claudio, *young lord of Florence*

➤ Benedick, *young lord of Padua*

➤ Leonato, *governor of Messina*

➤ Antonio, *his brother*

➤ Balthasar, *Don Pedro's attendant*

➤ Conrade, *follower of Don John*

➤ Borachio, *follower of Don John*

➤ Friar Francis

➤ Dogberry, *a constable*

➤ Verges, *a headborough*

➤ Sexton

➤ Boy

➤ Hero, *Leonato's daughter*

➤ Beatrice, *Leonato's niece*

➤ Margaret, *gentlewoman attending Hero*

➤ Ursula, *gentlewoman attending Hero*

➤ Messengers, watch, lord, attendant, etc.

Much Ado About Nothing Is Much Ado About Something

Friendship is constant in all other things
Save in the office and affairs of love:
Therefore all hearts in love use their own tongues;
Let every eye negotiate for itself
And trust no agent.

—*Much Ado About Nothing*

Will villainy stop a wedding? Will deception create love out of nothing? Eavesdrop on the truth in one of Shakespeare's most popular comedies. Based on a short story by the Italian Renaissance writer Bandello, *Much Ado About Nothing* satirizes human nature while conjuring up scenarios of tragicomic romance—with men dishonored and women undone.

The title "Much Ado About Nothing" sounds offhand and apologetic; you might expect the play that follows such a beginning to be a sweet piece of fluff and not much more. However, the play and the title itself are weightier than they initially seem. There is certainly "much ado" in this romantic comedy—it's very much "about" the ultimate risk of our lives: losing our pride and living in love. Let's see how by looking at the story itself.

The play is set in Sicily, where Don Pedro, Prince of Arragon, has recently defeated his half-brother, the illegitimate Don John, in a military engagement. Apparently reconciled, they return to the capital, Messina, as guests of the Governor, Leonato.

Sweets to the Sweet

Don John in *Much Ado About Nothing* is a first draft of the envious, malicious man who turns out to be Iago in *Othello*.

Count Claudio, a young nobleman serving in Don Pedro's army, falls in love with Hero, Leonato's daughter, whom Don Pedro woos on his behalf. The play's central plot, written mainly in verse, shows how Don John maliciously deceives Claudio into believing that Hero has taken a lover on the eve of her marriage, causing Claudio to repudiate her publicly, at the altar.

Don John's deception, with its tragicomical resolution, is offset by a parallel plot written mainly in prose, portraying another, more light-hearted deception, by which Hero's cousin, Beatrice, and Benedick (a friend of Don Pedro and Claudio) are tricked into acknowledging their love. That's the outline; now connect the dots with me.

Stack the Deck

> Sigh no more, ladies, sigh no more,
> Men were deceivers ever,—
> One foot in sea and one on shore,
> To one thing constant never.

> —*Much Ado About Nothing*

In the first part of the play, Claudio's friend Don Pedro volunteers to woo Hero on his friend's behalf, but no sooner has he begun than Don John plants the rumor that Don Pedro has whisked off Hero. As a result, Claudio drops Hero faster than a hot potato. After Don Pedro clarifies the situation, Leonato announces the wedding of Claudio and Hero. Not to be undone, the conspirators hatch a scheme to discredit Hero publicly. One of Don John's accomplices, Borachio, pretends to woo Hero while Claudio and Don Pedro look on from their hiding place. Borachio has asked his friend Margaret to stand in for Hero.

Meanwhile, Beatrice and Benedick continue to amuse the others with their delightful antagonism. Here's an example of their banter:

Benedick:	What, my dear Lady Disdain! Are you yet living?
Beatrice:	Is it possible disdain should die while she hath such meet food to feed it as Signior Benedick? Courtesy itself must convert to disdain, if you come in her presence.

As you can see, Benedick starts the insult by saying that he could inspire disdain, but Beatrice gives it right back to him by saying that he could inspire disdain in anyone.

Turning Tricks

Another trick is prepared, this one with a very different purpose: Don Pedro and Claudio will have a conversation about Beatrice's undying love for Benedick while Benedick is within earshot. Meanwhile, Hero and Margaret will do the same for Beatrice, describing how deeply Benedick loves her. This "labor of Hercules" succeeds as the conspirators bring "Signior Benedick and the lady Beatrice into a mountain of affection, the one with th' other."

However, on the very day of their planned wedding, Claudio denounces Hero as unfaithful. Borachio's performance has succeeded. Chaos ensues: Hero faints from shock, for even her father believes the false accusation and curses her. An objective observer, the Friar, advises Leonato to say that Hero died of grief and then hope the truth will prevail.

In a comical interlude involving Dogberry, a local constable, and his deputies, Borachio and Conrade are captured and brought to Leonato. Borachio's confession prepares the way for a reconciliation. Leonato extracts a pledge from Claudio to pay homage at Hero's "tomb," and take the hand of his "niece" in marriage. Since *Much Ado About Nothing* is a comedy, it ends with the "miraculous" return of Hero, masked as Leonato's "niece." She is quickly reunited with Claudio.

Benedick and Beatrice also join hands and the company celebrates the happy turn of events in a festive dance. Finally, news is brought that Don John has been captured and will be punished for his deeds.

Star Quality

The stars come out in Kenneth Branagh's version of *Much Ado About Nothing*—Emma Thompson, Denzel Washington, and Kenneth Branagh himself. There's even Keanu Reeves and Michael Keaton. Branagh (Benedick) and Thompson (Beatrice) are as close to perfection as it gets.

Stars abound in the film version of Much Ado About Nothing.

Who Gets Top Billing?

For it so falls out
That what we have we prize not to the worth
Whiles enjoy it, but being lack'd and lost,
Why, then we rack the value; then we find
The virtue that possession would not show us
Whiles it was ours.

—*Much Ado About Nothing*

When the composer Victor Berlioz turned *Much Ado About Nothing* into an opera in 1861, he retitled it *Beatrice et Benedict*. Even King Charles I, never noted for his subtle literary bent, changed the title in his personal copy of the play just as Berlioz had done. Both men were far more interested in the witty lovers than their romantic opposites. Berlioz and King Charlie had a lot of company, as it turns out.

From the start, critics have obsessed about the plot focus in *Much Ado About Nothing*—is it the Claudio plot or the Benedick–Beatrice plot? It's clear that most of the action is devoted to Claudio and Hero, who are eventually brought together despite numerous obstacles, chief among them being the deliberate chicanery of Don John, Borachio, and Conrade, and Claudio's own naïveté and willingness to believe in false rumors.

Benedick:	Do you not love me?
Beatrice:	Why, no; no more than reason.
Benedick:	Why, your uncle, and the prince, and Claudio Have been deceived—they swore you did.

Beatrice:	Do you not love me?
Benedick:	Troth, no; no more than reason.

—*Much Ado About Nothing*

But the play's real center of interest lies in the relationship between the witty pair of lovers, Beatrice and Benedick, who delight in bickering with one another and declaring their "immunity" to love's charms until an elaborate ruse succeeds in drawing out their love for each other.

The Least You Need to Know

➤ *As You Like It* satirizes pastoral life and people who are artificial and overly sentimental when in love.

➤ Jaques's "The Seven Ages of Man" speech from *As You Like It* is very famous, beginning with the oft-quoted line "All the world's a stage."

➤ If you're up for a screwball romantic comedy, *Much Ado About Nothing* is one of Shakespeare's most hilarious.

➤ *Much Ado About Nothing* turns on the love of two pairs of lovers: Beatrice and Benedick and Claudio and Hero.

Chapter 12

Twelfth Night and The Merry Wives of Windsor

In This Chapter

➤ Who's who in *Twelfth Night*

➤ The plot of *Twelfth Night*

➤ Shakespeare's songs

➤ Who's who in *The Merry Wives of Windsor*

➤ The plot of *The Merry Wives of Windsor*

If music be the food of love, play on;
Give me excess of it, that, surfeiting,
The appetite may sicken, and so die.
That strain again! it had a dying fall:
O, it came o'er my ear like the sweet sound
That breathes upon a bank of violets,
Stealing and giving odour!

—*Twelfth Night*

And, boy, do they ever play in *Twelfth Night*. The title refers to the play's reported premier on January 6, the twelfth day of the Christmas season marked by the Feast of Epiphany. Twelfth Night was a time of rejoicing and holiday high-jinks. Tricks and jokes were the order of the day, and the ordinary rules of life were temporarily suspended. We're talking a great blow-out here, kids.

Fun and games aside, *Twelfth Night* is the most carefully plotted and expertly written of Shakespeare's romantic "Golden Comedies." It's a miracle of musical form and balance. The festive, gently satirical comic plot centers around a series of practical jokes and mistaken identities.

The Merry Wives of Windsor is unique among Shakespeare's comedies because of its setting: It's the only comedy with a recognizable setting, and the only nonhistory play to be set in England. It depicts ordinary, middle-class life—just like you and me before we win the lottery. And since it's a tale of the suburbs, it centers around sexual misadventure and mistaken identity. (Doesn't *everyone* in the suburbs fool around?) So listen up for two great stories.

Who's Who in *Twelfth Night*

Some are born great, some achieve greatness, and some have greatness thrust upon 'em.

—*Twelfth Night*

Will Power

Twelfth Night, or *What You Will*, is the only Shakespeare play that has a subtitle.

In Sir Toby Belch, Shakespeare was creating another character like the popular Sir John Falstaff, who was such a hit in *Henry IV, Parts I and II*. Like Falstaff, Toby is a knight with a great fondness for merrymaking of all kinds.

Further, all the main comic characters of *Twelfth Night*—Sir Toby, Sir Andrew Aguecheek, Maria, Malvolio, and Feste—are (like Falstaff) caricatures of the representative personality types of Elizabethan England. These include the jolly knight (Sir Toby), the weak-minded coward (Sir Andrew), the clever, flirtatious servant (Maria), and so on. We still have these types today; you probably work with most of them.

Meet the rest of the cast:

➤ Orsino, *Duke of Illyria*

➤ Sebastian, *Viola's brother*

➤ Antonio, *a sea captain, Sebastian's friend*

➤ Sea Captain, *Viola's friend*

➤ Valentine, *gentleman attending on the Duke*

➤ Curio, *gentleman attending on the Duke*

➤ Sir Toby Belch, *Olivia's uncle*

➤ Sir Andrew Aguecheek

➤ Malvolio, *Olivia's steward*

➤ Fabian, *Olivia's servant*

➤ Feste, *a clown, Olivia's servant*

➤ Olivia, *a rich countess*

➤ Viola, *Sebastian's sister*

➤ Maria, *Olivia's gentlewoman*

➤ Lords, priests, sailors, officers, musicians, gentlewoman, servant, and other attendants

The Mother of All Parties: *Twelfth Night*

A noble-born twin sister and brother, Sebastian and Viola, are separated from each other when their ship is wrecked in a storm at sea. Each fears the other has drowned. Rescued by the captain, Viola arrives in the kingdom of Illyria and decides for safety's sake to disguise herself as a boy, "Cesario," which will protect her from unwanted sexual advances, and work for Duke Orsino, the ruler of the country. Orsino has been vainly courting the Countess Olivia, who has consistently rejected him because she has decided to mourn her brother's death for seven years. Viola gets the job and soon finds herself delivering the Duke's declarations of love to the Countess.

Gender Bender

> I am all the daughters of my father's house,
> And all the brothers too.
>
> —*Twelfth Night*

Olivia falls in love with "Cesario" (Viola); Viola falls in love with Orsino. Meanwhile, Viola's twin brother Sebastian has also been rescued from drowning by Antonio, a kindly sea captain. Of course, Sebastian and Antonio head for Illyria, where the action is.

In the meantime, Sir Toby Belch, Olivia's fat, jolly, hard-drinking cousin, urges Sir Andrew

Fire at Will

Although Illyria was, in fact, a real place on the east coast of the Adriatic sea in Europe, Shakespeare used the name to give an exotic flavor to what was really an imaginary kingdom. Like most Elizabethan dramatists, Shakespeare was fond of setting his romantic comedies in faraway places with strange-sounding names. He never tried to make these places realistic, however.

Sweets to the Sweet

Disguised as Cesario, Viola suggests that things are not always as they seem. Gender scholars argue that identity is fluid in this play, for Viola does not simply impersonate a man but rather seems to become a eunuch. Some scholars don't have enough to fill their days.

Aguecheek's hopeless attempts to woo Olivia. Sir Toby, Andrew, Feste, and Maria are carousing one night when the priggish Malvolio bursts in to scold them for their merry ways. Determined to revenge themselves, the barflies send Malvolio an anonymous love letter, knowing he'll assume it's from Olivia.

Meanwhile, Olivia's passion for Cesario has become so intense that she declares her intentions openly, much to Viola's discomfort. Sebastian and Antonio have arrived in Illyria. Antonio hides at an inn while Sebastian hits the hot spots in town.

Take a Letter, Maria

By now Malvolio has followed the instructions of the false love letter, and, crazily costumed, he makes a fantastic approach to Olivia. The Countess, supposing him mad, asks Sir Toby to lock him up as a lunatic. With Malvolio out of the way, she resumes her courtship of Cesario (Viola).

Here's Malvolio, Sir Andrew Aguecheek, and Feste in the Lake George Opera Festival's 1968 performance of Twelfth Night.

Olivia's attentions to the Duke's "man" have so enraged Aguecheek that the cowardly knight actually challenges Cesario to a duel. Though both are anxious to avoid any real fighting, Sir Toby and Fabian (another servant) egg them on to the point where bloodshed is only avoided by Antonio's sudden appearance. Thinking Viola is Sebastian, Antonio draws his sword in his/her defense and ends up battling Sir Toby himself. A group of police officers arrest Antonio. The beleaguered captain then asks "Sebastian" (Viola) for a purse he's lent the real Sebastian earlier. When Viola doesn't know what he's talking about, he accuses her of ingratitude, calling her by her brother's name as the officers lead him away. Viola now realizes that her twin must be alive and in Illyria, and she goes off very excited.

Star Quality

Shakespeare's sources for the romantic plot of *Twelfth Night* include an Italian comedy called *Gl'Ingannati* (*The Deceived*), published in 1537.

Soon Sebastian himself wanders in. Of course, he's mistaken for Cesario (just as Viola was taken for him). The gang of dolts attack him; however, this time they find themselves opposed by a young man who spiritedly defends himself. Sebastian is on the verge of soundly beating the fools when Olivia arrives. Supposing Sebastian to be "Cesario," she scolds her cousin for fighting with him and lovingly invites Sebastian into her house.

While Sebastian and Olivia are ripening their relationship in one part of the house, Feste the jester disguises himself as Sir Topas, a priest, and visits Malvolio in jail. After tormenting Malvolio, Feste drops his disguise and provides Malvolio with pencil and paper so he can write to Olivia, informing her of his plight.

In the Dark, All Cats Are Gray

He does it with a better grace, but I do it more natural.

—*Twelfth Night*

Will Power

On the comic level, the tension between the Puritanical Malvolio and the roistering Toby is the play's chief dramatic conflict. Malvolio, the moralistic, self-made man, threatens Toby and by extension the entire class of idle, drunken aristocrats. Thus Toby's words to Malvolio, "Dost think because thou art virtuous, there shall be no more cakes and ale," means "You'd better not expect that we're going to disappear."

In the meantime, Olivia persuades Sebastian to marry her at once. She still thinks that he's "Cesario" and wants to snare him while she can. Sebastian is aware that there must be some mistake in all this, but he doesn't care: Olivia is beautiful and rich, and he has no problem seizing the moment.

Accompanied by Viola, Orsino visits Olivia to renew his suit in person. When Olivia appears, she addresses "Cesario" as husband. Viola, of course, denies both Antonio's and Olivia's accusations. Orsino is ready to banish Viola when Andrew and Toby accuse "Cesario" of having beaten them. Viola again denies all knowledge of the affair. Sebastian himself at last appears onstage, and all the complications are satisfactorily resolved.

Will's Hit Parade

When that I was and a little tiny boy,
    With hey ho, the wind and the rain,
A foolish thing was but a toy,
    For the rain it raineth every day.

But when I came to man's estate,
    With hey ho, the wind and the rain,
'Gainst knaves and thieves men shut their gate,
    For the rain it raineth every day.

But when I came, alas, to wive,
    With hey ho, the wind and the rain,
By swaggering could I never thrive,
    For the rain it raineth every day.

But when I came unto my beds,
    With hey ho, the wind and the rain,
With toss-pots still had drunken heads,
    For the rain it raineth every day.

A great while ago the world began,
    [With] hey ho, the wind and the rain,
But that's all one, our play is done,
    And we'll strive to please you every day.

—*Twelfth Night*

Shakespeare's songs are among the loveliest Elizabethan lyrics, and the songs sung in *Twelfth Night* include some of his greatest hits. Often the songs suggest that love is sweet and life is short, and so lovers should make hay while the sun shines. Other times, the mood is melancholy, conveying life's sadness and uncertainty. Occasionally, the two ideas are combined: Life is sad, but love improves it. Certainly all these themes are appropriate to a romantic comedy like *Twelfth Night*, which emphasizes love and melancholy as much as wit and high spirits.

This mournful little ballad outlines the progress of the singer's life—from youth, to manhood, to death, repeating the melancholy refrain about the wind and the rain, ballad-fashion, at the middle and end of every stanza. After the romantic complications and the comic convolutions, these final poignant lyrics seem to ask what all the

Sweets to the Sweet

Twelfth Night is Shakespeare's most musical work. Almost every act contains one or more tunes sung by Feste or, in certain productions, Viola, with other characters frequently chiming in.

fuss was about. It was just some "midsummer madness," a brief dream of love and merrymaking—what you, the audience, will it to be.

Everyone has his or her own favorite Shakespearean song (okay, so maybe you don't, but you *should*). Since I'm writing this book, I get to pick my favorites. Here, then, are my personal Top 10 Favorite Shakespearean Songs:

10. "O mistress mine! Where are you roaming?" (*Twelfth Night*)

9. "It was a lover and a lass" (*As You Like It*)

8. "Fear no more the heat o' th' sun" (*Cymbeline*)

7. "Hark, hark the lark" (*Cymbeline*)

6. "Come unto these yellow sands" (*The Tempest*)

5. "Blow, blow, thou winter wind" (*As You Like It*)

4. "When daisies pied and violets blue" (*Love's Labor's Lost*)

3. "Tell me where is fancy bred?" (*The Merchant of Venice*)

2. "Under the greenwood tree" (*As You Like It*)

And my #1 favorite song from Shakespeare?

1. "Where the bee sucks, there suck I" (*The Tempest*)

Star Quality

Shakespeare's songs are widely available on CDs and cassettes. Some recordings even use instruments from Shakespeare's time, such as **lutes** (a half-pear-shaped guitar) and **sackbutts** (the forerunner to the trombone), to get authentic sounds. For a special treat, check out Aaron Copeland's brilliant arrangements of Shakespeare's songs.

Who's Who in *The Merry Wives of Windsor*

"Why, then the world's mine oyster,
Which I with sword will open"

—*The Merry Wives of Windsor*

You've met the cast of *Twelfth Night*, so let's get to know the jolly folks in *The Merry Wives of Windsor*.

141

- ➤ Sir John Falstaff
- ➤ Fenton, *a gentleman*
- ➤ Robert Shallow, *a country justice*
- ➤ Abraham Slender, *Shallow's cousin*
- ➤ Francis Ford, *gentleman of Windsor*
- ➤ George Page, *gentleman of Windsor*
- ➤ William Page, *a boy, George Page's son*
- ➤ Sir Hugh Evans, *a Welsh parson*
- ➤ Doctor Caius, *a French physician*
- ➤ Host of the Garter Inn
- ➤ Bardolph, *Falstaff's follower*
- ➤ Pistol, *Falstaff's follower*
- ➤ Nym, *Falstaff's follower*
- ➤ Robin, *Falstaff's page*
- ➤ Peter Simple, *Slender's servant*
- ➤ John Rugby, *Doctor Caius' servant*
- ➤ Mistress Alice Ford
- ➤ Mistress Margaret Page
- ➤ Mistress Anne Page, *Margaret Page's daughter*
- ➤ Mistress Quickly, *Doctor Caius' servant*
- ➤ Servants

A Merry Little Plot

> This is the short and the long of it.
>
> —*The Merry Wives of Windsor*

According to legend, Shakespeare wrote *The Merry Wives of Windsor* in two weeks because Queen Elizabeth wanted to see Shakespeare's popular character Falstaff in love. While no one has been able to prove this story, the play's structure *does* suggest that Shakespeare worked fast—there are odd subplots that are never tied together. Let's take a look at the story now.

Sir John Falstaff and his buddies Bardolph, Nym, and Pistol have been raising a little heck over at Shallow's place. Unfortunately for our good ol' boys, Shallow is a Justice of the Peace. Shallow threatens to press charges against Falstaff, but Master Page talks him out of it.

Star Quality

The '82 BBC production of *The Merry Wives of Windsor* is a gem. Starring Ben Kingsley as the frenzied Mr. Ford, Judy Davis as Mistress Ford, and Richard Griffith as Falstaff, the production draws intriguing parallels between Elizabethan and contemporary homemakers.

Richard Griffith starred in this 1982 BBC production of Shakespeare's The Merry Wives of Windsor.

Page has a daughter, Anne, whom the Justice wants to marry to his cousin, Abraham Slender. Unfortunately, Doctor Caius and Master Fenton also have designs on Anne. Although Slender is Master Page's choice, Anne is sweet on Fenton. All three suitors ask Mistress Quickly for help. No fool, she accepts money from all three men for her services. But when Doctor Caius discovers that he and Slender love the same woman, he challenges the parson to a duel. To prevent bloodshed, the Host of the Garter Inn sends the two men to opposite ends of the town and the duel is called off.

Meanwhile, Falstaff has a hankering for Mistress Ford *and* Mistress Page. He writes identical love letters to both of them. He then sends Pistol and Nym to deliver the letters but they suffer a sudden attack of scruples and refuse. Falstaff's page delivers the letters while Pistol and Nym get back at Falstaff by spilling the beans to Masters Ford and Page.

Girls Just Wanna Have Fun

When Mistress Ford and Mistress Page receive Falstaff's identical love letters, they decide the time has come to teach the knight a lesson. In the meantime, Ford is afraid that his wife will fall for Falstaff; Page, in contrast, thinks the whole affair is a hoot and trusts his wife completely. To test his wife's virtue, Ford disguises himself, taking the name "Brook," and pays Falstaff to procure Mistress Ford for him.

Just as Falstaff starts to put the moves on Mistress Ford, her friend Mistress Page brings word that Ford is arriving. Hiding in a basket of dirty laundry, Falstaff is carried past Ford and dumped into a muddy stream—as the merry wives had planned. Delighted at their success, the wives plot another trick. To that end, they send a message to Falstaff suggesting another meeting with Mistress Ford.

Passionate Heart Seeks Same

Again, Ford visits Falstaff, finds out about the meeting, and once again plots to catch his wife with the portly knight. Sure enough, Falstaff and Mistress Ford are together when Mistress Page dashes in to announce Ford's arrival. This time, the ladies dress Falstaff in a dress that belonged to the Witch of Brentford, a woman Ford hates. Sure enough, Ford is tricked by the disguise and so he thrashes Falstaff. The women then reveal their tricks and suggest one last attempt to teach Falstaff a lesson.

The wives invite Falstaff to disguise himself with horns as the ghost of Herne the Hunter and meet them in Windsor Forest. Mistress Anne is disguised as a fairy, and children play her subjects. The women pinch and burn Falstaff until he begs for mercy. The plot ends happily (after all, it *is* a comedy): Mistress Anne marries Fenton, the man she loves, and Slender and Caius get tricked into running off with disguised boys. Best of all, Ford learns to trust his wife.

The Least You Need to Know

➤ *Twelfth Night* is the most carefully plotted and expertly written of Shakespeare's romantic "Golden Comedies."

➤ *Twelfth Night* centers around a series of practical jokes and mistaken identities.

➤ Shakespeare's songs are among the loveliest Elizabethan lyrics.

➤ *The Merry Wives of Windsor*, Shakespeare's only comedy set in a recognizable locale, concerns mistaken identity and sexual misadventure.

Part 3
Problem Plays

After 1600, when a more sober mood took hold in England, the tone of Shakespeare's plays changed as well, resulting in the three "problem" plays: All's Well That Ends Well, Troilus and Cressida, *and* Measure for Measure.

What's the "problem" in these "problem plays"? They're not comedies, and they're not tragedies. There's no clear resolution at the end: The sinners don't become saints.

Since scholars long ago couldn't put a label on these three plays, they called 'em as they saw 'em—hence, "problem play." Today we'd likely call these plays "black comedies" or "satires" because they poke fun at the darker side of human nature: corruption, greed, stupidity, a little illicit nooky, and so on.

Chapter 13

All's Well That Ends Well

In This Chapter

➤ Who's who in *All's Well That Ends Well*

➤ The plot of *All's Well That Ends Well*

➤ The play's ambiguity

➤ *All's Well That Ends Well* as a "problem play"

Mitzi's husband had been slipping in and out of a coma for several months, yet she stayed by his bedside every single day. When he came to, he motioned for her to come nearer. As she sat by him, he said:

> "You know what? You have been with me all through the bad times. When I got fired, you were there to support me. When my business failed, you were there. When I got shot, you were by my side. When we lost the house, you gave me support. When my health started failing, you were still by my side.
>
> "When I think about it now, you know what? I think you bring me bad luck."

We all have problems, right? Never fear, dear reader—*All's Well That Ends Well* won't be one of yours, even though it *is* classified as a "problem play." I promise.

Besides, it's only a "problem play" because the action seems to be more tragic than comic. In fact, about the only reason that *All's Well That Ends Well* can be called a "comedy" is that it ends happily for the central characters. Stay tuned for the whole story.

Who's Who in *All's Well That Ends Well*

Before you can figure out the plot, take a look at the players. The head weenies at this roast are Bertram, the Count of Rossillion; and Helena, a gentlewoman protected by Bertram's mother, the Countess of Rossillion. I hesitate to call these two the "hero" and the "heroine" because it's not that simple here. We'll just call them the main characters. I'll let you judge their merits later.

Here's the rest of the gang:

- ➤ King of France
- ➤ Duke of Florence
- ➤ Bertram, *Count of Rossillion*
- ➤ Lafew, *an old lord*
- ➤ Parolles, *a parasitical follower of Bertram*
- ➤ Two French Lords (the brothers Dumaine)
- ➤ Rinaldo, *a steward for the Countess of Rossillion*
- ➤ Lavatch, *a clown for the Countess of Rossillion*
- ➤ Page, *for the Countess of Rossillion*
- ➤ Gentleman
- ➤ Countess of Rossillion, *Bertram's mother*
- ➤ Helena, *gentlewoman protected by the Countess*
- ➤ Old Widow of Florence
- ➤ Diana, *the Widow's daughter*
- ➤ Violenta, *the Widow's neighbor and friend*
- ➤ Mariana, *the Widow's neighbor and friend*
- ➤ The usual assortment of lords, officers, and servants

Star Quality

In 1978, the BBC and Time/Life, Inc., announced their ambitious plan to deliver the Bard's entire canon to the folks in TV land. The jury is still out on the overall success of the project, but everyone agrees that *All's Well That Ends Well* is an intelligent and sophisticated winner. Try to catch it in reruns.

Bad Boys and the Women Who Love Them

It's a bleak opening: Everyone in Rossillion is mourning the recent death of Bertram's father, the Count. As a result of his father's death, Bertram is now under the King's guardianship. Lafew, a kind and worldly courtier, has come to take Bertram to the King's court in Paris. Bertram and his mother are unhappy at their parting. They're not alone in their sorrow; Helena, the orphaned daughter of the deceased physician to the Rossillion family, cannot accompany Bertram. Brought up like a sister to the young Count, Helena worships the ground he walks on—and a whole lot more. Even though he really is too big a fish to consider landing, Helena has not yet given up hope of reeling him in.

Helena has a few tricks up her sleeve. Upon learning that the King of France is ill with an ulcerous sore, she recalls that her father, a famous healer, had a cure for just such a complaint. She decides to travel to Paris in an attempt to cure the King of his complaint—and to win Bertram's heart and hand. She hopes that this show of kindness will convince Bertram that she's good wife material, even though she's not to the manner born. The old Countess encourages Helena's plan by revealing that she would welcome her as a daughter-in-law.

Working Without a Net

A young man married is a man that's marr'd.

—*All's Well That Ends Well*

When Helena arrives at court, the King of France does not fully trust her skill, despite his knowledge of her father's reputation as a healer. So she makes a bargain with him—she wagers her life on a cure. If she fails she will be executed; if she succeeds, she will be allowed to select her own husband from among the ranks of the eligible men at court.

Lay the smart money on Helena—she cures the King. Bet you can't guess which young man she picks for her hubby. The path of true love is rarely smooth, however: Bertram isn't thrilled about making the cut. He objects to Helena's lowly birth, lack of nobility, and poverty. Sticking to his side of the bargain, the King removes some roadblocks by making Helena a noble and giving her a rich dowry. Nonetheless, Bertram refuses to budge. Finally, the King pulls rank and insists that Bertram marry Helena.

Will Power

Despite our current views on the social status of a doctor, a physician in the sixteenth century was considered merely a superior tradesman, unless, of course, he was of noble birth. And that was *before* managed care.

Hello Kitty Meets Hello Sailor?

Our remedies oft in ourselves do lie,
Which we ascribe to Heaven.

—*All's Well That Ends Well*

Deciding he'd rather be a fighter than a lover, Bertram plans to run away to the Tuscan wars. He sends Helena back to Rossillion, promising to join her, but takes a left and ends up in Italy. Tuscany was a happening place even then.

Bertram sends Helena a letter with his conditions for marriage:

1. She must obtain his ancestral ring. Naturally, he always wears it on his finger.

2. She must have his child.

In Bertram's own words:

> When thou canst get the ring upon my finger, which never shall come off, and show me a child begotten of thy body that I am father to, then call me husband: but in such a "then" I write a never.

Bertram also drops a line to his mother explaining that he won't return to France or his home as long as Helena is alive. Understandably shocked, the Countess sides with Helena.

Meanwhile, Helena has been blaming herself for the "sin" of sending Bertram off to the wars. To do penance, she sets off on a pilgrimage to the shrine of St. James. Arriving in Florence, she hears that Bertram's friend Parolles has led him into licentious, piggy behavior. A Widow who invites Helena to stay with her passes on the news that Bertram has been soliciting her daughter, Diana, to be his mistress. Diana is less than thrilled by this turn of events.

Fire at Will

Initially, critics panned the play, recoiling in horror from the bed-trick it contains. Subsequent critics jeered the play's poetry and dramatic structure. Recently, however, scholars have applauded Shakespeare's description of the redemptive quality of love.

Fire at Will

All's Well That Ends Well marks the first time Shakespeare used the "bed-trick," the substitution of one woman for another in bed in order to deceive a lover.

Trick or Treat

The web of our life is of a mingled yarn,
good and ill together.

—*All's Well That Ends Well*

Helena suggests that Diana pretend to agree to Bertram's request, but Helena will take Diana's place in bed in order to fulfill his conditions. The Widow agrees, and Helena has Diana obtain Bertram's ring before she agrees to the appointment. She tells the girl to promise that the ring will be replaced by another when they are in bed together.

Everything goes according to plan. Helena takes Diana's place, offers herself to Bertram, and puts a ring back on his finger. She also conceives, fulfilling each of Bertram's supposedly impossible requests—without his knowledge.

When Bertram returns to the camp, he finds that his braggart soldier friend, Parolles, is to be tested for his courage. Of course, Parolles turns out to be an utter coward. When Parolles thinks he has been captured by the enemy, he offers to tell his captors everything they want to know—including the inside scoop on Bertram's extra-curricular activities. Bertram realizes that he has been a cement-head and starts to mature.

Helena, Diana, and the Widow return to the court in Paris. In the meantime, Bertram has also returned and believes, as does everyone else, that Helena is dead. According to the rector of Saint Jacques le Grand, Helena died of grief while on her pilgrimage. As a result, he now begins to appreciate her virtue. Isn't it always the way, girls?

Lafew presents his daughter Maudlin to Bertram, and the King approves the match. Since Bertram has learned to be obedient, he agrees to the match and offers for the engagement the ring that "Diana" had given him in bed. The King immediately recognizes the ring as the one he had given to Helena. The King asks how Bertram obtained it, and when the young man lies frantically, he accuses him of having killed Helena.

In a letter, Diana asks for justice since Bertram has not kept his promise to marry her. She then enters and tells her story, supported by her mother. Bertram tries to wriggle out of his difficulty and is saved only by Helena, who announces that she has fulfilled all his conditions. Bertram willingly accepts Helena as his wife, Diana is offered a large dowry and the promise of suitable husband, and *All's Well That Ends...Okay.*

Sweets to the Sweet

Shakespeare based Parolles on the stock character of the braggart soldier who is eventually exposed as a lout. Bawdy and rather unappealing, Parolles leads Bertram into evil. His punishment is well deserved, and his character is useful as a means of displaying Bertram's growing maturity.

Will Power

Shakespeare based the play on Boccaccio's tale of Giletta de Nerbona in the *Decameron*. Boccaccio's early sixteenth century story revolves around Giletta of Narbona, the daughter of a wealthy and respected physician. Like Helena, Giletta falls in love with young count (Beltramo), follows him to Paris where she remedies the King's incurable disease, and because of her newly acquired royal favor, is granted the right to demand a husband: Beltramo. You get the picture.

Reality Bites

> The bitter past, more welcome is the sweet.
>
> —*All's Well That Ends Well*

So what's the problem in this problem play? *All's Well That Ends Well* differs from many of Shakespeare's other comedies in its dark overtones:

➤ Shakespeare gives us the problems at court but provides no ideal world.

➤ We get a love story without any action.

➤ The heroine is equivocal—is she Snow White or the Wicked Witch?

➤ The hero is a callow jerk, a poster boy for immaturity.

➤ The fairy-tale ends happily only if we suspend our disbelief to allow for Bertram's speedy conversion.

In large part, it's the debate surrounding Helena and Bertram that has earned *All's Well That Ends Well* the label "problem play." It's clear that Shakespeare has left it up to us to decide their characters. Let's shine the spotlight on Helena first.

Humble Pie

> I dare not say I take you, but I give
> Me and my service, ever whilst I live,
> Into you guiding power. This is the man.
>
> —*All's Well That Ends Well*

So says Helena to Bertram in Act II, throwing herself at his feet. This is seriously humble. As a result, some critics regard Helena as a genuine romantic heroine—resourceful, but also virtuous, feminine, charming, and modest. She never behaves cynically, and her motives are above reproach. In her first monologue, for example, Helena is quick to set Bertram up as her "bright particular star" while she regards herself as too base to occupy "his sphere" and must be content to view this heavenly body from below.

Not so fast...

Playing for Keeps

Check out the following interchange between Helena and the Widow:

Helena: ...The Count he woos your daughter,
           Lays down his wanton siege before her beauty,
           Resolv'd to carry her. Let her in fine consent,

As we'll direct her how 'tis best to bear it.
Now his important blood will nought deny
That she'll demand. A ring the county wears,
That downward hath succeeded in his house
From son to son, some four or five descents,
Since the first father wore it. This ring he holds
In most rich choice; yet in his idle fire.
To buy his will, it would not seem too dear,
Howe'er repented after.

Widow: Now I see
The bottom of your purpose.

Helena: You see it lawful then. It is no more
But that your daughter, ere she seems as won,
Desires this ring; appoints him an encounter;
In fine, delivers me to fill the time,
Herself most chastely absent. After,
To marry her, I'll add three thousand crowns
To what is pass'd already....
Why then to-night
Let us assay our plot, which if it speed
Is wicked meaning in a lawful deed,
And lawful meaning in a lawful act,
Where both are not sin, and yet a sinful fact.

Hmm...This conversation seems to reveal that Helena is a cunning little vixen. After all, she plots with Diana's mother, the Widow, to catch Bertram through the devious bed-trick. This is cold, calculating pursuit; Bertram doesn't stand a chance against a woman this determined. Whether she's motivated by love, sex, or ambition, Helena sets out to trap Bertram, succeeds, and—when he flees her—captures him again.

Is Helena a conniving schemer? A feminist? A clever wench? An ingratiating doormat? Is Bertram a wimp? A creep? Secretly in love with Parolles?

As a result of this ambiguity, Shakespeare's tale resonates for contemporary audiences, all of us who steadfastly deny that we've been weaned on talk shows that feature "Wimps and Feminazis I Have Loved."

Fire at Will

In this play, Shakespeare seems disillusioned about human virtue and love seems degraded into lust. Even though the play ends well as a result of the cool trick and enemies are reconciled, the tone is sad. No one is dancing in the aisles at the end of this one, folks.

The Least You Need to Know

➤ *All's Well That Ends Well* is a "problem play" because it fails to provide an unqualified happy ending. It has a dark tone, explicit portrayal of sexual dishonesty, and a realistic atmosphere.

➤ This play marks the first time Shakespeare used the "bed-trick."

➤ Most critical debate centers around the interpretation of the two main characters, Bertram and Helena. Is he wussy or wounded? Is she a put-upon or putting upon?

Chapter 14

Troilus and Cressida

> ### In This Chapter
>
> ➤ Who's who in *Troilus and Cressida*
>
> ➤ The plot of *Troilus and Cressida*
>
> ➤ *Troilus and Cressida* as a problem play
>
> ➤ *Troilus and Cressida* as political satire
>
> ➤ An unsavory cast of characters

All lovers swear more performance than they are able, and yet reserve an ability that they never perform; vowing more than the perfection of ten, and discharging less than the tenth part of one.

—*Troilus and Cressida*

Troilus and Cressida's unconventional form—a satirical comedy-drama-tragedy-history—and pessimistic tone appeal to today's cynical audiences. A brilliant vision of a world without values and coherence, *T & C* is so popular with contemporary theater-goers that it's being produced almost continuously around the world. See for yourself what all the fuss is about.

Who's Who in *Troilus and Cressida*

His heart and hand both open and both free;
For what he has he gives, what thinks he shows;
Yet gives he not till judgment guide his bounty.

—*Troilus and Cressida*

The headliners get top billing: Troilus (Priam's hunky son) and Cressida (Calchas's fine but cold daughter). Meet the rest of the cast:

➤ Priam, *King of Troy*

➤ Hector, *Priam's son*

➤ Troilus, *the youngest of Priam's five sons*

➤ Paris, *Priam's son*

➤ Deiphibus, *Priam's son*

➤ Helenus, *Priam's son*

➤ Margarelon, *Priam's illegitimate son*

➤ Aeneas, *Trojan commander*

➤ Antenor, *Trojan commander*

➤ Calchas, *a Trojan priest, taking part with the Greeks*

➤ Pandarus, *Cressida's uncle*

➤ Alexander, *Cressida's servant*

➤ Servant and Boy, *Troilus' servants*

➤ Servant, *Paris' servant*

➤ Agamemnon, *the Greek general*

➤ Menelaus, *his brother*

➤ Nestor, *Greek commander*

➤ Ulysses, *Greek commander*

➤ Achilles, *Greek commander*

➤ Ajax, *Greek commander*

➤ Diomedes, *Greek commander*

➤ Patroclus, *Greek commander*

➤ Thersites, *a deformed and scurrilous Greek*

➤ Servant, *Diomedes's servant*

➤ Helen, *Menelaus's wife*

➤ Andromache, *Hector's wife*

➤ Cassandra, *Priam's daughter, a prophetess*

➤ Cressida, *Calchas' daughter*

➤ Assorted Trojans and Greek soldiers

Will Power

Shakespeare took the material for *Troilus and Cressida* from Chaucer's *Troilus and Creseyde* (1386), Caxton's translation of *The History of the Destruction of Troy* (1471), Lydgate's *Troy Book* (1413), and Chapman's translation of *The Iliad* (1596–1598).

What's Love Got to Do with It?

Lechery, lechery; still wars and lechery; nothing else holds fashion.

—*Troilus and Cressida*

156

Time: Four to five days, around 1193 B.C.

Place: The Trojan and Greek camps

When he goes off to war, Calchas, Cressida's father, leaves her in the care of his brother Pandarus, a notorious procurer (as his name not-so-subtly suggests). Beautiful as well as shrewd, Cressida becomes an asset to her uncle's business. He introduces her to Priam's son, Troilus, who falls fast and hard for her beauty. However, Troilus doesn't want his father and eldest brother (Troy's great hero, Hector) to know about his love for Cressida because he knows that they will object to the match.

When the play opens, Troilus tells his uncle, Pandarus, that he is not in the mood to go to battle because he has "such cruel battle here within" to win Cressida's love.

She's So Fine

The Trojan War erupted when the Trojan stud Paris kidnapped the luscious Helen, a Spartan, from her husband King Menelaus. Kings rarely welcome wife-snatching, although today we usually take to the courts rather than to arms for satisfaction.

Shakespeare picks up the story seven years down the line. The soldiers are bored and realize that their cause is yesterday's news. The Greek general Nestor has asked Priam to release Helen so they can all get on with their lives. In discussing the Greek proposal, Priam and his older sons, Hector and Helenus, the priest, and their sister Cassandra argue that too much Trojan blood has already been shed so it's clearly time to mail Helen home. Cassandra even prophesies the burning of the city if they don't put an end to the situation now.

Troilus, in contrast, argues that releasing Helen will result in a loss of prestige. He sneers that "reason and respect / Make livers pale and lustihood suspect."

Hector reveals that he has challenged the Greeks to a duel. Everyone is astonished at his bravery and daring. Ajax, a pompous warrior, is chosen to accept Hector's challenge. The Greek's great warrior,

Forsooth!

Ilium was Priam's famous palace. Its many towers could be seen from a distance so that it appeared to be "wrought up unto the heavens."

Will Power

The 10-year Trojan War ended when the Greeks pretended to withdraw, leaving behind a large wooden horse with a raiding party inside. When the Trojans brought the horse into the city, the Greeks popped out and sacked Troy.

Fire at Will

Even though the play's complete title is *The History of Troilus and Cressida*, it's a comedy, not a history. But don't push the point—*T & C* squeaks through as comedy on a technicality. The two stars are alive at the end.

Achilles, sulks in his tent and refuses to be involved in the duel or anything having to do with the war. Ulysses tries to jolly him out, but no go.

'Til Death Do Us Part?

Troilus and Cressida's romance is interrupted by Agamemnon's announcement that he will exchange the Trojan general Antenor for Cressida. The lovers swear to remain faithful to each other. They exchange tokens of their love, but Troilus has a strong suspicion that Cressida is as false as Burt Reynold's hair.

Forsooth!

A **courtesan** was the medieval equivalent of a call girl, but one who was highly trained and educated. She would cater only to the most wealthy and powerful men. In many cases she wielded considerable power herself.

When Cressida arrives at the Greek camp, she gets the once-over from Agamemnon and his generals. They each greet her with a kiss—and she greatly enjoys their smooching.

Only Ulysses refuses to be won over by her charms. Recognizing Cressida for the courtesan she is, he condemns her: "Fie, fie upon her! / There's language in her eye, her cheek, her lip; / Nay, her foot speaks; her wanton spirit look out / At every joint and motive of her body." Cressida plays both ends toward the middle to make sure that she gets what she wants.

His grousing is cut short when Hector and Troilus, armed for the duel, follow Cressida and Diomedes. The duel ends in a draw because Hector refuses to kill his cousin Ajax. Agamemnon and his commanders invite Hector to their tents for a banquet. Achilles asks Hector to visit when he leaves Agamemnon.

Triolus lovingly gazes at Cressida in the PBS presentation of Triolus and Cressida—*the poor guy!*

Frailty, Thy Name Is Woman

Let it not be believe'd for womanhood!
Think he had mothers, do not give advantage
To stubborn critics, apt without theme
For depravation, to square the general sex
By Cressid's rule.

—*Troilus and Cressida*

Meanwhile, Troilus gets Ulysses to help him find Cressida's tent. As he spies on his love, Troilus gets more than he bargained for: Diomedes is in love with Cressida, and she's not playing hard to get. To show her eagerness to play footsie, Cressida gives Diomedes Troilus' love token. We see that Cressida is shallow and deceitful.

Shattered at Cressida's unfaithfulness, Troilus vows to get revenge on Diomedes in battle the next day. It's a two-for-one deal. By killing Diomedes, Troilus not only saves his honor but also robs Cressida of her lover.

Billy, Don't Be a Hero

As Hector gets ready for the battle, his wife Andromache and his sister Cassandra plead with him not to go since they have had upsetting dreams that he will be killed. But Hector insists that he must fight to uphold his honor.

Meanwhile, Achilles orders his Myrmidons to slaughter Hector. They eagerly comply. News of Hector's death unsettles the Trojans. If such a great warrior could be killed so easily, what hope do the rest of the troops have? Troilus swears vengeance on Achilles: "Hope of revenge shall hide our inward woe!"

Forsooth!

The **Myrmidons** were a warlike tribe that followed Achilles.

Neither Fish Nor Fowl

You know that *Troilus and Cressida* is classified as a "problem play" because it doesn't fit neatly into the comedy or tragedy shelves.

It's not a tragedy because:

➤ Tragedy deals with a hero's fall in a world of absolute good and evil. The world described in *Troilus and Cressida* is morally wishy-washy, steeped in vice.

➤ Tragic heroes learn from their suffering and realize the reason for their downfall. Troilus, in contrast, is only diminished by his experiences.

It's not a comedy because:

➤ There's nothing amusing about the situation.

➤ It's too caustic. Nobody's chuckling over Cressida's infidelity or Troilus' betrayal.

There's little doubt that *Troilus and Cressida* can be classified as a political satire, however.

As you learned in the first part of this book, Shakespeare's age roiled with political intrigue, gossip, and betrayal. (See? The more things change, the more they stay the same.) The Trojan War provided Shakespeare with some delicious parallels to current events. For example:

➤ Many people in Shakespeare's day believed that, like Troy, Elizabethan London had gone too far off track to be saved.

➤ Like Homer's warriors, Elizabethan courtiers ignored warnings of degeneracy, such as frequenting prostitutes.

➤ Like the Greeks, the Elizabethans believed in order and degree in government, commerce, and families.

The subject of the Trojan War allowed Shakespeare to castigate corruption in his society without stepping on too many toes. Ulysses' speech in Act I, scene iii is one of the most famous passages in Shakespeare. Traditionally used to illustrate the Elizabethan world picture, it describes how society, like a stringed instrument, becomes "untuned" if a single string is broken. The result? All harmony collapses and chaos reigns. Here's an excerpt:

Fire at Will

Although it is still produced around the world, its unappealing characters and unsatisfactory outcome make *Troilus and Cressida* one of Shakespeare's least popular plays. Don't look for this one on the marquee at the multiplex though.

The heavens themselves, the planets, and this center
Observe degree, priority, and place,
Insisture, course, proportion, season, form,
Office, and custom, in all line of order;
And therefore is the glorious planet Sol
In noble eminence enthron'd and spher'd
Amidst the other; whose med'cinable eye
Corrects the ill aspects of planet evil,
And posts like the commandment of a king,
Sans check, to good and bad. But when the planets
In evil mixture to disorder wander,
What plagues and what portents, what mutiny!...
O, when degree is shak'd,
Which is the ladder of all high designs,
The enterprise is sick.

Guess Who's Not Coming to Dinner?

Think you have some creepy friends? The characters in *Troilus and Cressida* are a real laugh riot.

➤ *Cross off Cressida.* Although her wit has the sparkle of Portia and Beatrice, Cressida is too cold and calculating to be appealing as they are. Watching her in action, Thersites says, "How the devil Luxury, with his fat rump and potato finger, tickles these together! Fry, lechery, fry!"

➤ *Jettison the Greeks.* They're a coarse, ignoble, and opportunistic group.

➤ *Abolish Achilles.* So much for the traditional heroes of legend. Here, the noble Achilles has been reduced to a whiny wuss who spends his days pouting in his tent with, as Mr. Shakespeare puts it, his "masculine whore." (Yes, you read that right. A "masculine whore" was what we today would call a "gay lover.")

➤ *Ax Ajax.* He's a brainless clod.

➤ *Nix on Nestor.* Shakespeare has transformed wise Nestor into a long-winded nuisance.

The only heroic character is Hector, and he's killed by Achilles' thugs. The triumph of the cynical characters over the idealistic ones makes this one of Shakespeare's most puzzling and intriguing plays.

> The end crowns all,
> And that old common arbitrator, Time,
> Will one day end it.
>
> —*Troilus and Cressida*

The Least You Need to Know

➤ *Troilus and Cressida* takes place during the Trojan War.

➤ Troilus loves Cressida, but she is unfaithful and calculating.

➤ War and love are shown to be equally vicious and destructive.

➤ The play is filled with despair, disgust, and disillusionment. That's why it's perfect for today.

➤ The editors of the 1632 folio placed *Troilus and Cressida* between the Histories and the Tragedies. Whether the play is a comedy or a tragedy is still being debated. That's why it's a called a "problem play."

Chapter 15

Measure for Measure

In This Chapter

➤ Who's who in *Measure for Measure*

➤ The plot of *Measure for Measure*

➤ The source of *Measure for Measure*

➤ *Measure for Measure* as a Christian allegory

➤ *Measure for Measure* as a "problem play"

Three buddies die in a car crash and go to heaven to an orientation. They are all asked, "When you are in your casket and friends and family are mourning upon you, what would you like to hear them say about you?"

The first guy says, "I would like to hear them say that I was a great doctor and a great family man."

The second guy says, "I would like to hear that I was a wonderful teacher who made a huge difference in our children of tomorrow."

The last guy replies, "I would like to hear them say...Look! He's *moving*!"

Wouldn't we all? *Measure for Measure* is obsessed with death. In fact, much of the action takes place in a prison. This is the story of a corrupt governor who twists justice to gratify his own lust and is the only one of Shakespeare's comedies that has sparked as much controversy over interpretation as his tragedies. Find out why now.

Who's Who in *Measure for Measure*

The main characters are Vincentio (*Vin-chen'-see-oh*), the Duke of Vienna; Angelo, his Deputy; Claudio, a young gentleman; and Isabella, Claudio's sister. Here's the rest of the gang:

➤ Escalus, *an ancient lord*

➤ Lucio, *a fantastic (an eccentric)*

➤ Two other like gentlemen

➤ Provost

➤ Thomas, *a friar*

➤ Peter, *a friar*

➤ Justice

➤ Varrius

➤ Elbow, *a simple constable*

➤ Froth, *a foolish gentleman*

➤ Pompey, *a clown and servant to Mistress Overdone*

➤ Abhorson, *an executioner*

➤ Barnardine, *a dissolute prisoner*

➤ Mariana, *Angelo's fiancée*

➤ Juliet, *Claudio's beloved*

➤ Francisca, *a nun*

➤ Mistress Overdone, *a bawd (the woman who runs a house of prostitution)*

➤ The usual assortment of lords, officers, servants, and attendants

Star Quality

The Shakespeare Plays, (BBC/Time Life TV) did a smash job with the "problem plays," especially *Measure for Measure*. As a general rule of thumb with this series, the more obscure the play, the better the production. They're available on videocassette.

Who *Was* That Masked Man?

Condemn the fault, and not the actor of it?

—*Measure for Measure*

Time: 1500s

Place: Vienna

Vincentio, Duke of Vienna, pretends to leave Vienna and appoints Angelo, Mr. Virtue himself, as Deputy with full power to enforce the law. However, the Duke has gone nowhere—he's disguised himself as a friar to spy on Angelo. Why the ruse? The city is corrupt since the Duke has been lax about enforcing the laws.

Mistress Overdone explains that Claudio is in jail awaiting execution. His crime: fornicating with his fiancée Juliet before marriage, thus violating Angelo's determination to stamp out pre- and extramarital sex.

Escalus, the Duke's aged advisor, urges leniency. Meanwhile, Claudio begs his friend Lucio to appeal to his sister Isabella for help; a religious novice on the verge of entering the convent, her plea should carry weight. Isabella reluctantly agrees to visit Angelo and plead her brother's cause. After all, "The miserable have no other medicine, / But only hope."

As Isabella's plea for mercy becomes more and more passionate, Angelo gets turned on. Her appeal is famous:

> O, it is excellent
> To have a giant's strength; but it is tyrannous
> To use it like a giant...
> Could great men thunder
> As Jove himself does, Jove would ne'er be quiet,
> For every pelting, petty officer
> Would use his heaven for thunder;
> Nothing but thunder! Merciful Heaven,
> Thou rather with thy sharp and sulphurous bolt
> Split'st the unwedgeable and gnarled oak
> Than the soft myrtle: but man, proud man,

Will Power

The disguised ruler theme is an old, widespread folktale device: A ruler disguises himself and roams among his subjects to do good and wipe out evil. King Arthur, Ulysses—all the big men on campus have played this game.

Fire at Will

Measure for Measure is one of Shakespeare's most controversial works. The play has been praised as superb comedy and damned as tragedy badly adapted to comedy.

Dress'd in a little brief authority,
Most ignorant of what he's most assured,
His glassy essence, like an angry ape,
Plays such fantastic tricks before high heaven
As make the angels weep; who, with our spleens,
Would all themselves laugh mortal.

Ignoring her appeal, Angelo gradually gets the virginal Isabella to realize that he is propositioning her: her brother's life for her company in bed. Horrified, she stalks out, threatening to denounce him. She firmly believes that her brother will gladly die to save her virginity.

Poor Isabella!

Die Hard

Some rise by sin, and some by virtue fall.

—*Measure for Measure*

She's wrong: Claudio has no intention of dying for his sister's virtue. Claudio's response is one of Shakespeare's most famous meditations on death:

Ay, but to die, and go we know not where;
To lie in cold obstruction and to rot;
This sensible warm motion to become
A kneaded clod; and the delighted spirit
To bathe in fiery floods, or to reside
In thrilling region of thick-ribbed ice;
To be imprison'd in the viewless winds,
And blown with restless violence round about
The pendant world; or to be worse than worst
Of those that lawless and incertain thought
Imagine howling? 'tis too horrible!
The weariest and most loathed worldly life
That age, ache, penury and imprisonment
Can lay on nature is a paradise
To what we fear of death.

Claudio sees his spirit drowned in fiery lakes, locked in ice, blown about by invisible winds. The most miserable life on Earth is better by far than death. With a view of the afterlife like this, can you blame the guy for wanting to hang on?

Isabella is not sympathetic. She calls him a beast, a coward, a dishonest wretch who will choose life from her sin: "Is't not a kind of incest, to take life / From thine own sister's shame?" Ouch.

Fire at Will

We've come a long way, baby, so Isabella emerges to the contemporary sensibility as the ultimate prude. It's hard to sympathize with her.

This Is Just a Test

The Duke tells Claudio and Isabella that Angelo was only testing Isabella when he made his sex-trade proposal. Angelo has abandoned his fiancée Mariana, who still loves him nevertheless. The Duke wants Isabella to return to the Deputy and pretend to consent to the trade of body for brother; however, in a clever bed-trick, Mariana will slip into bed in the darkness. Mariana agrees to the plan.

Angelo does indeed dally with Mariana—whom he thinks is Isabella—yet still orders Claudio's execution. The Duke/Friar suggests Barnardine, the most stubborn prisoner, be executed instead and his head presented to Angelo. As Shakespeare comments:

But man, proud man,
Drest in a little brief authority,
Most ignorant of what he's most assured,
His glassy essence, like an angry ape,
Plays such fantastic tricks before high heaven
As make the angels weep.

Star Quality

King James loved *Measure for Measure* for its obvious allusions to his royal person, including his reputation for righteous virtue. The all-powerful Duke of Vienna, making wrongs right, had considerable appeal to the good Scottish king.

Not surprisingly, Barnardine refuses to cash in his chips quite that fast. He's saved when the pirate Ragozine, conveniently already dead, contributes his head. The Duke tells Isabella that Claudio is dead; she is given a letter for a Friar Peter asking for a meeting with him.

Lucio has impregnated and deserted the whore Kate Keepdown. When he's not busy with Kate, Lucio provides much of the bizarre humor and exaggerated comic language. Often vile and satiric, he attacks our frailties, especially our sexual excesses.

Fire at Will

Some critics find the comic parts of *Measure for Measure* disgusting and the tragic parts horrible. Others criticize Angelo's marriage to Mariana and the lack of poetic justice.

At the city gates, Isabella and Friar Peter accuse Angelo before the Duke, who is now ruling. Lucio, Angelo, and the Duke accuse Friar Lodowick of heading the conspiracy to defame Angelo. Mariana tells all, but Angelo denies just as much. The judgments: Angelo must marry Mariana, Claudio must marry Juliet, Vincentio offers to marry Isabella, and Lucio must marry Kate Keepdown.

As the Duke concludes:

The very mercy of the law cries out
Most audible, even from his proper tongue,
"Angelo for Claudio, death for death!"
Haste still pays haste, and leisure answers leisure;
Like doth quit like, and Measure Still For Measure.

In Life, as in Literature

As usual, Shakespeare took from outside sources in constructing *Measure for Measure*. But as we know, it's what he did with the raw material that counts. Only Shakespeare could spin gold from straw.

Here, the straw concerns a true incident. In 1547, a young wife in Milan prostituted herself to save her condemned husband. The judge (who had forced the woman to yield her virtue) executed her husband nonetheless. Eventually, he was forced to marry the widow and then put to death for his crime against her.

The story got around.

A Higher Court

> Why, all the souls that were, were forfeit once;
> And He that might the vantage best have took
> Found out the remedy. How would you be,
> If He, which is the top of judgment, should
> But judge you as you are?
>
> —*Measure for Measure*

There's a tidy little contingent who argue that *Measure for Measure* is a Christian allegory. The title itself comes from the Bible: "Judge not, that ye not be judged: and with what measure ye mete, it shall be measured unto you again" (Matthew 7:1 and 7:2).

Here's how the allegory shakes out:

➤ The Duke = God

   Like Superman, the Duke does good and uncovers evil. He's divine, Christian Providence.

➤ Isabella = the soul or the Church

➤ Angelo = Satan

Angelo, a devil disguised as an angel (Angelo = angel) is out to corrupt the soul of a pure virgin. Just as Christ was tempted in the desert by Satan, so is Isabella. Like the Devil in his arguments, Angelo applies false principles to ethical arguments.

Sweets to the Sweet

Critic G. Wilson Knight says the play symbolizes the Sermon on the Mount and the forgiveness of sin. The Biblical quote Shakespeare used as the source of his title does suggest that mercy and sympathy should temper justice.

He asks what Isabella would do if some powerful person could release her brother with the proviso that she lay down her body to him. "Better," she replies, "it were a brother died at once / Than that a sister, by redeeming him, / Should die for ever." Angelo's counter-argument is clever: She has called the law tyrannical and her brother's crime nothing but a casual slip, so she is contradicting herself.

Measure for Measure as a Problem Play

> They say, best men are moulded out of faults,
> And, for the most, become much more the better
> For being a little bad.
>
> —*Measure for Measure*

By 1604, when Shakespeare wrote *Measure for Measure*, King James was in power and very fond of Shakespeare's acting company, which he showered with money and calls for personal appearances. As a result, Shakespeare was rolling in dough. Why, then, the note of near tragedy, bitter cynicism, satire, and dark irony in *Measure for Measure*?

The optimism and patriotism of the Elizabethan Age had by now evaporated. The new king was aristocratic and imperial in his taste; he was not interested in the great unwashed as Elizabeth had been. The middle class was horrified by the way their tax money was frittered away on the King's excesses. The stiff-necked Puritans were being persecuted by the haughty Scottish king, so much so that many fled into exile or went underground. As the price of theater admissions soared, many of the workers who had filled The Globe pit no longer could afford the admission charges.

Sweets to the Sweet

The famous quote "What's mine is yours, and what is yours is mine" comes from *Measure for Measure*.

As the audience changed, Shakespeare started aiming his plays higher, to people like today's theater crowd who delight in satire, irony, and sophisticated wit. Hence, the "problem play," that curious mix of comedy, tragedy, and satire.

The Least You Need to Know

➤ Angelo = villain; Duke = hero; Escalus = good man.

➤ The theme of the play is tempering justice with mercy.

➤ Some critics read *Measure for Measure* as a Christian allegory. It's your call.

➤ *Measure for Measure* is the best of the three "problem" comedies because of great characters like Isabella, Claudio, the Duke, and Angelo.

Part 4
Tragedies

Hamlet's famous suicide speech:

> *To be, or not to be, that is the question:*
> *Whether 'tis nobler in the mind to suffer*
> *The slings and arrows of outrageous fortune,*
> *Or to take arms against a sea of troubles,*
> *And by opposing end them. To die, to sleep—*
> *No more, and by a sleep to say we end*
> *The heartache and the thousand natural shocks*
> *That flesh is heir to; 'tis a consummation*
> *Devoutly to be wish'd. To die, to sleep—*
> *To sleep: perchance to dream—ay, there's the rub,*
> *For in that sleep of death what dreams may come,*
> *When we have shuffled off this mortal coil,*
> *Must give us pause…*

Hamlet *as performed at the Brooklyn Shakespeare Festival:*

> *"To be, or what?"*

In this section, you'll survey Shakespeare's tragedies: Titus Andronicus, Hamlet, Romeo and Juliet, Julius Caesar, Othello, The Moor of Venice, King Lear, Macbeth, Antony and Cleopatra, Coriolanus, *and* Timon of Athens.

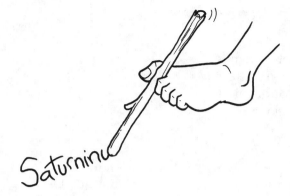

Chapter 16

Saturninus

Titus Andronicus

In This Chapter

➤ The Elizabethan revenge tragedy

➤ Who's who in *Titus Andronicus*

➤ The plot of *Titus Andronicus*

➤ Why *Titus Andronicus* is important

Vengeance is in my heart, death in my hand,
Blood and revenge are hammering in my head.

—Titus Andronicus

Go ahead, make my day.

—Dirty Harry

What do Titus Andronicus, Hamlet, and Dirty Harry have in common? The answer is they're all out for revenge.

Revenge tragedies were Elizabethan blockbusters, the sixteenth century equivalent of "nuke-'em-'til-they-glow" summer spectaculars. Revenge may be a dish best served cold, but as time has demonstrated, we haven't lost our taste for bloody and ruthless retribution. Read on to discover how Shakespeare created his own twist on the revenge tragedy in his first play, *Titus Andronicus*. In the following chapter, you'll see how he does it in one of his greatest plays, *Hamlet*.

The Elizabethan Revenge Tragedy

> Do me some service ere I come to thee.
> Lo by thy side where Rape and Murder stands;
> Now give me some surance that thou art Revenge—
> Stab them, or tear them on thy chariot-wheels,
> And then I'll come and be thy waggoner.
>
> —*Titus Andronicus*

Most Elizabethan revenge plays follow a set formula: The hero sets off to avenge a crime committed against a family member or to avenge a personal injustice. Like the "family" members in the *Godfather* saga, the hero of an Elizabethan revenge play pulls out all the stops to maintain personal and family honor. Not surprisingly, the hero usually has to take the law into his own hands and work outside the traditional power structure. Thus the hero becomes romanticized—a champion of the sensitive, misunderstood individual over the cold, uncaring system. Think Charles Bronson in *Death Wish 1, 2*, etc.

The revenge tragedy also has two other features. The person seeking revenge…

➤ Feigns madness

➤ Delays in achieving his vengeance

Both Titus and Hamlet feign madness (more on that later) and both take their sweet old time getting vengeance.

In a revenge tragedy, the playwright crams as much torture as possible into the five acts. By the end of the play, there's a heap of corpses on the stage—including the hero's. To add a little spice to this grim stew of blood and guts, Shakespeare (and his cohorts then and now) throw in a little incest, some poisoning, a dab of dismemberment (remember the strangulation scenes in *The Godfather*?), and a ghost or two.

But how can you keep 'em down on the farm once they've seen Paree? As with the James Bond movies, you've got to make the brutality more and more extravagant to keep the audience coming back for more. The results can be surprisingly amusing, as the following excerpt from *Titus Andronicus* shows:

> Even now I curse the day, and yet I think
> Few come within the compass of my curse,
> Wherein I did not some notorious ill:
> As kill a man, or else devise his death;
> Ravish a maid, or plot the way to do it;
> Accuse some innocent, and forswear myself;
> Set deadly enmity between two friends;
> Make poor men's cattle break their necks;

Set fire on barns and haystalks in the night
And bid the owners quench them with their tears.
Oft I have digged up dead men from their graves
And set them upright at their dear friends' door.
Even when their sorrows almost was forgot,
And on their skins, as on the bark of trees,
Have with my knife carved in Roman letters
'Lest not your sorrow die, though I am dead.'
But I have done a thousand dreadful things
As willingly as one would kill a fly
And nothing grieves me heartily indeed
But that I cannot do ten thousand more.

Fire at Will

The high priest of twentieth century poetry, T. S. Eliot, called *Titus Andronicus* "one of the stupidest and most uninspiring plays ever written." The critic Edward Ravenscroft even claimed that Shakespeare could never have written this "heap of rubbish."

Who's Who in *Titus Andronicus*

Titus Andronicus fits the bill as an action hero. He is brave, cunning, and loyal. So what if he's also ruthless and cruel? A man's gotta do what a man's gotta do. Here's the rest of the gang:

➤ Saturninus, *son of the late Emperor of Rome, afterwards Emperor*

➤ Bassianus, *Saturninus' brother*

➤ Titus Andronicus, *a noble Roman, general against the Goths*

➤ Marcus Andronicus, *Titus' brother, tribune of the people*

➤ Lucius, *Titus Andronicus' son*

➤ Quintus, *Titus Andronicus' son*

➤ Matrius, *Titus Andronicus' son*

➤ Mutius, *Titus Andronicus' son*

➤ Young Lucius, *Lucius' son, a young boy*

➤ Aemilius, *a noble Roman*

➤ Publius, *Marcus Andronicus' son*

➤ Sempronius, *Titus' kinsman*

➤ Caius, *Titus' kinsman*

➤ Valentine, *Titus' kinsman*

➤ Alarbus, *Tamora's son*

➤ Demetrius, *Tamora's son*

➤ Chiron, *Tamora's son*

➤ Aaron, *Tamora's lover*

➤ Captain

➤ Messenger

➤ Tribune

➤ Clown

➤ Tamora, *Queen of the Goths*

➤ Lavinia, *Titus Andronicus' daughter*

➤ Nurse and a black child

➤ Usual assortment of attendants, officers, soldiers; this time around, throw in some Romans and Goths as well

Star Quality

Titus Andronicus was one of Shakespeare's most famous plays when it was new. As the decades wore on, however, it fell into disfavor for its extreme violence. It wasn't seriously staged again until Peter Brooks' famous 1955 production with Laurence Olivier and Vivien Leigh at Stratford. The production was so vivid that some members of the audience had to be carried away in ambulances every night.

Make My Day

What can I say about a tragedy that contains the stage directions: "Enter the Empress' sons [Demetrius and Chiron] with Lavinia, her hands cut off, and her tongue cut out, and ravish'd" (II, iv)? I'll let you judge for yourself.

Place: Ancient Rome

Time: The action covers four days

The Emperor has died, and his sons Bassianus and Saturninus want the throne. As the play opens, a crowd has gathered in front of the capitol to hear each son plead with the Roman people to support his claim to the throne. Titus Andronicus' brother Marcus interrupts the campaigning to announce that Titus has conquered the Goths.

Amid great fanfare, Titus enters and addresses the Romans. He explains his sacrifices on behalf of the Roman cause, most notably the death of 20 of his 24 sons in battle. To honor Titus, Marcus' sons, led by Lucius, announce they will sacrifice Titus' greatest prisoner, Alarbus, son of the Queen of the Goths. Titus chops off Alarbus' limbs and throws him into the fire. Hey, it was Shakespeare's first play; the kid wanted a hit, and the audience ate it up.

Laurence Olivier takes a turn as Titus Andronicus in the celebrated 1955 production at Stratford-upon-Avon.

Marcus urges Titus to throw his hat into the political ring, but Titus declines; after 40 years in battle, he feels it's time for a little R&R. Titus chooses Saturninus as the new emperor. As his first official act, Saturninus chooses Lavinia as his queen. Since she's in love with Bassianus, Lavinia is less than thrilled, but she accepts nonetheless.

Some Days It's Just Better to Stay in Bed

Bassianus, no schlub, seizes Lavinia. In the ensuing dispute, Titus stabs the guard Mutius, his own son, feeling that he has been dishonored. Saturninus grabs Tamora, the Queen of the Goths, as his bride.

Titus' sons denounce him for killing Mutius. Still angry at his brother for the loss of Lavinia, Saturninus lays the blame on Titus' "dishonorable sons."

Meanwhile, Titus has brought the Moor Aaron to Rome as a prisoner. After the lovers Tamora and Aaron do the horizontal cha-cha, Aaron plots with Tamora's sons to kill Bassianus, seize Lavinia, rape and maim her, and frame Lavinia's brothers for the crime. The plan goes as arranged: Tamora's sons kill Bassianus and carry off Lavinia. After the rape, they slice out Lavinia's tongue and chop off her hands so she can't identify her rapists.

Titus asks to be his sons' "bail," but Saturninus refuses. Tamora's sons mock the badly maimed Lavinia. Her uncle Marcus bemoans her hideous disfigurement, a sight "to make thy father blind."

Fire at Will

By Act II, there are 10—count 'em, 10—murders. And that's only Act II.

Titus pleads before the tribunal for the lives of his sons, but to no avail. Aaron declares that the Senate will spare Titus' sons if he or Marcus or Lucius cuts off his hand and sends it to the Emperor. Titus chops off his hand, but his sons are executed anyway. Their heads and his hand are returned, giving rise to the famous stage direction, "Enter Messenger with two heads and a hand." Titus directs Lucius, his last surviving son, to raise an army of Goths against the Emperor.

Titus bids farewell to a hand.

I'll Be Back, Baby

Lavinia sort of fingers (no pun intended) her attackers by writing their names on the ground with a staff. The stage directions read: "She takes the staff in her mouth, and guides it with her stumps, and writes." Titus and Marcus vow revenge. Tamora has a son by Aaron and orders the baby killed. Instead, Aaron kills the nurse and takes his son to the Goths.

Pretending to be insane, Titus shoots arrows with messages into the Emperor's yard. Saturninus gathers up the arrows and decides it's time to take Titus out of the action. As Titus' son Lucius marches the Goths into Rome, Tamora decides to play with Titus' mind by pretending to be Revenge "sent from below / To join with him and right his heinous wrongs."

The Horror! The Horror!

In the final act, Lucius finds Aaron and forces him to reveal the entire plot. Aaron begs Lucius to spare his infant son. Lucius and his chief generals come to Titus' home for a banquet.

The banquet is a bloodbath. Titus, dressed as a cook, kills Tamora's sons, grinds their bones, bakes their heads in a pie, and serves the results to Tamora. When Tamora realizes what's on the menu (and after she eats the pie), Titus gives her the recipe and wholesale slaughter follows— including Titus. Only three are left alive: Lucius, his young son, and Marcus.

Lucius condemns Aaron to a lingering death. Marcus asks the Romans to accept Lucius as their governor and reveals what has happened to his family. The Romans overwhelm him with shouts of "Rome's gracious governor!" and Lucius takes the job.

Sweets to the Sweet

Looking for a new party sensations? Here's the recipe Titus uses for pot pie a la Sweeney Todd: "Lavinia, come, / Receive the blood, and when they are dead, / Let me go grind their bones to powder small, / And with this hateful liquor temper it, / And in that paste let their vile heads be bak'd."

No Pain, No Gain?

[*Where are Chiron and Demetrius?*]
Why, where they are, both baked in this pie;
Whereof their mother daintily hath fed,
Eating the flesh that she herself hath bred.
'Tis true, 'Tis true, witness my knive's sharp point.

[*He stabs the Empress.*]

Okay, so *Titus Andronicus* is a bloody melee, without the redemption of *King Lear* or the awareness of *Hamlet*. There's no salvation and not a whiff of self-knowledge. Let's not beat around the bush: *Titus Andronicus* is an orgy of gratuitous violence. So why bother reading or watching it?

First, *Titus Andronicus* is great entertainment. Crude and cruel, it gives modern audiences a taste of what it must have been like to be a member of Shakespeare's audience in his day. And call me shallow, callow, what have you—Shakespeare knew what to give his audience to keep them riveted to their seats. You don't take a popcorn break when you're watching *Titus Andronicus*.

Second, *Titus Andronicus* offers a fascinating glimpse at Shakespeare in the making. *Titus Andronicus* contains the seeds of Lady Macbeth (in Tamora), Hamlet (in Lucius), and King Lear (in Titus himself).

The Least You Need to Know

➤ Elizabethan revenge tragedies feature heroes who take the law into their own hands (and blast everyone in their path) to avenge an injustice.

➤ Titus Andronicus is a victorious Roman general who avenges his daughter Lavinia's rape and mutilation.

➤ *Titus Andronicus* prefigures Shakespeare's greatest dramas.

Chapter 17

Hamlet

In This Chapter

➤ Who's who in *Hamlet*

➤ The plot of *Hamlet*

➤ Hamlet and madness

➤ Famous Hamlets of stage and screen

➤ A *Hamlet* parody

A hit, a very palpable hit.

—*Hamlet*

That's *Hamlet* all right: the greatest play by the world's greatest playwright. Here are some fun facts to use to dazzle your friends at your next cocktail party:

➤ *Hamlet* has been performed more than any other play in the world.

➤ There has been more criticism written about *Hamlet* than any other work of literature.

➤ *Hamlet* has been translated more than any other play.

➤ There are nearly 50 movie versions of *Hamlet*, more than 25 ballets, six operas, and dozens of assorted musical compositions.

➤ Hamlet's lament "To be or not to be" is the most quoted phrase in English.

➤ *Hamlet* is the longest of Shakespeare's plays.

Are you terrified yet? "No way I'll get through *this* baby," you mutter. Not to worry; it's a smashing story that's surprisingly contemporary and easy to read and understand. Have I lied to you yet?

Who's Who in *Hamlet*

Hamlet gets top billing. The son of the King of Denmark, Hamlet is a student of indeterminate age (somewhere between 18 and 30 years old) who returns from school to find that Daddy's dead and Mommy's married Uncle Claudius less than two months after the funeral. Of course, Claudius has seized the throne of Denmark. (And you thought *your* job was insecure.)

Here's the whole cast:

➤ Bernardo, *officer*

➤ Francisco, *soldier*

➤ Horatio, *Hamlet's friend*

➤ Marcellus, *officer*

➤ Ghost of Hamlet's father

➤ Hamlet, *son of the former king/Claudius' nephew*

➤ Claudius, *King of Denmark*

➤ Cornelius, *courtier*

➤ Gertrude, *Queen of Denmark/Hamlet's mother*

➤ Polonius, *Lord Chamberlain*

➤ Laertes, *Polonius' son*

➤ Ophelia, *Polonius' daughter*

➤ Reynaldo, *Polonius' servant*

➤ Players, *actors*

➤ Voltemand, *courtier*

➤ Guildenstern, *courtier*

➤ Rosencrantz, *courtier*

➤ Osric, *courtier*

➤ Fortinbras, *Prince of Norway*

➤ A Norwegian Captain

➤ Gravediggers, *two clowns*

➤ English Ambassadors

➤ The usual assortment of attendants and courtiers

Will Power

Shakespeare's source for *Hamlet* is known as the *Ur-Hamlet,* a play now lost that was popular in the late 1500s. It comes from a ninth century saga about Amleth, a pre-Viking prince, who assumed a mask of madness to protect himself from his uncle, who had killed his father. After avenging his father's death, Amleth went on to other heroic deeds.

The twentieth century certainly hasn't cornered the market on dysfunctional families: Kenneth Branagh as Hamlet at his mother and uncle's wedding.

To Be or Not to Be

'Tis now the very witching time of night.

—*Hamlet*

The play begins on the outer ramparts of Elsinore castle. It's nearly midnight—the witching hour—and bitterly cold. Bernardo, a guard, is on duty waiting for Francisco to relieve him from his watch. Bernardo is nervous because the previous two nights he and Francisco had seen what appeared to be the ghost of the recently deceased King. Hamlet's closest friend, Horatio, comes to check out the situation. As Horatio dismisses the idea of a ghost, it suddenly appears before them. Horatio tries to address the ghost, but it vanishes.

The next scene takes place in the court, with the new King Claudius celebrating his wedding to Hamlet's mother, Gertrude, a scant two months after the death of her first husband, King Hamlet. Everyone is partying, except Prince Hamlet—he sits off to the side, dressed in black.

Claudius conducts business and urges Hamlet to stay in Denmark instead of returning to school in Wittenberg. Hamlet agrees to stay, even though he believes that Claudius is "a little more than kin, and less than kind."

Sweets to the Sweet

Remember that Elizabethans firmly believed in things that go bump in the night. Ghosts were thought to return to Earth if they had unfinished business and so could not rest easily in their graves.

Alone, Hamlet delivers his first famous soliloquy. It starts:

O, that this too too sullied flesh would melt,
Thaw, and resolve itself into a dew,
Or that the Everlasting had not fixed
His canon 'gainst self-slaughter. O God, God,
How weary, stale, flat, and unprofitable
Seems to me all the uses of this world!

—*Hamlet* (I, ii)

The scene shifts to Laertes saying good-bye to his sister Ophelia before he leaves for school. We learn that Hamlet is involved with Ophelia. Laertes tries to warn Ophelia that Hamlet can never marry her because he is destined to become King and so must marry someone of royal blood. She promises to be careful. Polonius enters and lectures his son on his conduct. Try his famous advice when your teenager goes off to college (*before* you hand over the credit card):

Sweets to the Sweet

Hamlet has spawned more famous quotes than any other Shake-spearean play. Here are some you can memorize while you're stuck in line at the ATM:

➤ "Sweets to the sweet: farewell!"

➤ "Brevity is the soul of wit."

➤ "The time is out of joint: O cursed spite, / That ever I was born to set it right!"

➤ "Frailty, thy name is woman!"

➤ "Get thee to a nunnery, go."

➤ "This above all, to thine own self be true."

…Give thy thoughts no tongue,
Nor any unproportioned thought his act.
Be thou familiar, but by no means vulgar.
Those friends thou hast, and their adoption tried,
Grapple them unto thy soul with hoops of steel;
But do not dull thy palm with entertainment
Of each new-hatched, unfledged courage. Beware
Of entrance to a quarrel, but being in,
Bear't that th' opposed may beware of thee…
Costly thy habit as thy purse can buy,
But not expressed in fancy; rich not gaudy,
For the apparel oft proclaims the man…
Neither a borrower not a lender be,
For loan oft loses both itself and friend,
And borrowing dulls th' edge of husbandry.
This above all, to thine own self be true,
And it must follow as the night the day,
Thou canst not then be false to any man.

Polonius, like Laertes, doesn't trust Hamlet's intentions. Although Ophelia has no reason to distrust Hamlet, she's a good little Renaissance girl and so agrees to break off the relationship.

Something Is Rotten in the State of Denmark

The ghost appears on the battlements, identifies itself as Hamlet's father, and asks Hamlet to revenge his "most foul, strange, and unnatural murder." The ghost reveals that King Hamlet was poisoned by his brother Claudius in his sleep. Hamlet swears revenge and warns his friends that he will put on an "antic disposition"—feign madness—until he can avenge his father's death.

Ophelia tells Polonius that Hamlet, in complete disarray, came to see her. Silently, he grabbed her hand and studied her at arm's length. Convinced that Hamlet is still madly in love with Ophelia, Polonius believes his request that Ophelia cut the relationship has sent Hamlet 'round the bend.

The Tweedledum and Tweedledee of Shakespeare

Two months later, Claudius sends for Hamlet's friends Rosencrantz and Guildenstern to see if they can figure out why Hamlet is acting so strangely. Rosencrantz and Guildenstern admit to Hamlet they are spying on him.

Hamlet decides to get proof of Claudius' guilt before proceeding further. A band of roving actors arrives, and Hamlet arranges for them to add some lines to their play that will prove Claudius' guilt. "The play's the thing / Wherein I'll catch the conscience of the king," he believes.

Star Quality

In the mid-'60s, the modern British dramatist Tom Stoppard wrote a famous (and funny) play called *Rosencrantz and Guildenstern Are Dead* after the line in *Hamlet* announcing that R & G had shuffled off this mortal coil. About 25 years after the play was created, in 1991, it was turned into a film starring Tim Roth and Gary Oldman and won honors at the Venice Film Festival. Next time you're at a loss as to what to rent on a Saturday night, check this movie out.

Polonius sets up a meeting between Hamlet and Ophelia. Hamlet expresses his despair in the play's most famous soliloquy:

> To be, or not to be, that is the question:
> Whether 'tis nobler in the mind to suffer
> The slings and arrows of outrageous fortune,

Or to take arms against a sea of troubles,
And by opposing end them. To die, to sleep—
No more; and by a sleep to say we end
The heartache, and the thousand natural shocks
That flesh is heir to. 'Tis a consummation
Devoutly to be wished—to die, to sleep—...

—*Hamlet* (III, i)

After Hamlet rebukes Ophelia for her betrayal, the play, called *The Mousetrap*, is staged. When the murder scene is enacted, Claudius calls for lights and storms out. Hamlet and Horatio are now convinced that the ghost told the truth—Claudius did indeed kill his brother.

Hamlet enters while Claudius is at prayer and overhears Claudius admit to the murder. Although this is the perfect opportunity for Hamlet to kill Step-Daddy Dearest, our hero refuses to do it; he fears that because Claudius is praying, his sins will be forgiven.

Fire at Will

"There are more things in heaven and earth, Horatio / Than are dreamt of in your philosophy." There's a whole group of scholars who argue that Hamlet and Gertrude had an incestuous relationship. This is a key scene in the argument.

Question: Did Hamlet sleep with his mother?
Answer: Only in the New York company.

—John Barrymore

Hamlet tries to convince his mother Gertrude to stop making nice with Claudius. Polonius is hiding behind a curtain. When Hamlet attacks his mother, she screams, Polonius yells, and Hamlet stabs at the sound, killing Polonius. Unable to understand why his mother can forget King Hamlet so easily, Hamlet berates her so violently that the ghost appears. Showing itself to Hamlet only, the ghost reminds Hamlet to leave Gertrude's fate to God. Fed up and fearful, Claudius decides to send Hamlet to England, where he will be killed.

Her father's death at her former lover's hand has sent Ophelia spinning into madness. Laertes returns to Denmark after he hears of his father's death, and Claudius manipulates him into seeking his revenge on Hamlet.

We learn that while at sea, Hamlet had Rosencrantz and Guildenstern killed in his place. Correctly perceiving that Hamlet's on to him, Claudius plots with Laertes to kill Hamlet during a dueling exhibition. As an insurance policy, they'll poison Laertes' sword and offer our hero a poisoned goblet of wine.

"Good Night, Sweet Ladies; Good Night"

Gertrude brings the sad news that Ophelia had drowned. Later, the gravediggers discuss the inappropriateness of Ophelia being buried in a Catholic cemetery after she killed herself. In one of Shakespeare's famous "comic relief" scenes, Hamlet and

Horatio, strolling through the cemetery, joke with the gravediggers. Hamlet finds the skull of his childhood friend the court jester: "Alas, poor Yorick! I knew him Horatio—a fellow of infinite jest, of most excellent fancy."

Mel Gibson starred as Hamlet in the 1990 film version of Shakespeare's famous play. The movie also starred Glen Close, Alan Bates, Ian Holm, and Helena Bonham-Carter.

Hamlet is startled to see Ophelia's funeral; he did not know that she had died. In his grief, Hamlet grapples with Laertes in Ophelia's grave. Not only does this reveal Hamlet's continued love for Ophelia, but it also foreshadows his death.

Hamlet apologizes to Laertes for Polonius' death, saying "I have shot mine arrow o'er the house, / And hurt my brother." Despite Hamlet's humility (and the beauty of his poetry), Laertes insists that honor demands that the duel go on. Hamlet scores the first and second hits. Gertrude toasts Hamlet's success with the poisoned wine. Both Hamlet and Laertes are wounded with the poisoned sword.

Sweets to the Sweet

In the Catholic religion, people who commit suicide are not permitted a proper Catholic burial.

> The expectancy and rose of the fair state,
> The glass of fashion and the mould of form…

—Hamlet

Gertrude dies, but not before revealing that she had been poisoned by Claudius' wine. Laertes reveals Claudius' plan and then dies. Hamlet stabs Claudius with the poisoned sword and then forces him to drink the poisoned wine—double revenge! As he dies, Hamlet gives the nod to Fortinbras for king of Denmark. "Good night, sweet prince," Horatio says. "The rest is silence," Shakespeare notes.

A Prozac Moment: Was Hamlet Mad?

> Though this be madness, yet there is method in 't.
>
> —*Hamlet*

As with the question of Michael Jackson's gender, the issue of Hamlet's madness keeps people up nights. Was Hamlet really mad or was he just pretending madness in the great tradition of revenge heroes? Chew on these ideas:

Hamlet *is* mad because:

➤ He speaks "wild and whirling words" when he hears of his father's murder (I, v, 127–134).

➤ He tells Laertes that he was the only one who truly loved Ophelia, but he told her that he never loved her when she returned his letters and gifts.

➤ His mood changes abruptly throughout the play.

➤ He alone sees his father's ghost in his mother's chamber (III, iv, 105).

➤ He tells Laertes that he killed Polonius in a "fit of madness" (V, ii, 236–250).

Hamlet is *not* mad because:

➤ He tells Horatio that he is going to "feign madness" (I, v, 166–180).

➤ His madness only manifests itself when he is with Polonius, Claudius, Gertrude, Ophelia, Rosencrantz, and Guildenstern. He acts normally with Horatio, Bernardo, Francisco, the Players, and the gravediggers.

➤ Claudius says that Hamlet's "actions although strange, do not appear to stem from madness" (III, i, 165–167).

➤ Polonius admits that Hamlet's actions and words have a "method" to them; they're logical (II, ii, 206–207).

➤ He tells Gertrude that he is not mad, "but mad in craft" (III, iv, 188–199).

Role of the Lifetime

> A heck of a part, tosh.
>
> —Richard Burton

Every actor yearns to play Hamlet, regardless of age, size, shape, and even gender. Here are some notable actors who have made the cut.

1. Edmund Kean (1787–1833)

   Kean was such a powerful Hamlet that during the intermission, members of the audience ran out of the theater and dragged their friends in for the second half.

2. Sarah Bernhardt (1844–1923)

   "The Divine Sarah," as she was called, played the tortured Dane in the 1900 French silent film by Clement Maurice. It is unlikely the film still exists, but the tradition of female Hamlets continues; recently, Diane Venora took a stab at the role in a New York production.

3. John Barrymore (1882–1942)

   One of the best Hamlets of his generation, Barrymore painted certain parts of his anatomy green when he played Hamlet on stage in 1922. (And no, I'm not telling *which* parts he selected.)

4. Sir John Gielgud

   Gielgud played Hamlet first in 1930 and again in the famous film version. His portrayal is considered the definitive Hamlet, but Mel Gibson gets my vote.

5. Jack Benny

   The ageless one played a Polish actor who specializes in Hamlet in a 1942 version called *To Be or Not to Be.*

6. Laurence Olivier (1907–1989)

   The premier actor of his generation, Olivier revitalized interest in Shakespeare through the visually stunning 1948 black-and-white film version of the play.

7. Grigori Kozintsev (1905–1973)

   In 1964, this Kiev-born Ukrainian wrote and directed a black-and-white version that created the definitive mood of *Hamlet.* Accompanied by a Dimitri Shostakovich's romantic score, Kozintsev's *Hamlet* is a must see.

8. Richard Burton

   Directed by John Gielgud in 1964, Burton's *Hamlet* became the longest-running Shakespeare play on Broadway. Wearing black "rehearsal clothes," Burton was an intense, sexy Hamlet.

*Laurence Olivier as
Hamlet.*

9. Nicol Williamson

   Williamson plays a high-strung Hamlet who knows the Establishment is bankrupt. Anthony Hopkins got Claudius, and Marianne Faithfull had a turn as Ophelia in this 1969 movie.

10. Kevin Kline

    Kline played Hamlet in two New York Shakespeare productions, first in 1986 and again in 1990. The critics' response was mixed, but I loved both versions.

12. Mel Gibson

    Mad Max made a surprisingly effective Insane Dane in Franco Zeffirelli's 1990 version. Alan Bates is Claudius, Glenn Close is Gertrude, and Helena Bonham-Carter is Ophelia. The scene between Hamlet and Gertrude is steamy and simply yummy.

13. Christian Bale

    A favorite of the Internet and no stranger to Shakespeare, this Welsh actor appeared in the Danish *Prince of Jutland* made in 1994.

14. Ralph Fiennes

   In 1995, this Brit took London and Broadway by storm in the Almeida Theatre Company's production of *Hamlet*.

15. Kenneth Branagh

   Although it's over four hours long, Branagh's film version of *Hamlet* is spectacular. Interestingly, it's set at the close of the nineteenth century.

A Thin Slice of Ham-let

Hamlet has inspired more parodies than *Saturday Night Live*. Just for fun (and to help you along with some of that Elizabethan language), here's a hard-boiled detective story rundown of Shakespeare's most famous play:

Something was rotten in Denmark, rank and gross, as rotten as a dame named Gertrude in bed with her husband's killer while the caterer recycled the funeral baked meats for the wedding reception, at which bride did not wear white. Hamlet was a sharp prince, good with a knife, but not sharp enough to handle his old man kicking the bucket with an earful of murder. My name's Horatio, Hamlet's gumshoe buddy, trying to stay clean in a dirty castle.

A grizzled ghost pleaded the Fifth when I gave him the third degree, then split the scene when the cock crew, like a guilty man before a marshal serving summons. King Claudius, cool as a cucumber after offing his brother, twisted nephew Hamlet's arm not to return to college at Wittenberg, Caltech having yet been built.

The ghost came again. It was Hamlet's father's spirit. His tale would freeze blood and make your hair stand on end like porcupine quills. He demanded revenge for murder most foul. The snake that killed him wore the crown. Me and Hamlet took the case. Hamlet's main squeeze, Ophelia, a green girl, griped that Hamlet was as pale as his shirt, in dirty sox, acting weird. Fortinbras was gang-banging Polacks. Hamlet played mad, but when the Santa Ana blew, he knew a hawk from a handsaw. A bunch of non-Guild actors showed up for the castle venue. "To be or not to be," mused Hamlet, thinking of a one-way ticket to the morgue. At the play, the King freaked. Polonius hid behind Queen Gertrude's bedroom curtain, but Hamlet smelled a rat and stabbed him dead. "I'll lug the guts into the neighbor room," he said, the corpse where worms ate brunch and didn't leave a tip. Laertes found his sister Ophelia drowned in muddy death.

Hamlet and Laertes got to business with a couple of long knives while the Queen gulped some poison Pinot Noir the King meant for Hamlet. The Queen fell. Hamlet and Laertes cut each other up, then Hamlet swigged from the deadly cup and stabbed the killer King stone cold dead. Instant karma, I guess. Fortinbras stomped into Denmark with his gang and lots of drums. I was the last guy left. I heard a gunshot. I looked off into the distance, toward beautiful La Jolla, a solid heavy man like a rock.

You get the picture.

The Least You Need to Know

➤ *Hamlet* is Shakespeare's most famous play.

➤ Hamlet thinks too much, but he still gets the job done, avenging his father's murder. Everyone dies, but that's why it's called a tragedy.

➤ Critics debate whether Hamlet is really deranged or just pretending to be the Insane Dane.

➤ Every actor wants to play Hamlet. In our day, Laurence Olivier, Richard Burton, Nicol Williamson, Kevin Kline, Mel Gibson, Ralph Fiennes, and Kenneth Branagh got the nod.

Chapter 18

Romeo and Juliet

In This Chapter

➤ Who's who in *Romeo and Juliet*

➤ The plot of *Romeo and Juliet*

➤ Shakespeare's mature poetry

➤ A tragedy of fate or character?

➤ *Romeo and Juliet* on film

On a transatlantic flight, a plane passed through a severe storm. The turbulence was awful, and things went from bad to worse when one wing was struck by lightning. A woman stood up in the front of the plane and started screaming.

"I'm too young to die!" she wailed. "Well," she screamed, "if I'm going to die, I want my last minutes on Earth to be memorable! Is there *anyone* on this plane who can make me feel like a real woman?"

For a moment there was silence. Forgetting their own peril, everyone stared, riveted, at the desperate woman in the front of the plane.

A man stood up in the rear of the plane. "I can make you feel like a woman," he said. He was gorgeous: tall, dark, and handsome. He started to walk slowly up the aisle, unbuttoning his shirt one button at a time. No one moved. The woman was breathing heavily in anticipation as the stranger approached. He removed his shirt. Muscles rippled across his chest as he reached her and extended the arm holding his shirt to the trembling woman. He whispered:

"Iron this."

Is it any wonder we keep returning to *Romeo and Juliet*? Who wants reality when we can have a *real* romance? *R & J* has it all: love, passion, mad blood stirring—and no Kenneth Starr snooping around in the end.

Who's Who in *Romeo and Juliet*

It's the young and the restless, Elizabethan style. You know that Romeo is a hunka hunka burning love; Juliet, a rare flower of budding womanhood. What about the rest of the ensemble? Meet them now:

➤ Chorus

➤ Escalus, *Prince of Verona*

➤ Paris, *a young nobleman, the Prince's kinsman*

➤ Montague, *Capulet's enemy*

➤ Capulet, *Montague's enemy*

➤ An old man of the Capulet family

➤ Romeo, *Montague's son*

➤ Mercutio, *the Prince's kinsman and Romeo's friend*

➤ Benvolio, *Montague's nephew, Romeo's friend*

➤ Tybalt, *Lady Capulet's nephew*

➤ Petruchio, *Tybalt's follower*

➤ Friar Lawrence, *Franciscan monk*

➤ Friar John, *Franciscan monk*

➤ Balthsar, *Romeo's servant*

➤ Abram, *Montague's servant*

➤ Sampson, *Capulet's servant*

➤ Gregory, *Capulet's servant*

➤ Clown, *Capulet's servant*

➤ Peter, *servant to Juliet's nurse*

➤ Page, *to Paris*

➤ Apothecary

➤ Three musicians

➤ Lady Montague, *Montague's wife*

➤ Lady Capulet, *Capulet's wife*

➤ Juliet, *Capulet's daughter*

➤ Nurse, *to Juliet*

➤ Usual assortment of citizens, gentlemen and gentlewomen, pages, guards, watchmen, et. al.

Star Quality

Although a common fire escape replaced the noble balcony, the Bernstein/Robbins 1961 reworking of *Romeo and Juliet* as *West Side Story* became an American classic. Starring Natalie Wood as Maria/Juliet and Richard Beymer as Tony/Romeo, the film exploded with emotion. Be sure to catch it; you'll be humming "Tonight" and "America" for days.

Eternal Love

As the Chorus informs us in the beginning:

> Two households, both alike in dignity
> In fair Verona, where we lay our scene,
> From ancient grudge break to new mutiny,
> Where civil blood makes civil hands unclean,
> From forth the fatal loins of these two foes
> A pair of star-cross'd lovers take their life;
> Whose misadventur'd piteous overthrows
> Doth with their death bury their parents' strife.

What's *this*? We get the play's ending at the very beginning? Yes, you read that right. It's part of Shakespeare's brilliance that foreknowledge of the tragic conclusion adds to the drama rather than reduces it. Why?

The Chorus suggests that the lovers are fulfilling their destiny—their deaths are not an end but rather the continuation of their love. By dying in their bloom, Romeo and Juliet achieve eternal love.

Saturday Night Fever

The action opens on the streets of Verona, a pleasant little Italian town. For years, the peace has been periodically disturbed by the feuding of two families, the Montagues and the Capulets, who bear an ancient grudge. At the start of the play, the feud flares up again because of servants spoiling for a fight.

That very evening the Capulets are holding a traditional family party. Romeo, a Montague, decides to crash the party with some of his friends. He is in love with Rosaline, but since she doesn't return his love, a fella's entitled to a little shopping around.

At the party, Romeo looks across the room, glimpses Juliet, and you guessed it—falls instantly in love. Here's what Romeo gasps when he glimpses Juliet for the first time:

Sweets to the Sweet

As the play opens, Romeo is a stereotype of the romantic Renaissance lover. He writes poetry and revels in sorrow, tears, secrecy, and isolation. He speaks in flowery rhymed couplets (pairs of lines), not commonly found in Shakespeare's blank verse.

O, she doth teach the torches to burn bright!
It seems she hangs upon the cheek of night
As a rich jewel in an Ethiop's ear—
Beauty too rich for use, for earth too dear!
So shows a snowy dove trooping with crows,
As yonder lady o'er her fellows shows.
The measure done, I'll watch her place of stand,
And touching hers, make blessed my rude hand.
Did my heart love till now? Forswear it, sight!
For I ne'er saw true beauty till this night.

Unfortunately, the object of Romeo's love is the daughter of his family's arch-enemy. To complicate matters, Juliet returns Romeo's love. And you thought your teenagers were driving you nuts?

Claire Danes and Leonardo DiCaprio star as the famous star-crossed lovers in the 1996 film version of Romeo and Juliet.

Balcony Sales Soar

After the party, the young couple woo each other in Capulet's orchard. Amazed by Juliet's beauty, Romeo delivers his famous soliloquy:

Romeo: But, soft! what light through yonder window breaks?
           It is the east, and Juliet is the sun.
           Arise, fair sun, and kill the envious moon

196

Who is already sick and pale with grief
That thou, her maid, art far more fair than she.
Be not her maid, since she is envious...
It is my lady, O, it is my love!
O that she knew she were!...
　　　She speaks!
O, speak again, bright angel, for thou art
As glorious to this night, being o'er my head,
As is a winged messenger of heaven
Unto the white-upturned wond'ring eyes
Of mortals that fall back to gaze on him,
When he bestrides the lazy puffing clouds,
And sails upon the bosom of the air.

Juliet:　　　O Romeo, Romeo, wherefore art thou Romeo?
Deny thy father and refuse thy name;
Or, if thou wilt not, be but sworn my love,
And I'll no longer be a Capulet.

Here's where Juliet declares that "that which we call a rose / By any other name would smell as sweet / So Romeo would, were he not Romeo call'd" (II, ii). As this breathtaking poetry shows, *Romeo and Juliet* marks the beginning of Shakespeare's mature period.

After gorgeous poetry like this, you know it's going to be a short courtship. Sure enough, the kids agree to be secretly married the next day. But it's more than mere hormonal overdrive: These kids have the real thing.

Meanwhile, Lord and Lady Capulet are discussing a match between Juliet and the wealthy, noble Paris. Lady Capulet approaches marriage as a transaction, common in Shakespeare's day: "So shall you share all that he doth possess, / By having him making yourself no less."

Heaven on Earth

Romeo rushes to his priest, Friar Lawrence, to arrange the wedding ceremony. Romeo informs Juliet of the time and place by giving a message to her Nurse, and the couple meet and are married

Fire at Will

"O Romeo, Romeo, wherefore art thou Romeo?" is the most misunderstood sentence in all of Shakespeare. It means "*Why* are you Romeo?" not "*Where* are you, Romeo?"

Will Power

Mercutio's "Queen Mab" speech in Act I, scene iv is a Shakespearean tour de force. Both impassioned and alienated, the speech shows Shakespeare's genius with language.

197

that very afternoon. The Friar counsels moderation and wisdom: "These violent delights have violent ends, / And in their triumph die, like fire and powder, / Which as they kiss consume." He cautions Romeo to love moderately, so that he may love long.

But the kids revel in their love and by pushing their luck, taunt death. Who can blame them? Love this strong burns bright. Besides, can we really see Romeo and Juliet gumming their cereal as they compare cellulite? No. Their love is destined to speed by faster than a speeding bullet.

> **Sweets to the Sweet**
>
> Escalus represents law, order, and justice. He appears at each of the three crucial points in the play: when the feud breaks out anew, at Mercutio's death, and at the fateful climax of the lovers' sacrificial death. He shows that the forces of rational order are useless against passion.

After the ceremony, Romeo and Juliet decide that Romeo will come to Juliet's bedroom at nightfall. Romeo impatiently passes the intervening hours with his friends, among them the swift-witted Mercutio. As they walk, Tybalt Capulet appears. Tybalt is insulted that Romeo attended the Capulet party and so challenges him to a duel. Romeo, however, is unwilling to fight his new cousin. Mercutio fights in Romeo's place and is killed. Romeo jumps in, kills Tybalt, and flees to the safety of the Friar's cell. Romeo is punished with exile.

Mercutio's death is the play's turning point; from now on, Romeo and Juliet's love will hurtle them to doom.

A Plague o' Both Your Houses!

> Good night, good night! parting is such sweet sorrow,
> That I shall say good night till it be morrow.
>
> —Romeo

The lovers, wretched at this turn of events, spend their first and last night together and part sadly. No sooner has Romeo left than Juliet learns that her parents have arranged for her to marry Paris. We have every reason to believe that Paris would, under other circumstances, have made an excellent, loving husband for Juliet, but these aren't other circumstances.

Since everything happens fast in this play, the wedding is scheduled for the next day. Unwilling to reveal her secret marriage or agree to double-dipping, Juliet causes a huge family quarrel by refusing to marry Paris. Her father threatens to throw her out of the house if she does not change her mind, and Juliet hurries to the Friar for advice.

The Best-Laid Plans...

Juliet and the Friar concoct a desperate plan: Juliet will pretend to consent to the marriage, but the night before the wedding she will swallow a sleeping potion that will make her appear dead. Her parents and Paris will mourn for her and put her in the family vault. The Friar will inform Romeo, who will run away with Juliet when she awakens.

The plan complete, Juliet returns to her parents. Later that night, she swallows the potion. The next morning, she is discovered, believed dead, and mourned pitifully. So far, so good. But as chance would have it, the Friar's message never reached Romeo.

When Romeo hears the news that his bride is dead, he decides to go to her tomb and kill himself there. For this purpose he brings poison. At the last minute, the Friar discovers that his message has not been delivered and decides to go to the tomb and fetch Juliet.

Fire at Will

They may not be hard on the eyes, but don't be misled by their beauty: The characters in *Romeo and Juliet* are firmly earthbound. This play abounds with sexual puns, double-entendres, and other bawdy references. Be sure to get a copy of the play that explains *all* the references.

Arriving at the tomb, Romeo meets Paris, who has come to mourn Juliet. Paris tries to arrest Romeo for breaking his exile. In the ensuing fight, Paris is killed. Romeo says his farewell to the sleeping Juliet and takes the poison. "O true apothecary! / Thy drugs are quick. Thus with a kiss I die."

A Day Late and a Dollar Short

> When he shall die,
> Take him and cut him out in little stars,
> And he will make the face of heaven so fine
> That all the world will be in love with night,
> And pay no worship to the garish sun.
>
> —Juliet

Seconds after Romeo's death, the Friar arrives and Juliet awakens. The Friar cannot persuade Juliet to leave Romeo's body. The Friar leaves, and Juliet kills herself with Romeo's dagger. The watchmen arrive, find the three corpses, and sound the alarm.

The Friar comes forward and explains what has happened. His story is corroborated by a farewell letter Romeo has sent to his father. Seeing how the feud has brought such tragedy, the Capulets and the Montagues decide to call an end to their battle, and peace is restored to Verona.

Calling the two feuding families to him, the Prince admonishes, "See what a scourge is laid upon your hate, / That heaven finds means to kill your joys with love." The Prince himself has lost two relatives by not punishing the feuding families harshly enough to make them stop. Capulet and Montague, each pledging gold statues of the other's child, shake hands and vow to feud no more. The play ends on a note of "glooming peace": "The sun for sorrow will not raise his head." The Prince challenges everyone to think this over and closes the play with the words, "Never was a story of more woe, / Than this of Juliet and her Romeo." The play has come full circle and completed itself as was foretold in the Prologue.

Elizabethan Star Wars

What strange kind of tragedy do we have here? In Shakespeare's other tragedies, the calamity comes about because the hero has a tragic flaw that causes his downfall. But Romeo and Juliet are trapped in a situation they didn't create. After all, it's not their fault that their parents have been doing a Hatfield and McCoy for generations. They don't have any apparent tragic flaws, so how can we explain their fate?

Shakespeare calls them "star-crossed," born under the wrong stars. Remember that the Elizabethans were great believers in the influence of the stars and planets on a person's life. They believed that a person's fate was determined in large part by the arrangement of stars at the time of his or her birth. Any half-competent astrologer could determine a baby's personality, life, and even death from the configuration of the sky and stars at the exact moment of birth.

Is *Romeo and Juliet* a tragedy of fate or a tragedy of character? I'll vote for fate. The tragedy is created through bad luck, poor timing, blunders, and tragic misunderstandings. The teenage lovers also have to deal with their parents, who are too absorbed in their petty hatreds to cope with reality.

Sweets to the Sweet

Oh, how time flies: Romeo and Juliet meet, fall in love, and die in less than a week.

Will Power

Romeo and Juliet are surely Shakespeare's most famous pair of "star-crossed" lovers, but they are far from the only ones. In *Henry VI, Part II*, as the Duke of Suffolk is about to be murdered aboard a ship, he recalls, "A cunning man did calculate my birth / And told me that by water I should die." When Benedick in *Much Ado About Nothing* is having trouble writing a love poem, he comforts himself with the knowledge that "I was not born under a rhyming planet." In *Two Gentlemen of Verona*, Juliet puts all her faith in astrology.

Child Brides

Actress Ellen Terry once claimed: "As soon as a woman is old enough to understand Juliet, she's too old to play her." Unfortunately, most Juliets are far above the age of consent. Here are a few of the most famous:

➤ Norma Shearer was 36 years old in the 1936 movie; her Romeo, Leslie Howard, was middle-aged. They're so good you can almost forget they're too old for the roles—almost, but not quite. (Howard was the third choice for the role: Clark Gable, 34, was the first choice.)

➤ Susan Shentall made an astonishingly forgettable Juliet to Laurence Harvey's equally blah Romeo. Who knows how old they are? Who cares? Forget this 1954 gobbler.

➤ Margot Fonteyn and Rudolph Nureyev danced their way through their 1966 version. The zoom lens reminds us that they're too old to be teenage lovers, but they sure can trip the light fantastic.

Not surprisingly, the best version of *Romeo and Juliet* is Franco Zeffirell's 1968 film. Seventeen-year-old Leonard Whiting and 15-year-old Olivia Hussey come closest to capturing the essence of Shakespeare's star-crossed young lovers. Critics complained that their blank verse was blank indeed, but the chemistry is there.

Star Quality

The 1961 film version of *West Side Story*, starring Natalie Wood, Richard Beymer, and Rita Moreno, is a vivid adaptation of the landmark Broadway musical, updating *Romeo and Juliet* to the youth gang atmosphere of New York City in the late 1950s. The movie won 10 Academy Awards, including Best Picture, Best Direction, and Supporting Actor and Actress.

The 1996 Claire Danes/Leonardo DiCaprio version got the lovers' ages close, but the post-modern '90s view gets old really fast. Even though all the words are there (in the right places, too), there are only so many MTV images you can take before your brain short circuits.

The Least You Need to Know

➤ In *Romeo and Juliet*, the world's most famous lovers play out the world's worst run of luck.

➤ Unique among Shakespeare's tragedies, *Romeo and Juliet* is tragedy of fate, not character.

➤ The poetry is gorgeous, richer and deeper than anything that Shakespeare had written before.

➤ *Romeo and Juliet* is the classic tear-jerker.

Chapter 19

Julius Caesar

In This Chapter

➤ Who's who in *Julius Caesar*

➤ The plot of *Julius Caesar*

➤ The play's real hero

What better place to set the stage for a story chock-full of heroes and villains than in ancient Rome? William Shakespeare knew a great backdrop when he saw it, all right, and boiled up a tale full of trouble with a capital T. Who are the troublemakers? Who's *not*? It all started with a little envy, some ambition, and a grudge or two. Read on to get the scoop on one of Shakespeare's most popular and enduring plays—*Julius Caesar*.

Who's Who in *Julius Caesar*

> Let me have men about me that are fat,
> Sleek-headed men, and such as sleep o' nights:
> Yond Cassius has a lean and hungry look;
> He thinks too much: such men are dangerous.

"Men at some time are masters of their fates": Surely this is true of the emperor himself, Julius Caesar, the character who gets top billing in this tragedy. Caesar knows the kind of men he wants on his side, and he's onto Cassius, a rat if ever there was one. It's no surprise that this power-hungry usurper-to-be conspires against Caesar.

Meet the rest of the gang:

➤ Octavius Caesar, *triumvir after the death of Julius Caesar*

➤ Mark Antony, *triumvir after the death of Julius Caesar*

➤ M. Aemilius Lepidus, *triumvir after the death of Julius Caesar*

➤ Cicero, *senator*

➤ Publius, *senator*

➤ Popilius Lena, *senator*

➤ Marcus Brutus, *conspirator against Julius Caesar*

➤ Casca, *conspirator against Julius Caesar*

➤ Trebonius, *conspirator against Julius Caesar*

➤ Caius Ligarius, *conspirator against Julius Caesar*

➤ Decius Brutus, *conspirator against Julius Caesar*

➤ Metellus Cimber, *conspirator against Julius Caesar*

➤ Cinna, *conspirator against Julius Caesar*

➤ Falvius and Murellus, *tribunes*

➤ Artemidorus of Cnidos, *teacher of rhetoric*

➤ Soothsayer

➤ Cinna, *a poet*

➤ Another poet

➤ Lucilus, *friend of Brutus and Cassius*

➤ Titinius, *friend of Brutus and Cassius*

➤ Messala, *friend of Brutus and Cassius*

➤ Young Cato, *friend of Brutus and Cassius*

➤ Volumnius, *friend of Brutus and Cassius*

➤ Flavius, *friend of Brutus and Cassius*

➤ Varrus, Clitus, Claudio, Strato, Lucius, Dardanius, *Brutus' servants*

➤ Pindarus, *Cassius' servant*

➤ Calphurnia, *Caesar's wife*

➤ Portia, *Brutus' wife*

➤ Senators, citizens, guards, etc.

Will Power

The Booths belonged to one of the most distinguished acting families of the nineteenth century. Their lives were inextricably entwined with Shakespeare in general and with *Julius Caesar* in particular. The patriarch of the clan, Junius Brutus Booth, was named after Brutus, the assassin who killed Julius Caesar. On April 14, 1864, John Wilkes Booth assassinated Abraham Lincoln, whom he considered a tyrant along the lines of Caesar. After shooting the president, Booth leaped from Lincoln's box onto the stage screaming, "Sic Semper Tyrannis" ("Thus Be It Ever to Tyrants").

Caesar Salad Days

As the play opens, the Roman people are lining the streets to cheer the triumphal return of Caesar from his victory over Pompey, a member of the first triumvirate and champion of the Republic. Flavius and Murellus, two tribunes, disperse the crowds, arguing that Caesar's triumph in civil war is no cause for celebration and that the people would be better off crying for Pompey, whom they had formerly worshipped.

Amid much hoopla, Caesar arrives to witness the race traditionally held on the Feast of Lupercal, which is being celebrated that day. A soothsayer warns Caesar to beware the ides of March, but Caesar ignores him: "He is a dreamer; let us leave him," he says. Meanwhile, Cassius has some issues about Caesar's growing power. He tells his buddy Brutus about his concerns. As Caesar emerges from the race, he eyes Cassius and tells Antony that he does not trust him. Casca joins Brutus and Cassius and describes how Caesar has refused the crown that Mark Antony has offered him three times. Brutus promises to consider Cassius' fear that Caesar's ambition is a danger to the democracy of Rome and agrees to meet him the next day. Casca is invited to join them.

Forsooth!

Tribunes were officers appointed to protect the interests of the people from possible injustice at the hands of patrician magistrates.

Sweets to the Sweet

During the Feast of Lupercal, two young men carrying thongs made from a sacrificed goat raced around the Palatine. Women lined up along the path to be smacked by the thongs to ensure fertility. *Ouch.*

The Feast of Lupercal commemorated the suckling of Rome's founders, Romulus and Remus, by a wolf. Raised by wolves, were you?

Midnight Madness

It is the eve of the ides of March. Lightning flashes across the sky as thunder roars. Terrified by the storm, Casca tells Cicero that either there is "civil strife in heaven" or someone has really offended the gods. He then describes the amazing things he has seen that night. It *was* a doozy.

> A common slave—you know him well by sight—
> Held up his left hand, which did flame and burn
> Like twety torches join'd; and yet his hand,
> Not sensible of fire, remain'd unscorch'd.
> Besides—I ha' not since put up my sword—
> Against the Capitol I met a lion,
> Who glaz'd upon me, and went surly by,
> Without annoying me.

After Cicero leaves, Cassius arrives, explains the omens of the storm, and discusses a conspiracy against Caesar. After all, "The fault, dear Brutus, is not in our stars, / But in ourselves, that we are underlings." Together, they plot how to win Brutus over to their side completely, for he is already inclined against Caesar.

Alone in his garden, Brutus debates with himself over the threat that Caesar poses to the Republic. "It must be by his death," Brutus thinks, "and for my part, / I know no personal cause to spurn at him, / But for the general. He would be crown'd: / How that might change his nature, there's the question." At last he decides that Caesar must be killed because he might become a tyrant. He and the other conspirators (Cassius, Casca, Decius, Brutus, Cinna, Metellus Cimber, and Trebonius) agree to kill Caesar the next day when he is crowned.

After the conspirators leave, Portia, Brutus' wife, enters. Just as he is about to reveal the conspiracy to her, another conspirator, Ligarius, arrives and he and Brutus go out.

Forsooth!

On the ancient Roman calendar, the **ides** were the 15th day of March, May, July, or October, or the 13th day of the remaining months. According to *Brewer's Dictionary of Phrase and Fable*, the ides started with Caesar, when soothsayers gave the warnings, and that's where we got the "beware the ides..."

Fire at Will

For better or verse, *Julius Caesar* is numero uno with high school teachers. Why teach *JC* when the comedies are so much more fun? The answer is plain to those who deal with teenagers: *Julius Caesar* is one of Shakespeare's shortest plays, and it doesn't have any sex. See why people hate Shakespeare in high school?

Beware the Ides of March!

Meanwhile, Caesar isn't sleeping well. His wife Calphurnia begs him not to go to the Senate meeting that day because she has premonitions of evil—an unnerving dream that Caesar was a statue, spouting blood like a fountain. Caesar sends his servant to the soothsayers to make a sacrifice and to determine what the gods are trying to say. The augurers tell Caesar to stay at home, and Caesar decides to listen to them, especially since his wife has urged him so strongly. However, one of the conspirators, Decius Brutus, persuades him to go to the Senate by pointing out how ridiculous he would seem to listen to his wife's superstitions.

The same morning, Artemidorus, a teacher of rhetoric, sends Caesar a letter warning him of the conspiracy. The Soothsayer also prepares to stop Caesar outside the Capitol to warn him of harm. Portia, who now knows Brutus' plan, anxiously anticipates its outcome.

With Friends Like This, Who Needs Enemies?

> When beggars die, there are no comets seen;
> The heavens themselves blaze forth the death of princes.
>
> —Brutus

Caesar is given two warnings, but he ignores them both and goes into the Senate. In a speech before the Senators, Caesar arrogantly praises himself. He asserts: "I am constant as the Northern Star, / Of whose true-fixed and resting quality / There is no fellow in the firmament." Among men on Earth, Caesar continues, "Men are flesh and blood, and apprehensive; / Yet in the number I do know but one / That unassailable holds on his rank, / Unshaked of motion; and that I am he." Bad call, Caesar.

Star Quality

Add Shakespeare to Hollywood and what do you get? In the case of Joseph L. Mankiewicz's 1953 *Julius Caesar*, you end up with a static, talky movie—despite Marlon Brando as Mark Antony, James Mason as Brutus, and John Gielgud as Cassius.

Casca signals the attack, "Speak, hands, for me!" He stabs Caesar, and one by one, the other conspirators add their blows. Seeing Brutus among their number, the stricken Caesar cries, "Et tu, Brute?"—Then fall, Caesar.

Mark Antony, lured out of the Senate by Trebonius, returns after the murder and pretends to join the conspirators. When left alone with Caesar's body, however, Antony vows to avenge the murder, even if he has to throw all Italy into civil war to do it.

Marlon Brando in his Caesar salad days. The toga makes the man. Photo courtesy of MGM Turner.

O, pardon me, thou bleeding piece of earth,
That I am meek and gentle with these butchers!
Thou art the ruins of the noblest man
That ever lived in the tide of times. ...
A curse shall light upon the limbs of men;
Domestic fury and fierce civil strife
Shall cumber all parts of Italy...

Meanwhile, Octavius, Caesar's heir, arrives near Rome. Next to Caesar's body, Brutus tells the crowd that Caesar was killed because he was too ambitious. The crowd cheers Brutus and is ready to make him a second Caesar, but Brutus orders them to listen to Antony's funeral oration for Caesar before they're so quick to pick a new prez.

In a brilliantly ironic speech, Antony inflames the crowd against the conspirators. His words have become famous:

Friends, Romans, countrymen, lend me your ears!
I come to bury Caesar, not to praise him.
The evil men do lives after them,
The good is often interred with their bones;
So let it be with Caesar. The noble Brutus
Hath told you Caesar was ambitious:
If it were so, it was a grievous fault,
And grievously hath Caesar answer'd it.
Here, under leave of Brutus and the rest
(For Brutus was an honorable man,
So are they all, all honorable men),
Come I to speak at Caesar's funeral.
He was my friend, faithful and just to me;
But Brutus says he was ambitious,
And Brutus is an honorable man.
He hath brought many captives home to Rome,
Whose ransoms did the general coffers fill;
Did this in Caesar seem ambitious?
When that the poor have cried, Caesar hath wept;
Ambition should be made of sterner stuff:
Yet Brutus says he was ambitious,
And Brutus is an honorable man.
You all did see that on the Lupercal
I thrice presented him a kingly crown,
Which he did thrice refuse. Was this ambition?
Yet Brutus says he was ambitious,
And sure he is an honorable man.
I speak not to disprove what Brutus spoke,
But here I am to speak what I do know.
You all did love him once, not without cause;
What cause withholds you then to mourn for him?
O judgment! thou [art] fled to brutish beasts,
And men have lost their reason. Bear with me,
My heart is in the coffin there with Caesar,
And I must pause till it come back to me.

(III, ii, 74–107)

Thrilled by Antony's words, the crowd runs wildly through the streets, determined to burn the conspirators' houses. As they slash and burn, the mob encounters Cinna the poet. Since he has the same name as one of the conspirators, the mob tears him to pieces. Brutus and Cassius flee Rome. Antony, Octavius, and Lepidus unite forces, calling themselves the second triumvirate. They prepare to kill anyone they suspect will be hostile to their cause.

209

Great Caesar's Ghost

Meanwhile, back in Asia Minor, Brutus and Cassius have gathered their forces. Their destruction is apparent when they begin to argue with each other. Brutus reprimands Cassius because the latter has permitted an officer to take bribes and because he has not been sending money to Brutus, who has been unable to raise his own funds. His anger spent, Brutus apologizes for his outburst and tells Cassius that Portia has killed herself. During the night, Brutus sees Caesar's ghost, who says that they will meet again at Philippi.

Cassius and Brutus march to Philippi in Greece to meet the armies of Antony and Octavius. The generals meet and "dis" each other before the battle begins. Mistaking some horsemen for enemies, Cassius runs upon a sword held by his servant, Pindarus. Brutus finds Cassius' body and sends it away for burial. In the second battle, Brutus' forces are smashed.

Fire at Will

Julius Caesar contains Shakespeare's usual quota of bad puns. Here's a real groaner:

Cobbler: ...I am but, as you would say, a cobbler.

Murellus: But what trade are thou? Answer me directly.

Cobbler: A trade, sir, that I hope I may use with a safe conscience; which is, indeed, sir, a mender of bad soles.

Cowards die many times before their deaths;
The valiant never taste of death but once.
Of all the wonders that I yet have heard,
It seems to me most strange that men should fear;
Seeing that death, a necessary end,
Will come when it will come.

—Brutus

Brutus commits suicide with the aid of his servant, Strato. Standing over Brutus' body, Antony says:

This was the noblest Roman of them all.
All the conspirators, save only he,
Did that they did in envy of great Caesar;
He, only in a general honest thought
And common good to all, made one of them.

Antony concludes his eulogy of Brutus by describing his nature as gentle "and the elements / So mixed in him that Nature might stand up / And say to all the world, 'This was a man!'"

Octavius declares that Brutus will receive burial befitting his virtue and calls an end to battle as the play concludes.

Whose Tragedy Is It Anyway?

For hundreds of years, critics, readers, and scholars have been debating which character gets the nod as the hero of *Julius Caesar*. There are three contenders: Caesar, Brutus, or the theme of rebellion. I'll give you the evidence; you make the decision.

1. Caesar as hero
   - ➤ The play is called *Julius Caesar*, not *Marcus Brutus* or *Tragedy with a Great Theme, Kids.*
   - ➤ The Elizabethans were obsessed with Caesar.
   - ➤ The play centers around Caesar, whether he's dead or alive. The opening scene presents opposite views of Caesar, the tribunes' hatred and the mobs' love. Later, Caesar marches in triumph. All eyes are on Caesar when he opens the Senate on the fateful ides of March; after his assassination, Antony and Octavius carry on his success and ambition.

2. Brutus as hero
   - ➤ Do an about-face on Caesar: If Brutus is the hero, Caesar must be an arrogant tyrant. Therefore, Brutus is doing his duty to the Republic by assassinating him.
   - ➤ Brutus' tragedy is the tragedy of a man too true to his ideals to be good at the job of statecraft.
   - ➤ Brutus was an honorable man. Even Antony knew that Brutus "was the noblest Roman of them all."

3. Theme as hero
   - ➤ *Julius Caesar* explores rebellion and the evil that comes after, so there's no hero.
   - ➤ Through his arrogance in seeking the crown, Caesar tempts the gods and invites his own death.
   - ➤ The rebel Brutus commits an immoral act and brings disaster to the Republic.

Star Quality

Jason Robards walked through the 1970 film version, doing a curiously zombie-like Brutus. Charlton Heston, Richard Chamberlain, Robert Vaughn, and Diana Rigg also march through in their togas. And what's a Shakespeare film without John Gielgud?

The Least You Need to Know

➤ One of Shakespeare's most popular and accessible plays, *Julius Caesar* focuses on the themes of rebellion and ambition.

➤ Some great lines, some great scenes: *Julius Caesar* is one of Shakespeare's most-quoted plays.

➤ Is Brutus the real hero of the play? The debate is still raging.

Othello, the Moor of Venice

I have done the state some service, and they know 't.
No more of that. I pray you, in your letters,
When you shall these unlucky deeds relate,
Speak of me as I am; nothing extenuate,
Nor set down aught in malice. Then, must you speak
Of one that loved not wisely but too well;
Of one not easily jealous, but being wrought
Perplex'd in the extreme; of one whose hand,
Like the base Indian, threw a pearl away
Richer than all his tribe; of one whose subdued eyes,
Albeit unused to the melting mood,
Drop tears as fast as the Arabian trees
Their medicinal gum.

—Othello

People either love or hate *Othello*—there's no middle ground with this tragedy. The emotions are so strong and the action so dense that there's no room in the audience for dilly-dallying. And *Othello* has it all: an evil villain, touchy racial issues, fierce sexual jealousy, generational conflicts, blood, and guts. Step into this seamy world for yourself.

Who's Who in *Othello*

Othello, the great tragic hero of this play, is a professional soldier known for his skill on the battlefield and his great dignity. Conscious of his own worth, he is nonetheless not afraid to show his feelings: "I will wear my heart upon my sleeve / For daws to peck at," he says. Brains and brawn, sensitive and sensible—ladies, line up right here.

Meet the rest of the gang:

➤ Duke of Venice

➤ Brabantio, *a senator, Desdemona's father*

➤ Other Senators

➤ Gratiano, *Brabantio's brother*

➤ Lodovico, *Brabantio's kinsman*

➤ Othello, *the Moor, in the military service of Venice*

➤ Cassio, *an honorable lieutenant*

➤ Iago, *an ensign, the villain*

➤ Roderigo, *a gull'd (gullible) gentleman*

➤ Montano, *governor of Cyprus (before Othello)*

➤ Clown, *Othello's servant*

➤ Desdemona, *Brabantio's daughter and Othello's wife*

➤ Emilia, *Iago's wife*

➤ Bianca, *a courtesan*

➤ Gentlemen of Cyprus, sailors, officers, etc.

Fire at Will

Famed Irish playwright George Bernard Shaw dismissed *Othello* for what he called its "police-court mentality and commonplace thought."

Want a great version of Othello? *Try the 1983 BBC tape with Anthony Hopkins as Othello. It's not "Silence of the Bard." Photo courtesy of PBS.*

You Can't Judge a Book by Its Cover

Othello is a Shakespearean tragedy, without a doubt, but it's different from the rest of the pack. Remember what you learned in the first part of this book about Shakespeare crafting each play from scratch. No production line for the Bard. As a result, each play is unique. Here's what sets *Othello* off from the rest of Shakespeare's tragedies:

1. *Othello* is a domestic tragedy, not a national one. The act has no national repercussions—corpses don't rise from their graves, the heavens don't rain blood.
2. There's only one emotion—sexual jealously.
3. There's no subplot to divert our attention.
4. Ditto on comic relief—there isn't any. The clown didn't make the cut.
5. There's only two settings (Venice and Cyprus)—we're not shifting from city to country, battlefield to bedroom.
6. There's very little action, especially for a Shakespearean tragedy. Iago acts; the others react.

Now, let's look at the story itself.

I Can't Get No Satisfaction

Time: Not specified

Place: Venice; a seaport in Cyprus

When the play opens, Iago and Roderigo are engaged in a heated discussion. From them we learn that Othello, a Moor (a black man) in the service of the Duke of Venice, has just eloped with Desdemona, a white Venetian lady, who has refused Roderigo's offer of marriage. Later, Othello describes his marriage this way. It's a famous passage.

Forsooth!

Throughout the play, Iago is referred to as Othello's **ancient**—his second-in-command.

Sweets to the Sweet

The hierarchy of the Venetian army ran as follows: Othello, full general and supreme commander; Cassio, lieutenant-general and Othello's designated successor; Iago, third in the chain of command, chief-of-staff.

Most potent, grave, and reverend signiors,
My very noble and approv'd good masters,
That I have taken away this old man's daughter,
It is most true; true, I have married her:
The very head and front of my offending
Hath this extent, no more. Rude am I in my speech,
And little blessed with the soft phrase of peace:
For since these arms of mine had seven years' pith,
Till now some nine moons wasted, they have used
Their dearest action in the tented field,
And little of this great world can I speak,
More than pertains to feats of broil and battle,
And therefore little shall I grace my cause
In speaking for myself. Yet, by your gracious patience,
I will a round unvarnished tale deliver
Of my whole course of love.

We also learn that Iago hates his general, Othello, and despises a young Florentine captain named Cassio, who has been promoted over Iago as Othello's *ancient*, or lieutenant.

A Snake in the Grass

Iago says that he follows Othello only to serve his own purposes. He advises Roderigo to warn Brabantio, Desdemona's father and a Venetian senator, of his daughter's elopement. Brabantio complains to the Duke, charging that Othello has enchanted his daughter. Nonetheless, the Duke agrees to the marriage because Desdemona asks him to and because he urgently needs Othello's military service against the Turks in Cyprus. Iago advises Roderigo to sell his estate and join the expedition if he wishes to try to win Desdemona from Othello.

Iago and Desdemona arrive on Cyprus, where they are courteously greeted by Cassio, Othello's faithful lieutenant. Iago plots to discredit Cassio and work a double revenge against Othello, whom he claims seduced his own wife, Emilia. In addition, Iago plans to continue bilking Roderigo of money while pretending to help him woo Desdemona.

Othello lands at Cyprus and announces a big bash to celebrate the victory over the Turks (drowned at sea) and his belated honeymoon. Iago gets Cassio looped, sets Roderigo upon him, and involves the lieutenant in such a "barbarous brawl" that Othello fires Cassio on the spot. Iago tells Cassio to enlist Desdemona's aid to help him get his job back.

Desdemona promises to help Cassio. Her help is so persistent, however, that Othello gets suspicious. By the end of the third act, Othello thinks of his wife as a "fair devil" and has appointed Iago his new lieutenant in place of Cassio. Meanwhile, Emilia finds Desdemona's handkerchief, the first gift that Othello ever gave his wife. Many times Iago had asked Emilia to steal it, so she decides to give it to him now—although she has no idea what he plans to do with it. Of course, Iago plans evil. He hides the handkerchief in Cassio's room.

Psssst…Lawrence Fishburn as Othello, Kenneth Branagh as Iago. Photo courtesy of Columbia Studios.

Suspicion Tears Me Apart

> Trifles light as air
> Are to the jealous confirmations strong
> As proofs of holy writ.
>
> —Iago

Othello's suspicions are confirmed when he sees Cassio holding the handkerchief Othello gave Desdemona before their marriage. "Excellent wretch! Perdition catch my soul, / But I do love thee! and when I love thee not, / Chaos is come again," he says, but it's too late. Enraged, Othello strikes Desdemona in front of her relative, Lodovico, who has just arrived with messages from Venice. Roderigo pounces on Iago's suggestion to kill his alleged rival, Cassio. During the fight, Cassio wounds Roderigo, but Iago intervenes in the dark, wounds Cassio, and finishes off Roderigo without being caught.

It took Orson Welles four years to film his 1952 version of Othello *(he ran out of money)—in contrast to the 23 days it took him to film* Macbeth. *Wells played the title role. It's brilliant and audacious, a* Citizen Kane *in Shakespearean English. Photo courtesy of Turner/UA.*

Squeeze Play

Jealous beyond reason, Othello smothers Desdemona in her bed. The climax is violent and disturbing. "Kill me tomorrow; let me live tonight!" Desdemona begs, but Othello is merciless. Desdemona's frantic pleas are devastating:

Desdemona:	But half an hour!
Othello:	Being done, there's no pause.
Desdemona:	But while I say one prayer!
Othello:	It is too late. [*Smothers her.*]

When Emilia knocks at the door, Othello contemplates his next move:

> ...Shall she come in? Were't good?
> I think she stirs again. No. What's best to do?
> If she come in, she'll sure speak to my wife.
> My wife, my wife, what wife? I have no wife.
> O insupportable! O heavy hour!
> Methinks it should be now a huge eclipse
> Of sun and moon, and th' affrighted globe
> Did yawn at alteration.

Emilia arrives in time to hear Desdemona forgive Othello, but since this is a tragedy, she's too late to save Desdemona's life. Quickly, Emilia figures out that Iago is behind the murder, calls for help, and implicates her husband in Desdemona's murder. Iago stabs Emilia and runs. Othello is caught, and Emilia dies.

By Act V, Iago is captured but refuses to speak at all. Othello wounds Iago and then stabs himself: "I took by the throat the circumcised dog, / And smote him, thus." Cassio is appointed governor of Cyprus, and "the censure of this hellish villain," Iago, is left to his charge.

Sweets to the Sweet

The smothering is symbolic as well as literal. As Othello swirls deeper and deeper into Iago's pit, no one can breathe—least of all Desdemona. Locked in the suffocating fantasy constructed by her husband's fantasies, she can only gasp for breath.

True Lies

The conflict between appearance and reality has been played out to its tragic end. In a world that's inherently deceptive, how can we tell the good guys from the bad guys?

Unfortunately, we can't. For example:

➤ "Honest" Iago is treacherous.

➤ Pure Desdemona gets branded a strumpet.

Since Shakespeare wants to make sure we don't miss his point, the irony is a little thick: Iago is called "honest" no less than 15 times. In fact, the word "honest" is mentioned a total of 42 times during the course of the tragedy.

This underscores the play's theme: appearance versus reality. Don't be misled by race—it's not the play's core at all. But that's not to say it isn't an issue...

Ebony and Ivory

Shakespeare is often touted for his universal appeal: Generations of high school teachers bludgeon their students into reading Shakespeare with the admonition, "It's good for you because the Bard speaks in Universal Truths." Miss Schmendrick, your eleventh grade English teacher, *was* correct: *Othello* once again proves Shakespeare's universality in its treatment of race.

Just as in *The Merchant of Venice*, the action revolves around Shylock's identity as a Jew, so now in *Othello* the action centers on Othello's identity as a Moor. When Iago wants to inflame Brabantio against Othello, he says:

> Even now, now, very now, an old black ram
> Is tupping your white ewe.

But Othello's color was meant to have romantic associations, linked to the medieval tradition shown in *The Adoration of the Magi* where a black man is presented as one of the Kings. He is quite removed from the impact of Puritanism, which relegated certain nationalities and races outside the pale.

Star Quality

Until the late 1700s, white actors played Othello in black-face. Othello changed to "tawny" in the 1800s to free the role from the deplorable connotations associated with slavery and to preserve the vision of a gallant, high-hearted man with a noble lineage.

Moor Than the Greatest Love the World Has Known

> O, beware, my lord, of jealousy!
> It is the green-eyed monster which doth mock
> The meat it feeds on.
>
> —Iago

The tragedy of the heroic, trusting Othello and the captivating, trusting Desdemona makes great theater, but it's the story of dastardly Iago that grips our guts. The most complex character in the play, Iago is a delight to dissect. Is he the embodiment of pure evil? A man only his mother could love? A real head case? Hmmm...

We can't deny that Iago has some legitimate motivation for his feelings. After all, Othello *did* promote Cassio over Iago. This relegated Iago to the position of Cassio's ensign.

But then we start going off the deep end. Suspicious by nature, Iago suspects that Othello has done the nasty with his wife, Emilia. "I hate the Moor," he says. "And it is thought abroad that 'twixt my sheets / He's done my office. I know not if't be true / But I, for mere suspicion of that kind, / Will do as if for surety."

But Iago also suspects that Cassio and Emilia are "making the beast with two backs," which leads readers to suspect that either Emilia is having a lot of extracurricular fun or Iago has a screw loose. Since Emilia never gives readers cause to suspect her virtue, it appears that Iago is jealous and suspicious by nature.

Fire at Will

According to some Freudian scholars, Iago is not jealous of Othello; rather, he is subconsciously in love with him. It's this homosexual attraction that led Iago to destroy Othello's marriage. It's your call—I'm not going *there*.

Star Quality

Paul Robeson's 1943 production of *Othello* on Broadway changed the course of American theater, breaking the color barrier. Tremendous theater, Robeson's performance as Othello drew people from all walks of life—taxi drivers and short-order cooks as well as blue-haired matrons. It ran for almost 300 performances, a Broadway record at the time for a Shakespeare play.

Further, Iago is one of those people who just hates to see others happy. After all, he's not happy himself, so why should anyone else be happy? Iago feels only contempt for others: Othello's jealousy and gullibility, Desdemona's innocence, Roderigo's stupidity, Cassio's drinking. And when he decides to destroy Othello, one excuse will do as well as another.

When his life lies in ruins, Othello demands to know Iago's motives. Iago refuses to say:

Othello:	Will you, I pray, demand that demi-devil Why he hath thus ensnared my soul and body?
Iago:	Demand me nothing; what you know, you know; From this time forth I will never speak word.

In Iago, Shakespeare created one of the first psychopaths—a charming man entirely without scruples, morals, or a conscience. "A nasty bastard," actor Bob Hoskins called him.

Othello's "Tragic Flaw"

Since he's a tragic hero, Othello *must* have a tragic flaw. According to the Big Daddy of Tragedy, Aristotle, the tragic hero must not be an entirely good man or one who is completely evil. Rather, he must be good but contribute to his own destruction by some moral weakness—the tragic flaw. After all, if an entirely good man is destroyed, we feel resentment, not sorrow. And if a nogoodnik gets his just desserts, we feel vindicated. But we pity the man who, having contributed in some way to his disaster, meets with a punishment out of all proportion to what he has done. That's why it's a tragedy.

Unfortunately, it's not easy to find Othello's tragic flaw. At first, he's noble and calm. In his dying speech he describes himself as "one not easily jealous," clearly the impression Shakespeare wishes to leave. His only flaw seems to be that he's human. This sets him off from many of Shakespeare's tragic heroes, who have clear flaws, such as Macbeth's overwhelming ambition or Hamlet's inability to exact his revenge in a timely fashion.

James Earl Jones and Diane Wiest made a heartbreaking Othello and Desdemona in a brilliant Broadway production, later filmed by PBS. Photo courtesy of PBS.

But as with all of Shakespeare's tragic heroes, Othello realizes what he has lost:

> Good name in man and woman, dear my lord,
> Is the immediate jewel of their souls:
> Who steals my purse steals trash; 't is something, nothing;
> 'Twas mine, 'tis his, and has been slave to thousands;
> But he that filches from me my good name
> Robs me of that which not enriches him
> And makes me poor indeed.

The Least You Need to Know

➤ The noble Moor Othello, his innocent wife Desdemona, and the loathsome villain Iago are the key players.

➤ *Othello* differs from Shakespeare's other tragedies because the tragedy is domestic, not national; there's only one emotion (sexual jealously); and there's no subplot or comic relief.

➤ *Othello*'s theme is the conflict between appearance and reality.

➤ *Othello* concerns racism as *The Merchant of Venice* concerns anti-Semitism; it's a factor, but not the main focus.

➤ Iago is truly evil, arguably Shakespeare's cruelest villain.

➤ What's Othello's tragic flaw? It seems to be only that he's human.

223

Chapter 21

King Lear

In This Chapter

➤ Who's who in *King Lear*

➤ The plot of *King Lear*

➤ A brutal world view

➤ The Fool

Blow, winds, and crack your cheeks! Rage! Blow!
You cataracts and hurricanes, spout
Till you have drench'd our steeples, drown'd the cocks!
You sulphurous and thought-executing fires,
Vaunt-courtiers to oak-cleaving thunderbolts,
Singe my white head! And thou, all-shaking thunder,
Smite flat the thick rotundity o' the world!
Crack nature's molds, all germens spill at once,
That make ingrateful man!

—Lear

As these lines show, *King Lear* is a real tear-jerker, kids. What could be more brutal than a sick old man thrown to the mercy of a fierce storm? Rejected by his daughters, stripped of his dignity, naked in the vicious wind—it tears your heart right out. Let me warn you right out of the gate that scholars consider *King Lear* to be Shakespeare's most pessimistic play. But there's a consolation prize for all the suffering: *Lear* may be Shakespeare's most savage play, but many claim that it's also his greatest one. So settle down and let Shakespeare bowl you over with bitterness and beauty.

Who's Who in *King Lear*

Ay, every inch a king.

—Lear

King Lear is the ruler of pre-Christian Britain. A vigorous, touchy man in his 80s, he expects absolute devotion from all his subjects, especially his three daughters, Goneril, Regan, and Cordelia. Although long eligible for membership in AARP, at the beginning of the play he's in good condition for his age. It's a *really* plum role.

Here's the cast in its entirety:

➤ Lear, *King of Britain*

➤ King of France

➤ Duke of Burgundy

➤ Duke of Cornwall, *Regan's husband*

➤ Duke of Albany, *Goneril's husband*

➤ Earl of Kent

➤ Earl of Gloucester

➤ Edgar, *Gloucester's son*

➤ Edmund, *Gloucester's bastard son*

➤ Curan, *a courtier*

➤ Oswald, *Goneril's steward*

➤ Old Man, *Gloucester's tenant*

➤ Doctor

➤ Fool, *to Lear*

➤ Captain, *employed by Edmund*

➤ Gentleman, *Cordelia's attendant*

➤ Herald

➤ Servants to Cornwall

➤ Goneril, *Lear's daughter*

➤ Regan, *Lear's daughter*

➤ Cordelia, *Lear's daughter*

➤ Knights, gentlemen, officers, messengers, and the usual group of unknown actors trying to break into the big time

Laurence Olivier (aka "Mr. Shakespearean Tragic Hero") as King Lear.

She Loves Me, She Loves Me Not

How sharper than a serpent's tooth it is
To have a thankless child!

—Lear

When the play begins, Lear has decided it's time to retire. He's going to give up his throne and divide Britain into thirds among his three daughters. First, however, he holds a "Can You Top This" contest, in which each daughter must declare how much she loves him. The winner gets the most goods. Goneril and Regan meet the challenge in hypocritically flowery terms, but when Cordelia's turn comes, she cannot bring herself to compete with her grasping sisters in flattering Daddy.

When Lear asks Cordelia—his favorite—what she has to say about her love for him, she replies, "Nothing, my lord." Lear is thunderstruck at this blow to his ego. "Nothing?" he blasts. "Nothing will come of nothing," he warns her. In other words, she will be disinherited if she can't find some praise for her father.

Sweets to the Sweet

An easy way to remember which evil daughter is married to which duke and which pair Lear visits first is to remember them alphabetically: Goneril's name begins with a G, which comes before the R of Regan's name. Goneril is married to Albany, whose name comes alphabetically before Cornwall, Regan's husband. Lear visits first the pair whose names come first in the alphabet: Goneril and Albany.

Fire at Will

Make no mistake: Lear is old but he's not dotty. His decision to cut off Cordelia is not an act of senility but rather the act of a man who will brook no opposition to his will.

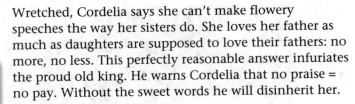

Wretched, Cordelia says she can't make flowery speeches the way her sisters do. She loves her father as much as daughters are supposed to love their fathers: no more, no less. This perfectly reasonable answer infuriates the proud old king. He warns Cordelia that no praise = no pay. Without the sweet words he will disinherit her.

Earl of Kent tries to mediate, but Lear warns him not to come "between the dragon and his wrath" and banishes him. Lear then banishes Cordelia from his sight and announces that the third of Britain that was supposed to go to her will instead be divided between Goneril and Regan and their husbands, the hen-pecked Duke of Albany and the cruel, power-hungry Duke of Cornwall.

Accompanied by a retinue of a hundred knights, Lear decides to spend one month alternately with each daughter. Remember what Ben Franklin said about fish and house guests: after three days, they both begin to stink. Even as Daddy packs his bags, the two vicious sisters plot to diminish his power.

In the Meantime...

Time shall unfold what plaited cunning hides.

—Cordelia

Next Shakespeare introduces the subplot concerning the Earl of Gloucester and his two sons: good-natured, naive Edgar and his vicious, calculating illegitimate brother, Edmund. Edmund cooks up a cruel but clever plot to disinherit Edgar; he forges a letter that "proves" Edgar is out to kill his father. Gullible Gloucester goes for the bait. On Edmund's advice, Edgar disguises himself as a mad beggar, Tom of Bedlam, and hides.

Getting the Bum's Rush

Lear's stay at Goneril's castle starts off on the wrong foot when she insists that he downsize his retinue of one hundred knights. He refuses because the men represent his former power and authority. Backed up by her faithful servant, Oswald, Goneril makes Lear miserable. Lear is comforted when Earl of Kent returns, disguised, from his banishment and serves him faithfully again. Lear's court jester, the Fool, tries to cheer up the King with his quips and riddles. At the same time, the Fool impresses on Lear the mistake he has made in dividing his kingdom.

Lear is so incensed by Goneril's constant nagging about his retainers that he curses her and storms out of the castle to seek shelter with Regan.

Travel Lite

Regan and her husband Cornwall have gone to Gloucester's castle on a visit. Kent beats Oswald, Goneril's servant, for his rudeness to Lear. Cornwall and Regan punish Kent by putting him in the stocks. Although he disapproves of what is going on in his own home, Gloucester is powerless to stop the combatants.

When Lear approaches the castle, he is shocked to see Kent in the stocks. He questions Regan about it, but she is on her sister's side and tells Lear to return to Goneril until his month with her is up. Goneril arrives, and the two sisters argue with Lear about his retainers, while he curses them both.

Any Port in a Storm

Lear leaves his ungrateful daughters and rushes out into a storm. Raging against the tempest, he defies the winds to crack their cheeks with blowing and calls out for cataracts to drown the earth and for thunderbolts to singe his white head. In this great speech (quoted at the beginning of this chapter), Lear says that Nature, even at her most violent, is not as cruel as his daughters. The violent storm shows that the world has been turned upside down: Daughters rule their fathers, a fool has more wisdom than his king, a bastard (Edmund) becomes legitimate, madmen lead the blind, and truth gets perverted.

In his misery, Lear feels his "wits begin to turn"—he is going mad. However, he agrees to find temporary shelter, even in a peasant hovel, because necessity "can make vile things precious."

In a crude shelter he meets the Fool, Kent, and Edgar, disguised as a mad beggar. Lear has become a "poor, infirm, weak, and despised old man." This wrenching scene brings us completely over to Lear's side.

Will Power

Crippled beggars and retarded people were common figures in Shakespeare's day because Henry VIII closed the monasteries, forcing these people to seek alms on the open road. Bedlam, the insane asylum, was so crowded that almost any lunatic who preferred to beg alms outside was permitted to do so. Thus Edgar's choice of a disguise is reasonable.

Will Power

British dukes, second in power only to princes, generally ruled the area that went by their name. Thus, the Duke of Cornwall ruled the southwestern part of England known as Cornwall. Dukes are of much higher rank than earls, like Kent and Gloucester. Cordelia is not married when the play opens, but she is being courted by two French noblemen, the Duke of Burgundy and the King of France.

Poor naked wretches, wheresoe'er you are,
That bide the pelting of this pitiless storm,
How shall your houseless heads and unfed sides,
Your looped and windowed raggedness, defend you
From seasons such as these?

Sweets to the Sweet

The great storm is often read as a metaphor of Lear's stormy emotions and approaching madness. In his madness, Lear paradoxically sees the true workings of the universe and his place in it.

Will Power

The famous modern Shakespearean scholar (and one of my teachers) Jan Kott paralleled Lear to the theater of the grotesque. In his famous book *Shakespeare: Our Contemporary* (1964), Kott sees the theme of Lear as "the decay and fall of the world." First there is the proud court and its attendants, but later only four beggars wandering in a storm. Lear loses not only his retainers and his kingdom, but also his identity as a king and a person.

A Poke in the Eye with a Sharp Stick

While Lear and his few friends are braving the storm, Cornwall has become furious with Gloucester for befriending the King. His anger is aided by Edmund's treachery. Edmund tells Cornwall that Gloucester is a traitor to Britain because he has had dealings with the French army to restore Lear to his throne.

In one of literature's most terrifying scenes, Gloucester is captured and Cornwall pokes out his eye. Blood-thirsty Regan insists that he gouge out the other eye, too. But before Cornwall can do so, one of his servants, unable to stand the spectacle, begs him to stop.

Cornwall and the servant draw swords and fight. The servant wounds Cornwall seriously, but before he can finish him off, Regan grabs a sword and stabs the servant in the back, killing him instantly. Then Cornwall screams, "Out, vile jelly!" and gouges out Gloucester's other eye. Cornwall dies from the wound he has received. When Gloucester is blinded, he learns the truth—that Edmund has plotted against him and Edgar is innocent.

The physical blindness reinforces Lear's moral blindness—he cannot judge which of his daughters really love him and which only pretend to love him. As with many of Shakespeare's tragic heroes, Lear mistakes appearance for reality. Much of the play is concerned with true vision, or insight into character, as opposed to surface vision, which can only see the outward shows of character.

The Last Step Is a Doozy

Gloucester decides to go to Dover, where Lear has gone to meet with Cordelia and the rescuing French army. On the way to Dover, Gloucester meets Edgar again, but he doesn't recognize his son, who has disguised his voice. In despair, Gloucester tries to leap off the Dover cliffs. Edgar fools him into thinking he is on the cliffs. Gloucester jumps, but only falls a few feet. Edgar tells him he has had a miraculous escape from death, so he ought to treasure life.

Meanwhile, Albany's sympathies have shifted from his wife to Lear. He berates Goneril for her cruelty to her father. Goneril despises her husband for being weak; besides, she has fallen for Edmund. Afraid that Edmund will marry her widowed sister Regan, Goneril plots to have Albany killed. Now that his father is branded a traitor, Edmund is the new Earl of Gloucester. Cornwall is slain by his servant as he was gouging out Gloucester's second eye.

It's a Mad, Mad, *Mad* World

Although Lear gets to the French camp at Dover, he feels too ashamed to meet Cordelia again because of the way he had treated her earlier. Cordelia bears no grudge, however, and sends some soldiers to find her father, who has gone completely mad under the stress of his night out in the storm.

Star Quality

The three top *King Lear* films are the 1970 Russian version, directed by Grigori Kozintsev; the 1971 version directed by Peter Brook (Paul Scofield as Lear); and the 1984 version directed by Michael Elliot (Laurence Olivier as Lear).

The armies of Albany and Cornwall, led by Edmund, meet to attack the French. Cordelia is reunited with Lear and assures him that she bears no hatred for his disinheriting her. On orders from Regan, Oswald tries to kill Gloucester. Edgar prevents him and kills Oswald instead.

Down for the Count

In the battle between the French and English armies, the French lose, and Edmund captures Lear and Cordelia.

The reunion between Cordelia and Lear provides a moment of exquisite gentleness before the brutal climax. As Lear awakens in Cordelia's arms, his madness lifts. The proud monarch who once demanded a retinue of a hundred is now content with a cell—if Cordelia is by his side:

No, no, no, no! Come, let's away to prison.
We two alone will sing like birds i'the cage;
When thou dost ask me blessing I'll kneel down
And ask of thee forgiveness; so we'll live,
And pray, and sing, and tell old tales, and laugh
At gilded butterflies, and hear poor rogues
Talk of court news; and we'll talk with them too—
Who loses and who wins, who's in, who's out—
And take upon's the mystery of things
As if we were God's spies; and we'll wear out,
In a walled prison, packs and sects of great ones
That ebb and flow by the moon.

A happy ending? Dream on.

The Tragic Climax

Albany accuses Goneril of adultery and challenges Edmund to a duel. Edgar enters, disguised, to fight the duel. He mortally wounds his brother and then reveals his identity. At death's door, Edmund tries to save Lear and Cordelia, but his message is too late. It rips your heart out.

Will Power

The story of King Lear is old and honored; as a result, Shakespeare wasn't the only one to crib from it. All told, there are more that 40 different versions of the story, all taken from *King Leir* (c. 1590). Curiously, however, all but Shakespeare's end as a fairy tale, with the noble Cordelia living happily ever after. Only Shakespeare's version of the story challenges our notion of justice.

Edmund dies soon after Goneril, who had poisoned Regan and then stabbed herself. Cordelia is hanged on Edmund's orders. The play ends with Lear bearing Cordelia's corpse. After recognizing his old retainer, Kent, Lear dies of a broken heart, and Edgar is left to rule the kingdom.

King Lear describes a world without pity. There's no God, no salvation—only illusion, blindness, and madness. Ironically, Lear dies a happy man because he thinks that Cordelia is alive: "Do you see this? Look on her! Look, her lips! / Look there! Look there!" [*He dies.*]

The last lines reinforce this hopelessness, as Edgar says:

The weight of this sad time we must obey,
Speak what we feel, not what we ought to say:
The oldest hath borne most; we that are young
Shall never see so much, nor live so long.

Fool Moon

The Fool is the most mysterious figure in the play. Essentially he is a court jester and not "foolish" at all.

He has four main functions in the play:

1. To teach Lear the magnitude of his folly. This he does with frequently cruel jokes. Thus he tells Lear, "thou madest thy daughters thy mother: for...thou gavest them the rod and puttest down thine own breeches." When Lear asks, "Dost thou call me fool, boy?" the Fool replies, "All thy other titles thou hast given away; that thou wast born with." As a Fool, he can say whatever he likes—even things that would be considered treason coming from anyone else.

2. To cheer the old King up.

3. To comment on the behavior of all the characters he meets in the play.

4. To state the play's themes.

Once the Fool performs these actions, he disappears from the play and is never heard from again. In Act III, scene vi, he disappears with the strange words, "I'll go to bed at noon," which seems to indicate that he knows he is going to die.

It's your call.

Fire at Will

At the end of the play Lear cries, "And my poor fool is hang'd!" Don't be fooled; Lear is referring to Cordelia, whom he calls "fool" as a term of affection. We never find out what happens to the Fool.

The Least You Need to Know

➤ When Lear decides to retire from the King biz, he asks his daughters to declare their love. When his favorite, Cordelia, rejects his demand, Lear (and the audience) enter Hell.

➤ The play's topics are as relevant today as they were 400 years ago: aging parents, sibling rivalries, homelessness, and suffering.

➤ *King Lear* describes a world without pity. There's no God, no salvation—only illusion, blindness, and madness.

➤ Lear has learned a lot, but the tuition was a killer.

Macbeth

Tomorrow, and tomorrow, and tomorrow,
Creeps in this petty pace from day to day,
To the last syllable of recorded time;
And all our yesterdays have lighted fools
The way to dusty death. Out, out, brief candle!
Life's but a walking shadow, a poor player,
That struts and frets his hour upon the stage,
And then is heard no more. It is a tale
Told by an idiot, full of sound and fury,
Signifying nothing.

—Macbeth

As James Thurber realized, *Macbeth* is a tale told by a genius, full of soundness and fury, and signifying many things. It's a drama about the success, the treachery, and the disintegration of a brave but flawed individual. Sound familiar? *Macbeth*'s diagnosis of evil is as timely today as it was when the King's Men first presented the play more than 400 years ago.

Besides, the play has everything a modern audience could want: witches, treachery, murder, and enough blood to qualify as a slasher flick. Stay tuned for the whole story.

Meet the Cast

Macbeth is courageous and intelligent, but also ambitious and murderous. And then there's the self-image problem. Even though Macbeth decides to murder his king for his kingdom, our hero nevertheless thinks of himself a good man. One of Shakespeare's most fascinating tragic heroes, Macbeth mirrors the contradictions most of us have experienced between duty and desire.

Here's the rest of the cast:

➤ Duncan, *King of Scotland*

➤ Malcolm, *Duncan's son*

➤ Donalbain, *Malcolm's son*

➤ Macbeth, *Scottish nobleman, general in the King's army*

➤ Banquo, *Scottish nobleman, general in the King's army*

➤ Macduff, *Scottish nobleman*

➤ Lennox, *Scottish nobleman*

➤ Ross, *Scottish nobleman*

➤ Menteith, *Scottish nobleman*

➤ Angus, *Scottish nobleman*

➤ Caithness, *Scottish nobleman*

➤ Fleance, *Banquo's son*

➤ Siward, *Earl of Northumberland, general of the English forces*

➤ Young Siward, *Siward's son*

➤ Seyton, *Macbeth's officer*

➤ Macduff's son

➤ An English doctor

➤ A Scottish doctor

➤ A Porter

➤ An Old Man

➤ Three murderers

➤ Lady Macbeth

➤ Lady Macduff

➤ Lady Macbeth's gentlewoman

Will Power

King James would have found *Macbeth* especially intriguing, since it's set in Scotland in the eleventh century, when James' family, the Stuarts, first ascended to the Scottish throne. Banquo, one of the most admirable characters in the play, is said to have been the father of the first Stuart king. And who said Shakespeare didn't know how to kiss up?

- ➤ Hecate
- ➤ Witches
- ➤ Apparitions
- ➤ Lords, Officers, and the usual assortment of wannabes

Witchy Women

Act I, scene i:

[*Thunder and lightning. Enter three witches.*]

Witch 1:	When shall we three meet again? In thunder, lightning, or in rain?
Witch 2:	When the hurly-burly's done, When the battle's lost and won.
Witch 3:	That will be ere the set of sun.
Witch 1:	Where the place?
Witch 2:	Upon the heath.
Witch 3:	There to meet with Macbeth.
Witch 1:	I come, Gramalkin.
Witch 2:	Paddock calls.
Witch 3:	Anon.
All:	Fair is foul, and foul is fair, Hover through the fog and filthy air.

Who could ask for a better opening? Three "weird sisters"—Men? Women? Something in between?—stir their vile potion on the wild Scottish heath. It's all so *delicious*.

"Fair is foul, and foul is fair" introduces the idea of moral relativity, of deceptiveness of appearances. You know that big Shakespearean theme from *Hamlet*, *Julius Caesar*, *Othello*, and *King Lear* especially.

My Hero

Then the scene shifts to a military camp. King Duncan of Scotland learns that during the fierce battle, "brave Macbeth" killed the traitor Macdonwald by ripping him open from the navel to the lips and cutting off his head, which he displayed on loyalists' castle.

Then came the king of Norway and another traitor, the Thane of Cawdor. Cawdor is sentenced to death, and Macbeth will get his title and lands. Duncan sums up the situation in the line, "What he [the Thane of Cawdor] hath lost, noble Macbeth hath won." But even though Cawdor was a cad, he knew how to die, as this famous line shows: "Nothing in his life / Became him like the leaving of it," says Malcolm.

The Witches drop by again, this time to do a little conjuring and greet Macbeth with three statements:

➤ All hail, Macbeth! Hail to thee, Thane of Glamis!

➤ All hail, Macbeth! Hail to thee, Thane of Cawdor!

➤ All hail, Macbeth, that shalt be king thereafter!

Is the witches' last statement a warning? A temptation? A prophecy? Shaken, Macbeth starts thinking about being king and the straightest line to the throne. Now let's think, boys and girls...

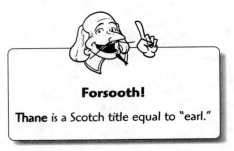

Forsooth!

Thane *is a Scotch title equal to "earl."*

The witches predict that Banquo will be "lesser than Macbeth and greater" and "not so happy, yet much happier." They also tell him that he will be the father of kings.

Told the story of Cawdor's disloyalty, Macbeth starts to believe the witches' prophecies. Banquo is not so credulous, however, and tells Macbeth that Satan's little helpers often fool us by first telling us truths to string us along.

Heir Today, Gone Tomorrow

Duncan names his son, Malcolm, "Prince of Cumberland." That gives Macbeth an instant motive for killing Duncan. "The Prince of Cumberland!" Macbeth says, "that is a step / On which I must fall down, or else o'erleap. / For in my way it lies."

Star Quality

Orson Welles' *Macbeth* (1949) stars Welles in the title role. More Welles than Shakespeare, this moody version was filmed entirely in bizarre interiors. The original version has the actors speaking with authentic Scottish accents.

Duncan decides to stop by Macbeth's castle for a little R&R. Notified by letter of the King's plans (and her husband's ambitions), Lady Macbeth worries that her hubby's character is "too full o' the milk of human kindness, / To catch the nearest way." Ever supportive, she asks the spirits to "unsex" her (take away her femininity) so she can help her beloved off their king.

Dial "Macbeth" for Murder

Macbeth arrives home, and he and the missus dance around the issue of murdering Duncan to move Macbeth up the ladder. Later, Macbeth contemplates killing his king:

> If it were done, when 'tis done, then 'twere well
> It were done quickly. If th' assassination
> Could trammel up the consequence, and catch
> With his surcease, success; but that this blow
> Might be the be-all and the end-all—here,
> But there, upon this bank and shoal of time,
> We'd jump the life to come…

Macbeth decides not to go through with it, but Lady Macbeth changes his mind. In one of the most blood-curdling images in the play, she says:

> I have given suck, and know
> How tender 'tis to love the babe that milks me;
> I would, while it was smiling in my face,
> Have pluck'd my nipple from his boneless gums,
> And dash'd the brains out, had I so sworn as you
> Have done this.

She then recounts the murder plan. When Duncan is asleep, she will get his attendants drunk. Then Macbeth and Lady Macbeth can murder Duncan and lay the blame on the drunken guards. Simple, but effective.

Hostess with the Mostess

After dodging Banquo on the way to Duncan's bedroom, Macbeth has a bout of insanity, during which he sees a floating dagger. Is the dagger there or not? Is this a physical representation of his guilt about his murderous intentions toward Duncan? Is he now just one short step away from wearing his underpants on his head?

Macbeth makes his way to Duncan's room, commits the murder, and staggers back to Lady Macbeth. Nervously, Macbeth explains that he thought he heard a voice say, "Sleep no more!…Glamis hath murdered sleep, and therefore, Cawdor / Shall sleep no more, Macbeth shall sleep no more!" Although rattled, Lady Macbeth recovers her composure, tells Macbeth that he must wash the blood from his hands, return to

Duncan's room, and smear the faces of the servants with blood. Macbeth refuses. Mocking his weakness, she takes the daggers and performs the task herself.

By murdering Duncan, Macbeth shatters human, natural, and divine laws. He has slain his king, his kinsman, and his guest. Getting down to brass tacks, he has murdered a good and innocent man in his sleep. That's just plain *wrong*. And sure enough, all of nature will revolt against his deed.

Orson Wells does Macbeth. Photo courtesy of Republic.

Knock, Knock. Who's There?

After the wicked deed comes the comic relief. In this famous scene, the drunken porter imagines himself the porter of hell. It's dramatic irony, comic relief, and foreshadowing all rolled into one.

Macduff discovers the body. The blame is indeed laid on the grooms, whom Macbeth has then murdered—out of love for Duncan, he claims. Malcolm and Donalbain decide that in the currently dangerous situation they had better hit the road—and fast. Naturally, people come to suspect Malcolm and Donalbain because they ran away. No white Bronco, though.

King for a Day

Macbeth is now King, but he can't rest easily. He fears Banquo because he's daring, discerning, and was there at the beginning. As insurance, Macbeth hires two murderers to kill Banquo and his son Fleance. Macbeth concludes his plan with the comment: "Banquo, thy soul's flight, / If it find Heaven, must find it out tonight."

Soon after, the scene shifts to the park. The two murders have been joined by a third. Banquo enters with Fleance. The murderers attack Banquo, who cries, "O, treachery! Fly good Fleance, fly, fly, fly!" (Love the pun on *Fleance* and *fly*.) He dies, and Fleance escapes.

Party Crasher

Back at the palace, Macbeth is hosting a huge banquet. The first murderer brings news of the night's murder. The murderer assures him that Banquo is "safe in a ditch / With twenty trenched gashes on his head."

Macbeth returns to the feast and in slips an uninvited guest—Banquo's bloody ghost. Of course, he plops (drifts?) into Macbeth's seat at the head of the table. Naturally, the others can't see the ghost. Forgetting his manners, Macbeth shouts at his guests, "Which of you have done this?" (Who has killed Banquo?) The guests don't have a clue what Macbeth is talking about. Macbeth shouts at the ghost, "Thou canst not say, I did it [the murder]; never shake / Thy gory locks at me." The ghost disappears.

Macbeth offers a toast "to our dear friend Banquo, whom we miss; / Would he were here!" He shouldn't have pushed it. Guess what? Banquo's ghost reappears. Macbeth shouts for it to leave his sight and the ghost disappears. Not surprisingly, the party breaks up. Given a choice between the ghost and the fruit cup, it's a no-brainer.

Alone, Macbeth feels so deep in blood "returning were as tedious as go o'er." Going back is as difficult as going forward—Macbeth's in so deep he might as well keep going. Lady Macbeth tells him he just needs a good night's sleep. She's off the mark because the banquet scene shows how Scotland has moved from order to chaos as a result of Macbeth's deed.

In another scene, Lennox and an unnamed lord discuss their suspicions about Macbeth. We learn that Macduff is out of favor because he has also voiced his suspicions.

Will Power

Elizabethan ghosts were nothing like our sheeted Halloween trick-and-treaters. As revitalized corpses, Elizabethan ghosts usually came back to Earth looking very much as they did when they left it: Banquo's ghost appears at the banquet with a bloody face, his wounds still oozing blood. In most cases, the ghost was only visible to the person he is haunting, which makes his appearance all the more terrifying. A ghost always had a mission when he returned to earth. Some wanted revenge; others wanted to warn the living, punish an evil-doer, or stir up some trouble.

Field Work

Macbeth visits the three witches to get some answers.

Using the blood of a sow who has eaten her young and the sweat that fell from a murderer as he was being hanged, the witches bring forth three apparitions.

1. The first, an armed head, tells Macbeth to beware of Macduff, the Thane of Fife.

2. The second, a bloody child, advises Macbeth that no one who was born of a woman can harm him. Since everyone is born of women, Macbeth figures that he's in the clear. Nonetheless, to make "double sure," Macbeth decides to kill Macduff anyway.

3. The third, a crowned child with a tree in his hand, tells Macbeth he will never be defeated until Birnam Wood (the forest) around his castle marches toward the castle.

The first apparition really shows Macduff beheading Macbeth, but we don't find this out until Act V. The second apparition foretells his death, his killer, and his supplanters. The third apparition signals the march from Birnam Wood to Dunsinane and the unnatural giving way to order.

Macbeth still wants one more answer: Will Banquo's descendants ever rule Scotland? The witches conjure a procession of eight kings, the last of whom holds a mirror that makes it seem as though the line of kings stretches endlessly. All of the kings in the procession resemble Banquo, and Banquo himself comes behind the line of eight, his hair caked with blood. Macbeth assumes Banquo's descendants will, in fact, rule Scotland. To cheer him up, the witches perform a wild dance and disappear. So considerate, these witches.

Macbeth decides to go further down the dark path of treachery. He'll start with a surprise attack on Macduff's castle at Fife to wipe out Macduff's whole family.

Star Quality

Roman Polanski's 1971 version of *Macbeth* is a gripping, extremely violent re-creation of Macbeth's lust for power, driven by his crazed wife.

Who's Who in Death and Gore

Macduff has run away from Scotland. Ross reassures Lady Macduff that her husband is a wise and trustworthy man. After Ross leaves, the murderers Macbeth has hired for the event break in and slaughter the entire family. We see how swiftly Macbeth carries out his revenge against Macduff.

In England, Malcolm tests Macduff's loyalty through a set of clever questions; that such a test is necessary shows the extent of Macbeth's depravity. Scotland lies in ruins, violence and death commonplace. "How does my wife?" inquires Macduff. "Why, well," replies Ross. "And all my children?" Macduff asks, to which Ross answers, "Well, too." Macduff then asks whether Macbeth has harassed his family. "No," says Ross, "they were well at peace, when I did leave 'em." Of course they were; they were dead.

Finally, Ross tells Macduff that Macbeth has had his wife and children "savagely slaughtered." Meanwhile, Siward is leading an invasion into Scotland.

Out, Damn'd Spot!

Back at Macbeth's castle, we learn that Lady Macbeth has gone mad from guilt. As she walks in her sleep, rubbing her hands together over and over, she mutters:

> Out, damn'd spot! Out, I say! One—two—why then 'tis time to do it. Hell is murky. Fie, my lord, fie, a soldier and afeard? What need we fear who knows it, and none can call our pow'r to accompt? Yet who would have thought the old man to have so much blood in him?

Inside his castle, Macbeth prepares for battle, "sick at heart," but nonetheless vowing to fight until his "flesh is hacked" from his bones. Lady Macbeth dies, although we are never told how, and Macbeth delivers the famous soliloquy quoted in the beginning of this chapter: "Tomorrow, and tomorrow, and tomorrow…"

In the Belly of the Beast

A messenger tells Macbeth something that seems unbelievable: "…I looked toward Birnam, and anon, methought, / The wood began to move." Malcolm's soldiers are using tree boughs as camouflage. Clever, eh?

On the battlefield, Macbeth kills Young Siward. Old Siward tells Malcolm that Macbeth will be forced to surrender without much fight since his men have defected to the other side.

In the field, Macduff confronts and challenges Macbeth. Macbeth warns Macduff that Macduff is

Sweets to the Sweet

Did you know that severed heads were probably the first soccer balls? If you ever direct the play, be sure to include this factoid in the playbill.

wasting time fighting because Macbeth leads "a charmed life" and cannot be defeated by "one of woman born." Macduff tells his adversary to give up hope, because "Macduff was from his mother's womb / Untimely ripped." Who would have guessed it's that old Caesarean birth trick?

Will Power

On April 25, 1057, Malcolm (known in Scottish history as Malcolm Canmore) and Saint Margaret founded Scotland's first dynastic succession.

Despite the fact that the conditions of his defeat as foretold in the prophecies have arrived, Macbeth vows to fight to the end. Placing his shield before him, Macbeth challenges Macduff, "...lay on, Macduff; / And damned be him that first cries. 'Hold, enough!'"

Malcolm, Old Siward, Ross, and their army enter Macbeth's castle victoriously. Macduff enters carrying Macbeth's head—guess who won *that* fight? Macduff hails Malcolm as king, points to Macbeth's head, and announces that now "the time is free." Giving thanks to all and inviting them to his coronation, Malcolm leads the actors off the stage. Order is restored.

What Does It All Mean?

Fair is foul and foul is fair. In *Macbeth*, things are seldom what they seem. The play is full of ambiguity and double meanings, starting with the prophecies. Here are some more ambiguities to chew on:

➤ The day is extremely foul (weather) and extremely fair (Macdonwald has been disemboweled).

➤ The witches claim Banquo is not so happy as Macbeth, yet much happier.

➤ Is the dagger a hallucination or a supernatural phantom?

➤ Ditto on Banquo's ghost.

➤ Is Ross playing both sides?

➤ Does Lady Macbeth commit suicide or die of cardiac complications?

Start with the theme of appearance versus reality. Then add the attraction to evil—yielding to the power of darkness leads to destruction. We see this from the beginning when Macbeth and Lady Macbeth regard the witches' greeting as prophecies. On their own, they decide to goose the prophecies by murdering the incumbent, Duncan.

But a story of an evil man who commits a terrible crime is not a tragedy—it's just a tale of corruption. *Macbeth*, in contrast, is about a good man who becomes evil, and that's the tragedy. At the end of the play, Macbeth remembers what he was and what he has thrown away:

I had almost forgot the taste of fears.
The time has been my senses would have cooled
To hear a night-shriek, and my fell of hair
Would at a dismal treatise rouse and stir
As life were in't. I have supped full of horrors:
Direness, familiar to my slaughterous thoughts,
Cannot once start me.

The Bloody Glove

Who was the third murderer? Trying to figure this out is a traditional Shakespearean game, like trying to decide why Shakespeare left his wife his "second-best bed." (Who got the "best" one?)

The first two murderers are Scottish gentlemen, previously Macbeth's enemies but now convinced that Banquo has wronged them. Okay, but what about murderer #3?

The third murderer is evidently somebody who knows Banquo and Fleance. The usual suspects include Macbeth, Lady Macbeth, or a servant or thane. But this theory doesn't hold water because all these people show up momentarily at Macbeth's dinner party—and without bloodstains.

Macbeth pays spies in each of his warlords' castles, so he has other people available to off an enemy here and there. It seems reasonable that he would send an experienced thug to help two amateur hit men kill a mighty warrior and his teenage son. It is also unlikely that he would want to introduce the assassins to each other ahead of time.

I've given you the evidence; the rest is up to you.

The Curse of "The Scottish Play"

Producing *Macbeth* on the stage is supposed to be unlucky. Past productions have been plagued by fires, botched lines, falls, and weapon injuries. Superstition requires those involved in a production of *Macbeth* to refrain from saying the play's title, but rather refer to it as "The Scottish Play."

How did the superstition get rolling?

➤ On August 7, 1606, during the play's first production, the boy who played Lady Macbeth died backstage.

➤ In 1849, more than 30 people were killed in a riot in front of the theater where *Macbeth* was being performed. The riot was caused by years of animosity between two Shakespearean actors.

➤ In one week in 1934, four actors playing Macbeth took sick.

➤ In the 1937 Laurence Olivier–Judith Anderson run, the theater's founder died, the director barely escaped death, and Olivier was nearly injured by falling scenery.

➤ The next year, a man lost both his legs in a parking lot accident outside the Stratford production of the play; the actress playing Lady Macbeth ran her car into a store window.

➤ Even critics can't escape the curse. Percy Hammond panned a performance and died a few days later of a "sudden illness."

Sweets to the Sweet

Some people think that the play's vision of evil, with witches, demonic familiars, and so forth, explains the bad luck.

Superstition aside, accidents are more common in *Macbeth* than in any other Shakespearean play because the stage is dark, there are fire scenes, the fog machine makes the stage slippery, there's more wielding of crude weapons by more people, and so forth. But hey, who knows?

The Least You Need to Know

➤ Spurred by his ambition and his ambitious wife, Macbeth murders his king, seizes his crown, and destroys his country.

➤ The play's themes concern appearance versus reality and the lure of evil.

➤ Play the Shakespearean parlor game: Who is the third murderer?

➤ To avoid the legendary *Macbeth* curse, refer to the play only as "The Scottish Play," never by the "M" word.

➤ *Macbeth* is a bloody, dark play, Shakespeare's contribution to film noir.

Antony and Cleopatra

There was a perfect man who met a perfect woman. After a perfect courtship, they had a perfect wedding. Their life together was, of course, perfect.

One snowy, stormy Christmas Eve, this perfect couple was driving along a winding road when they noticed someone at the roadside in distress. Being the perfect couple, they stopped to help. There stood Santa Claus with a huge bundle of toys. Not wanting to disappoint any children on the eve of Christmas, the perfect couple loaded Santa and his toys into their vehicle. Soon they were delivering the toys.

Unfortunately, the driving conditions deteriorated and the perfect couple and Santa had an accident.

Only one of them survived. Who was the survivor?

Answer: The perfect woman. (Everyone knows there is no Santa Claus and no such thing as a perfect man.)

[The male response: So, if there is no perfect man and no Santa Claus, the perfect woman must have been driving. This explains why there was a car accident.]

There aren't any perfect men and women in real life (Mel Gibson and Cindy Crawford aside, of course), but there *are* two in Shakespeare: Antony and Cleopatra. Okay, maybe they're not perfect, but their love certainly passes the litmus test. Read on to find out what makes them—and this play—so memorable.

Who's Who in *Antony and Cleopatra*

Airport fiction? Bodice rippers? Romance novels? Soap operas? They can't hold a candle to the heat in *Antony and Cleopatra*. Check out what Cleopatra says about her honey while he's away:

> Where think'st thou he is now? Stand he, or sits he?
> Or does he walk? Or is he on his horse?
> O happy horse, to bear the weight of Antony.
> Do bravely, horse, for wot'st thou whom thou mov'st?
> The demi-Atlas of this earth, the arm
> And burgeoner of men. He's speaking now,
> Or murmuring, "Where's my serpent of old Nile?"
> (For so he calls me.) Now I feed myself
> With most delicious poison. Think on me,
> That am with Phoebus' amormous pinches black,
> And wrinkled deep in rime? Broad-fronted Caesar,
> When thou wast here above the ground, I was
> A morsel for a monarch; and great Pompey
> Would stand and make his eyes grow in my brow;
> There would he anchor his aspect, and die
> With looking on his life.

Now, meet the whole cast:

➤ Mark Antony, *triumvir*

➤ Octavius Caesar, *triumvir*

➤ M. Aemilus Lepidus, *triumvir*

➤ Sextus Pompeius, *triumvir*

➤ Domitus Enobarbus, *Antony's friend*

➤ Ventidius, Eros, Scarus, Decretas, Demetrius, and Philo, *Antony's friends*

➤ Canidius, *Antony's lieutenant-general*

➤ Maegenas, Agrippa, Dolabella, Proculeius, Thidias, Gallus, *Caesar's friends*

➤ Taurus, *Caesar's lieutenant-general*

➤ Menas, Menecrates, Varrius, *Pompey's friends*

➤ Silius, *an officer in Ventidius' army*

➤ Schoolmaster, *acting as an ambassador from Antony to Caesar*

➤ Alexas, *Cleopatra's attendant*

➤ Mardian, *a eunuch, Cleopatra's attendant*

➤ Seleucus, *Cleopatra's attendant*

➤ Diomedes, *Cleopatra's attendant*

➤ Soothsayer, *Cleopatra's attendant*

➤ Lamprius, Rannius, Lucillius, *three Romans appearing as mutes*

➤ Clown

➤ Cleopatra, *Queen of Egypt*

➤ Octavia, *Caesar's sister and Antony's wife*

➤ Charmian, Iras, *Cleopatra's attendants*

➤ Assortment of officers, soldiers, messengers, etc.

Star Quality

The 1973 film of *Antony and Cleopatra,* starring Charlton Heston as Antony and Hildegard Neil as Cleopatra is slow-moving and middling. Chuck did a manly man Ben-Hur, but he's out of his league with Shakespeare's great lover.

See the Pyramids Along the Nile

Cleopatra:	If it be love indeed, tell me how much.
Antony:	There's beggary in the love that can be reckoned.
Cleopatra:	I'll set a bourne how far to be beloved.
Antony:	Then must thou needs find our new heaven, new earth.

We're talking a really high-maintenance relationship here. But the story of Antony's tragic love for Cleopatra begins long before the play starts. It is set against the background of a great political upheaval in a turbulent period of Roman history. The love affair shares the splendor of these events, and they are often referred to as the play progresses.

Here's the History Lite version: Julius Caesar, Gnaeus Pompeius, and Marcus Crassus formed the first Roman Triumvirate in 60 B.C. Seven years later, Crassus was murdered by Orodes. In 48 B.C., Caesar defeated Pompey in the battle of Pharsalia. Fearing Caesar's growing power, Marcus Brutus lent his efforts to the cabal that assassinated Caesar in 44 B.C. Caesar's avengers, Mark Antony, Octavius, and Lepidus, formed the second Triumvirate in 43 B.C. and divided the Roman Empire into three parts. Octavius Caesar took Italy and the western and northern provinces; Lepidus ruled over Africa—except for Egypt, which with all the conquered territories east of the Adriatic, was governed by Mark Antony.

Love at First Sight

Getting his ducks in a row for a war against the Parthians, Antony called Cleopatra to Tarsus to answer accusations that she had helped Brutus and Cassius in their war against the Triumvirate. The meeting didn't go quite as he planned, however, as Antony fell so hard for Cleopatra that he dropped everything—including his job and his wife Fulvia—to follow Cleopatra back to Alexandria. That's where Shakespeare takes up the story, as the couple is lounging in the ancient equivalent of a hot tub in Egypt.

Big Trouble in River City

You play, you pay: It doesn't take a rocket scientist to figure out how Mrs. Antony feels about her hubby doing the nasty with the Egyptian Queen. Octavius Caesar, in contrast, is enraged because Antony failed to help him fight against Fulvia's war and Sextus Pompey's conspiracy.

Sextus Pompey, the son of Gnaeus Pompey (one of the first Triumvirs) has inherited his father's resentment against Caesar and his heirs. And that's not all—he also claims his right to the imperial rule.

A proactive guy, Sextus Pompey has formed a conspiracy with the help of some notorious pirates who operate off the Italian coast. From their base in Sicily, they have raided the maritime provinces and smashed coastal shipping. Caesar is slipping in the polls and losing the people's allegiance. They've gone over to Pompey and flocked to the seacoasts, expecting an invasion.

Wake Up and Smell the Coffee

Caesar's political crisis, Fulvia's death, and the Parthian invasion shock Antony out of his lethargy. Once again the able statesman and general, he hot-foots it back to Rome to patch up his differences with Caesar by marrying his widowed sister Octavia. This frightens Pompey into a peace treaty.

But even in the midst of this activity, Antony knows he's not setting down roots. Acting on the advice of an Egyptian fortuneteller (don't we all?), he resolves to return to Cleopatra in Alexandria. In the meantime, Ventidius trounces the Parthian invaders, as Antony and his bride set out for Athens.

In her Egyptian court in Alexandria, Cleopatra has kept herself up to speed on Antony's affairs. When first she hears the report of his marriage, she flies into a rage, threatening to kill or maim the messenger who brings the news, beating him and frightening him away. When she calms down, she pumps him for information about Octavia's appearance and behavior. To save his neck, the messenger tells her the lies she wishes to hear. She resolves to win Antony back.

Liz Taylor burned up the screen and broke up at least one marriage as Cleopatra. Now, that was inspired casting. Photo courtesy of Fox.

Where There's a Will, There's a Way

In Athens, Antony also hears disturbing news from Italy: His brother-in-law Caesar has waged new wars against Pompey, made his will and read it publicly, and openly shown hostility toward his partner. Octavia insists on returning to Rome to patch up their differences before the breach widens beyond repair, while Antony readies his fleet to attack Caesar.

Her mission is unsuccessful. Only two reasons would be great enough to force Caesar into a war against Antony: to protect his sister against insult or injury or to protect himself against surprise attack. But Antony's return to Cleopatra in Egypt and his war preparations against Rome give Caesar both reasons, and he moves quickly to gain the advantage of surprise.

So I Changed My Mind. What's the Big Deal?

Before Antony even has time to finish his preparations, Caesar transports his entire army to the southwest coast of Italy and sails across the Ionian Sea to capture Toryne. Chief among these preparations is Cleopatra's insistence upon a sea battle and upon personally commanding her Egyptian navy in it. It's a terrific disaster: In the middle of the battle, Cleopatra decides to turn all her ships around and head home—and Antony follows her.

The defeat at Actium causes dissension in Antony's ranks, and much of his army desert him. Antony asks Caesar for terms of truce, but Caesar refuses and sends his ambassador Thidias to seduce Cleopatra to his side. Antony discovers them in time to prevent it.

Antony decides to fight to the death. Realizing his lord's judgment is impaired, Enobarbus, Antony's closest friend and subordinate, decides to jump to Caesar's side. Antony wins the next battle, which makes him overconfident. On the second day, he boldly decides to fight Caesar at sea again. This time his entire navy deserts him and surrenders to Caesar without a fight.

My Boyfriend's Back and You're Gonna Be Sorry

Broken, Antony accuses Cleopatra of betrayal and threatens to kill her. No fool, she locks herself in her mausoleum and sends him word she is dead. Hearing this news, Antony tries to commit suicide but succeeds only in wounding himself mortally. As he lies dying, another messenger from Cleopatra reveals the truth. Antony is carried to his mistress, where he dies in her arms.

Cleopatra decides she cannot live without Antony and refuses to be taken a prisoner by Caesar. She decides to kill herself by the bite of a venomous serpent, an asp. Caesar uses every means to prevent her, but she outwits him and dies with her maids. The scene is extraordinarily vivid:

Cleopatra:	[*To an asp, which she applies to her breast.*] With thy sharp teeth this knot intrinsicate Of life at once untie. Poor venomous fool, Be angry, and dispatch. O, couldst thou speak, That I might hear thee call great Caesar ass Unpolicied!
Charmain:	O eastern star!
Cleopatra:	Peace, peace! Dost thou not see my baby at my breast, That sucks the nurse asleep? [*Dies.*] ...

Charmain:	In this vile world? So fare thee well!
	Now boast thee, death, in thy possession lies
	A lass unparalleled. Downy windows, close,
	And golden Phoebus never be beheld
	Of eyes again so royal! Your crown's awry,
	I'll mend it, and then play—

Caesar discovers her body and orders a state funeral to bury the dead lovers together.

Tony the Tiger

Although into middle age, Antony is still a great soldier, reputed the most successful general and statesman of his time—the "triple pillar of the world." But his reputation does not stop there. He is notorious also for his dissolute life, his sensuality, and his vulgarity.

He spends his nights in drinking and carousing and his days in feasting and making love. He leaves the soldiering to his lieutenants like Ventidius, but not without being jealous of their success. He is cruel and conscienceless in marrying Caesar's widowed sister, purely for political expediency.

His other stupid moves include:

➤ Not adequately preparing against Caesar's less skillful but more alert generals

➤ Deserting the battle to follow his frightened mistress

But there's more to Tony the Tiger. A Stoic, he accepts Fulvia's death quietly, but with sadness, shame, and regret. A seasoned statesman and diplomat, Antony can out-talk and out-think even the great Caesar.

Above all he is kind. Despite all his callous cynicism, he is soft and generous. He treats Lepidus as an equal after Caesar has snubbed him; he releases his lieutenants from their loyalty after he has led them to defeat. He even offers them gold and letters of introduction. His supreme act of generosity is forgiving Enobarbus for deserting him.

Will Power

Asp is the common name applied to several unrelated poisonous snakes, including the European asp and the Egyptian cobra. The former is found from central France south to Sicily and east to the Balkans; the latter, throughout northern Africa and areas in the south. The asp that Cleopatra used to cause her death was probably either the Egyptian cobra or the horned sand viper. Now, aren't you glad you asked?

Norma Desmond of the Nile

Cleopatra is a male fantasy, both fear-inspiring and fantastic. A femme fatale, hard-nosed politician, tragic heroine, and brilliant queen, Cleopatra is every man's perfect woman because she's not the happy homemaker:

> Age cannot wither her, nor custom stale
> Her infinite variety. Other women cloy
> The appetites they feed, but she makes hungry
> Where most she satisfies; for vilest things
> Become themselves in her, that the holy priests
> Bless her when she is riggish.

There is no trick she won't use, no deceit she denies. Antony describes her as "cunning past man's thought." Enobarbus...

...saw her once
Hop forty paces through the public street;
And having lost her breath, she spoke, and panted,
That she did make defect perfection,
And breathless, pow'r breathe forth.

She and Antony enjoy endless nights of debauchery, drinking, carousing, and wearing each other's clothes. But does she exercise all of her charms and wiles to keep her lover or to deceive him? Does Cleopatra love Antony or merely use him?

Shakespeare leaves some doubt about the relationship between Antony and Cleopatra. After her treachery at Actium, Antony accuses Cleopatra of a triple infidelity: She left Julius Caesar for Pompey; she left Pompey when Antony conquered her; and now she will leave him for the next winner, Octavius Caesar.

Sweets to the Sweet

At the time of the action described in the play, Cleopatra is past her prime, her beauty somewhat faded. As a result, she must rely more and more on artifice and feminine wiles to attract her lover. While age makes Cleopatra more wily, however, it makes her more tragic and sympathetic to the audience.

Shakespeare never says clearly whether Cleopatra played a part in the mass surrender of Antony's troops in their final defeat. And her last hours in the monument are equally inconsistent.

Right after Antony's death, she claims that she is also resolved to die by her own hand—but then we find her trying to make some arrangements with Caesar.

Does she kill herself because she cannot live without Antony or because she cannot live with Caesar? This inconsistency enhances Cleopatra's cunning and her "infinite variety."

Liz Taylor and Rex Harrison as Cleopatra and Caesar. Photo courtesy of Fox.

It's the Poetry, Not the Plot

Antony and Cleopatra is celebrated more for its poetry than for its drama. Like a large dog, it sprawls: There are too many scenes trying to do too much. How many is too many? *Antony and Cleopatra* has 42 scenes, more than any other Shakespearean play.

The drama here comes from the conflict between Antony's love for Cleopatra and his sense of duty, the siren call of Egypt and the pressing demands of Rome. But its unity is established by the poetry.

In *Antony and Cleopatra*, Shakespeare's poetry achieves its greatest breadth and naturalness. There's breadth of experience and depth of emotion. To get the most from the play, here's what to focus on:

➤ Rhythm

➤ Images

➤ Figures of speech

➤ Sounds

Antony and Cleopatra marks a turning point in Shakespeare's poetic development. And with it he passes from the great tragedies to the romances.

The Least You Need to Know

➤ Antony and Cleopatra fall madly in love, destroy a few lives and kingdoms, and go down in a blaze of glorious poetry.

➤ Even though he is the victim of his own unbridled passion, Antony is still heroic.

➤ Cleopatra lives up to her rep: Although somewhat faded, she's still a fox.

➤ The play is most famous for its glorious poetry, not its drama or story line.

Chapter 24

Coriolanus and *Timon of Athens*

In This Chapter

➤ Who's who in *Coriolanus*

➤ The plot of *Coriolanus*

➤ Shakespeare's mature style

➤ Who's who in *Timon of Athens*

➤ The plot of *Timon of Athens*

➤ The style of *Timon of Athens*

Recognize from the start that both *Coriolanus* and *Timon of Athens* are not Shakespeare's headliners (so *that's* why you've never heard of them before). Not to worry, though—it *is* Shakespeare, after all.

Intensely intellectual, *Coriolanus* has a cold and austere tone. You can see this when you compare *Coriolanus* with another of Shakespeare's "Roman" plays, *Antony and Cleopatra*, which is noted for its gorgeous poetry. *Coriolanus*, in contrast, shows images used for their intellectual rather than emotional punch. Add an unsympathetic hero, and you don't have the makings of a crowd pleaser.

Then we come to *Timon of Athens*. A kind of morality play about worldly vanity, it's an acknowledged mess. The second half of the play is so shrill that some critics accuse Shakespeare of losing control. There's no doubt that he tinkered with the play, but it still lacks a true climax and is plainly unpolished.

Let's take a look at these two lesser-known works of the Bard. By the end of this chapter, you'll be madly in love with both of these plays. (Okay, maybe madly in *like* would be more accurate.)

Who's Who in *Coriolanus*

At last, a Shakespearean tragedy in which *both* sides repel us—the aristocratic Coriolanus with his contempt for the great unwashed masses and the scheming tribunes who play on their masters' folly and gullibility. Meet the cast:

➤ Caius Martius, *afterward Caius Martius Coriolanus*

➤ Titus Lartius, *general against the Volscians*

➤ Cominius, *general against the Volscians*

➤ Menenius Agrippa, *Coriolanus' friend*

➤ Sicinius Velutus, *tribune of the people*

➤ Junius Brutus, *tribune of the people*

➤ Young Martius, *Coriolanus' son*

➤ Roman Herald

➤ Nicanor, *a Roman*

➤ Tullus Aufidius, *Volscian general*

➤ Lieutenants to Aufidius and Coriolanus

➤ Conspirators with Aufidius

➤ Adrian, *a Volscian*

➤ Citizen of Antium

➤ Two Volscian guards

➤ Volumnia, *Coriolanus' mother*

➤ Virgilia, *Coriolanus' wife*

➤ Valeria, *Virgilia's friend*

➤ Gentlewoman, *attending on Virgilia*

➤ Assorted soldiers, senators, patricians, and so on

It's a Hard Knock Life

The play opens with a riot: The Roman citizens are grumbling that the patrician aristocrats don't care about the common folk. Caius Martius (later to receive the title of Coriolanus) is the worst of the bunch. He refuses to give the starving citizens grain from the public storehouses at a fair price. Martius believes that price cuts weaken the people's moral fiber. The bitter insults he hurls at the people suggest he does indeed deserve his reputation as a stink-pot.

The patrician Menenius Agrippa quickly pacifies the mob by his rather illogical tale of the belly and the members, an anecdote aimed to show the mob the place and function of all groups of citizens in government of the state. Not surprisingly, he insists that the patricians do feel the plebeians' pain.

Just when things seem to have quieted down, Caius Martius appears with news that another mob had appeared at the Senate chamber asking for food. They had been mollified with political representation rather than food. The plebeians now have five tribunes to represent them, though we never meet more than two in the play, Sicinius Velutus and Junius Brutus.

Fight Night

The Volscians, a neighboring tribe, have raised an army against Rome. Naturally, the senators raise an army to fight back. Martius immediately says that he will fight because he wants to do battle with the Volscian leader, Tullus Aufidius, a valiant warrior. Aufidius respects Coriolanus' military valor equally.

Meanwhile, the women wait for news from the battlefield. There's Volumnia, Caius Martius' mother, a trend-setter in the single-mother movement and defiantly in-your-face. Virgilia, Martius' wife, is a marked contrast to her assertive mother-in-law. She's meek and nonassertive.

Will Power

The events of the play cover about four years, 491 B.C. to 487 B.C. At that time, Rome had two classes, the Patricians and the Plebeians. The former were nobles and could send representatives to the Senate. The latter, the common people, suffered political, economic, and social discrimination and could not belong to the Senate. In 494 B.C., after a military mutiny, the Plebeians were given two Tribunes to look after their interests. Class hatred persisted between the Patricians and Plebeians, however, and about 20 years after the events of this play the Plebeians managed to gain some semblance of free voting for their Tribunes and therefore some real political power.

Good Help Is Hard to Find

> Had I a dozen sons, each in my love alike and none less dear than thine and my good Martius, I had rather eleven die nobly for their country than one voluptuously surfeit out of action.
>
> —Coriolanus

On the battlefield, Caius Martius insults the troops because they are too chicken to follow him into danger. He finally rushes the gates of Corioli and is shut inside, alone. Nevertheless, he manages to fight so valiantly and do such damage that the city surrenders. Then he goes in search of more killing, meets Aufidius and other soldiers, and vanquishes the whole lot.

> If you have writ your annals true, 'tis there
> That, like an eagle in a dove-cote, I
> Fluttered your Volscians in Corioli:
> Alone I did it. Boy!

For his bravery, Caius Martius is offered a large share of the booty. Since he hates to hear himself praised, he turns down everything except a good war-horse and the title "Coriolanus" in token of his victory.

Star Quality

Coriolanus is ideal for propaganda. As a result, in the 1930s, it was staged as a pro-Fascist parable in France. In the 1950s, it became a Marxist tool.

Letting It All Hang Out

> I thank you for your voices: thank you:
> Your most sweet voices.
>
> —Coriolanus

Back in Rome, the people rejoice. Coriolanus gets the ancient Roman equivalent of a ticker-tape parade. Rather than a key to the city, the senators decide to appoint him Consul. However, it is the custom that any candidate for that office must stand in the market place and show his wounds and scars to the people and ask for their votes. Coriolanus refuses to do this because he hates to be praised but also because he is too proud to humble himself before the common people.

Under protest, Coriolanus goes down to the marketplace and asks the people for their voices. However, he won't show his wounds, and his manner in asking for votes is by no means humble. The people do give their voices, but doubt remains. The tribunes Sicinius and Brutus persuade the people to revoke their consent.

While Coriolanus fumes, a mob calls for Coriolanus to be executed as a traitor. Coriolanus' friends try to persuade him to apologize to the Plebeians, but he refuses until his mother shames him into humbling himself. But again Coriolanus loses his temper and insults the mob. Now they call for his banishment. In a rage, Coriolanus curses the multitude and says that he refuses to be banished by them; instead he will banish Rome.

Sweets to the Sweet

Unlike most other tragic Shakespearean heroes, Coriolanus has only one notable soliloquy, just before he goes to Aufidius' house. As a result, we don't know exactly what's going through Coriolanus' mind; we only see what he says or does in a public situation. He's difficult to identify with since we do not understand his emotions.

Sore Loser

Seeking revenge on the entire population of Rome, Coriolanus offers to fight by the side of his former enemy Aufidius against his native city. Proud of Coriolanus' military prowess, Aufidius gives his former opponent joint command of the Volscian army.

But as time passes, Aufidius begins to feel jealous of Coriolanus' bravery. Aufidius' best soldiers flock to Coriolanus, who swells with pride. It is impossible for Coriolanus to remain in a subordinate position, and at times it is difficult to tell who is the senior man, Aufidius or Coriolanus. Nevertheless, the Volscian is a politic man and is prepared to wait until Rome has been captured to find some way to attack Coriolanus, accuse him of treason, and regain his old ascendancy among his own people.

Danger to Self and Others

The news of Coriolanus' alliance with the Volscians has struck terror to the Romans, who now try to reconcile with the man they had so willingly banished. Fat chance: Coriolanus refuses to speak to his old general, Cominius.

Then the three ladies in Coriolanus' life come to see him: Virgilia, his wife; Volumnia, his mother; and Valeria, their friend; together with Young Martius, his son. Virgilia says very little, but from her demeanor and Coriolanus' reaction, we can see that he is deeply touched by her words. Then Volumnia pleads with her son and finally gets him to understand that the noblest action is for him to follow the road of mercy and spare Rome. This he decides to do, though he seems quite sure that this action will be the cause of his death.

You're as cold as ice: Alan Howard as Coriolanus and Irene Worth as his mother. Photo courtesy of PBS.

Working Without a Net

Setting his plot in motion, Aufidius openly calls Coriolanus a traitor and then insults him by saying that he sold the chance to take Rome for a few tears from his mother's eyes. Unable to bear being taunted, Coriolanus threatens the Volscians. The people shout for his blood. In the confusion, Coriolanus is struck down and Aufidius stands on his corpse. Not exactly an honorable death.

> His nature is too noble for the world:
> He would not flatter Neptune for his trident,
> Or Jove for's power to thunder.

When Coriolanus dies, the Volscians celebrate his nobility. Arrangements are made for a splendid funeral, and Coriolanus' body is borne off with military honors. Ain't it always the way?

In this play, Shakespeare asks the question: What is the best form of government? The play strives to give an answer, but no one is sure what it is. One group claims that Shakespeare is being sympathetic toward the oppressed, while another claims that he shows the evils of government by the people.

Coriolanus doesn't offer any easy answers to the questions it poses, and Shakespeare takes pains to show us the faults and the virtues of both the citizens and Coriolanus. What we can't argue is the Elizabethan belief in order and balance. It's the failure of Coriolanus and the Romans to fulfill their duties that brings about confusion in the state.

A Lean, Mean, Poetry Machine

The play's poetry is characteristic of Shakespeare's mature style. The lines are closely packed with meaning and images are functional rather than decorative. As a result, they reveal character, attitude, and theme.

Further, the play's austere style suits its somber subject. Rhyme is very rare, and there's a considerable amount of prose, particularly when Menenius, the tribunes, or the common people are involved.

A few major images dominate the play, mainly those concerned with disease and the drastic action often needed to halt its spread. Then we get the animals, usually piggy ones, such as the ass, dog, cur, goose, cat, crow, goat, and mule.

But wait, there's more! Let's look at *Timon of Athens.*

Who's Who in *Timon of Athens*

Timon gets the nod as Mr. Misanthrope: There's scarcely a character in literature as cynical. The only one of Shakespeare's heroes to reject women, he goes mad when he realizes that he has been used and abused by his "friends." He's pathetic rather than sympathetic. Save your tears for Lear.

Can't tell the players without a scorecard? Here's the rundown on the characters in *Timon of Athens*:

➤ Timon of Athens

➤ Lucius and Lucullus, *two flattering lords*

➤ Sempronius, *another flattering lord*

➤ Ventidius, *one of Timon's false friends*

➤ Alcibiades, *an Athenian captain*

➤ Apemantus, *a churlish philosopher*

➤ Flavius, *Timon's steward*

➤ Falminius, Servilius, Lucilius, *Timon's servants*

➤ Caphis, Philotus, Titus, Hortensius, *servants to usurers*

➤ Poet, painter, jeweler, merchant

➤ Old Athenian

➤ Three strangers, one named Hostilius

➤ Page

➤ Fool

➤ Phrynia and Timandra, *Alcibiades' mistresses*

➤ Cupid

➤ Certain maskers (as Amazons)

➤ Assorted senators, servants, lords, et. al.

Sweets to the Sweet

Here, Apemantus is Shakespeare's mouthpiece. As with Lear's Fool, Apemantus is a brilliant and cruel opponent who argues with genuine wit and honesty.

This One's on Me

O you gods! what a number of men eats Timon, and he sees 'em not! It grieves me to see so many dip their meat in one man's blood, and all the madness is, he cheers them up too. I wonder men dare trust themselves with men.

Methinks they should invite them without knives:
Good for their meat, and safer for their lives.

—Timon of Athens

Fire at Will

Timon is trying to buy love and admiration. Deceived by appearance, he fails to see that everyone is greedy. Don't make the mistake of sympathizing with Timon, though; that's not Shakespeare's point.

Timon, a wealthy Athenian, is happy to spread the goodies around. Unfortunately, he's penny-wise and pound-foolish, and his largess soon empties his pockets. His faithful servant Flavius, the young general Alcibiades, and the cynic Apemantus have warned Timon about running up his credit, but he is totally convinced that his friends will help him out of the hole. To prove his point, Timon asks the government and those who have received gifts from him to cough a little back. Sure enough, everyone refuses.

Denied help by his "friends," Timon decides to give one last banquet. Instead of surf and turf, however, he serves warm water and throws stones at his guests. "Burn, house! Sink, Athens! Henceforth hated be / Of Timon, man, and all humanity!" he shouts. Then Timon decides to become a hermit and exile himself from Athens.

Heavy Metal

Seeking food, he digs for roots. To his astonishment, he unearths gold. Not surprisingly, when word gets around of his good fortune, people beat a path to his cave for a handout. Timon's steward Flavius is his only honest guest.

Star Quality

The general opinion of public officials has not improved with time. Centuries after Shakespeare smacked Athenian Senators in *Timon of Athens*, Mark Twain slammed U.S. Senators with, "Suppose you were an idiot and suppose you were a member of Congress. But I repeat myself," he said.

Help Is Not on the Way

I'll example you with thievery:
The sun's a thief, and with his great attraction
Robs the vast sea; the moon's an arrant thief,
And her pale fire she snatches from the sun;
The sea's a thief, whose liquid surge resolves
The moon into salt tears; the earth's a thief,
That feeds and breeds by a composture stolen
From general excrement: each thing's a thief.

—Timon of Athens

Several Athenian senators visit Timon and apologize for the shameful way they have treated him. Of course, it's not a simple social visit: no, they need his help against Alcibiades, who has been exiled over an argument with the Senate involving the execution of one of his soldiers. It's a lovely ironic reversal. Earlier, Timon had to ask the Senate for help; now, the Senate is forced to ask for his help. Not one to forgive and forget, Timon rejects their olive branch. He announces that he is planning to die soon and so is writing his epitaph.

When Alcibiades decides to invade Athens, he sends a messenger to Timon asking for help. As he is negotiating with the senators, the messenger returns with the news that Timon has indeed checked out. The messenger has made a wax impression of the epitaph on Timon's tomb. It reads:

> Here lies a wretched corse [corpse], of wretched soul bereft;
> Seek not my name: a plague consume you, wicked caitiffs left!
> Here lie I, Timon, who, alive, all living men did hate;
> Pass by and curse thy fill, but pass and stay not here thy gait.

Star Quality

Shakespeare took Timon's epitaph almost word-for-word from Plutarch's *Lives*.

The senators agree to Alcibiades' terms and surrender the city to him. He promises not to kill anyone...except for maybe a few who opposed him and Timon.

Timon of Athens has been relegated to the back row in the Shakespearean tragedy parade. It's not that the play is the bad boy of tragedies; rather, it just seems rough and unfinished when compared to the major tragedies such as *Macbeth*, *Hamlet*, and *King Lear*. Some scholars have theorized that the play we have is merely a draft; how else to explain the sloppiness?

The Least You Need to Know

➤ *Coriolanus* and *Timon of Athens* are minor tragedies in Shakespeare's canon. No need to memorize them.

➤ Coolly intellectual, *Coriolanus* boasts a proud and unsympathetic hero. But here, both sides are unappealing: the aristocratic Coriolanus and the scheming tribunes.

➤ When war hero Coriolanus refuses to show his wounds to the masses and ask for their votes, he is exiled. He joins the enemy, the Volscians, and is killed by a plot fomented by their leader, Aufidius. No one's sobbing.

➤ The play's poetry is characteristic of Shakespeare's mature style: packed lines and functional images.

➤ A morality play about worldly vanity, *Timon of Athens* is very rough around the edges. And in the middle, too.

➤ When Timon, the Mr. Got Rocks of Athens, loses all his money, his friends bolt. When he discovers gold, they return, but Timon has wised up. Crabbed and crotchety, he dies cursing his fellow citizens.

➤ *Timon of Athens* is always a bridesmaid, never a bride.

Part 5

Romances

Hot blood begets hot thoughts,
and hot thoughts beget hot deeds,
and hot deeds is love.

—Troilus and Cressida

Shakespeare's romances concern love, but they also concern a whole lot more. The last four plays: Pericles, Cymbeline, The Winter's Tale, *and* The Tempest *contain:*

➤ *Near-tragedy in the opening act or acts*

➤ *Loss of a child or exile*

➤ *Recovery and reconciliation*

➤ *A journey*

➤ *A great awareness of nature*

Think of the romances as tragedies in reverse; they open with all sorts of horrible stuff—dead children and wives, crazed husbands, shipwrecks—but end with happy reconciliations. The dead come back to life, lost children are found, endings become beginnings. So what if we need a little magic? Shakespeare does what it takes to rewind the death and destruction of the tragedies to create happy endings in the romances.

Chapter 25

The Tempest and The Winter's Tale

> ## In This Chapter
>
> ➤ Who's who in *The Tempest*
>
> ➤ The plot of *The Tempest*
>
> ➤ Critical interpretations of *The Tempest*
>
> ➤ Who's who in *The Winter's Tale*
>
> ➤ The plot of *The Winter's Tale*
>
> ➤ The themes of *The Winter's Tale*

The Tempest is one of Shakespeare's most beautiful and beloved plays. Here, even the monsters get great lines. Check out this stunning poetry from the grotesque monster Caliban:

> Be not afeard, the isle is full of noises,
> Sounds, and sweet airs, that give delight and hurt not.
> Sometimes a thousand twangling instruments
> Will hum about mine ears; and sometimes voices,
> That if then had wak'd after long sleep,
> Will make me sleep again, and then in dreaming,
> The clouds methought would open, and show riches
> Ready to drop upon me, that when I wak'd
> I cried to dream again.

The Winter's Tale, in contrast, is considered a lesser work. But as with *The Tempest*, it's filled with spectacular special effects and tremendous drama. What other play features a man chased by a bear?

Let's start with the wondrous *Tempest*.

Who's Who in *The Tempest*

Meet the cast:

➤ Alonso, *King of Naples*

➤ Sebastian, *his brother*

➤ Prospero, *the right Duke of Milan*

➤ Antonio, *his brother, the usurping Duke of Milan*

➤ Ferdinand, *the King of Naples' son*

➤ Gonzalo, *an honest old councilor*

➤ Adrian, Francisco, *lords*

➤ Caliban, *a savage and deformed slave*

➤ Trinculo, *a Jester*

➤ Stephano, *a drunken Butler*

➤ Master of a Ship

➤ Boatswain

➤ Mariners

➤ Miranda, *Prospero's daughter*

➤ Ariel, *an airy Spirit*

➤ Iris, Ceres, Juno, Nymphs, *spirits*

➤ Other Spirits attending Prospero

Star Quality

The Tempest has inspired a wide range of poetry, including Milton's "Comus," T. S. Eliot's "The Wasteland," and W. H. Auden's "The Sea and the Mirror."

Magical Misery Tour

The play opens in the midst of a violent storm at sea. A ship, furiously lashed by the wind and rain, is driven relentlessly toward shore. As the sailors battle the tempest, the royal passengers (King Alonso of Naples, his son Ferdinand, and Prospero's brother

Antonio, the usurping Duke of Milan) rush anxiously on deck with the rest of their party and urge the crew to do their best to save their royal necks. The royal party stays on deck for some time, but finally goes below to pray.

Meanwhile, Prospero and his 15-year-old daughter, Miranda, are stationed at the cave, which has been their home for the past 12 years. A master of magic, Prospero has created the storm to destroy the ship. Miranda begs her father to end the storm and save the passengers, and he assures her that everyone is safe. To pass the time before the relatives arrive, Prospero does the Facts of Life speech without the sex. Here, it's the story of their arrival on the island.

Prospero explains that he is the rightful Duke of Milan, who entrusted the government to his brother Antonio while he was busy studying. With the assistance of the King of Naples, Antonio seized the kingdom. Prospero and three-year-old Miranda were cast off in a leaky boat. Gonzalo, the nobleman appointed to carry out the banishment, took pity on Prospero and Miranda and stocked their small boat with food, water, and books. Prospero and Miranda were shipwrecked on a desolate island. Now, all of Prospero's enemies have been brought together on one ship within his power.

Prospero speaks to his servant Ariel, a spirit, who carries out his magic works. Ariel reports that everything has gone according to plan: the passengers have landed on the island. Prospero reminds Ariel that he rescued him (it?) from the witch Sycorax, who formerly ruled the island and once again promised to free Ariel (Ariel isn't holding out much hope; this is an old promise). Next we meet the monster Caliban, son of Sycorax, who has been enslaved by Prospero's magic. Caliban is part human, part fish, and part tortoise. Once treated kindly by Prospero, Caliban fell from grace when he attempted to rape Miranda.

Will Power

The Tempest was used to celebrate the engagement of King James' daughter, Elizabeth.

Control Freak

> O wonder!
> How many goodly creatures are there here!
> How beauteous mankind is! O brave new world
> That has such people in't!

—Miranda

Ferdinand and Miranda meet and fall instantly in love, as per Prospero's plan. It's not really *that* astonishing. While Ferdinand is handsome as well as royal, he's also the only other man Miranda has ever seen aside from her father, who doesn't count. To prevent the love affair from moving too fast, Prospero sets Ferdinand to work piling logs. Of course, teenagers being what they are, this just makes Miranda love him more.

Ain't love grand? Here are Pippa Guard as Miranda and Christopher Guard as Ferdinand. Photo courtesy of PBS.

Daze of Our Lives

The rest of the passengers are wandering around the island in a stupor. Convinced that Ferdinand has drowned, Alonso is grief-stricken and incapable of action. Ariel, invisible, put everyone but Sebastian and Antonio to sleep. Antonio convinces Sebastian to kill Alonso and Gonzalo while they sleep, so that Sebastian can seize the throne of Naples.

Just as the two conspirators are about to kill Gonzalo, Ariel awakens the old advisor. To explain their raised swords, the conspirators claim to have seen wild animals.

We have some comedy with Caliban, Trinculo, and Stephano, involving demon rum and a very large coat. Assuming that Stephano must be a god for bringing such a delicious drink, Caliban swears allegiance to him and gives Prospero two weeks' notice.

Miranda offers herself to Ferdinand as a wife. Spying on the sweetly innocent scene, Prospero approves of his machinations and their outcome. In another part of the island, Ariel bedevils Trinculo and Stephano. Caliban urges them to help him brutally kill Prospero. Ariel lures everyone off with a magical tune.

Meanwhile, the royal party is still searching for Ferdinand. Ariel makes some more trouble among the group. Happy that his enemies are busy trying to kill each other, Prospero stages a masque to honor Ferdinand and Miranda. The masque ends suddenly when Prospero remembers, thanks to his magical powers as a seer, that Caliban and his clownish cohorts are on their way to murder him.

Devil Dogs

Ariel has bewitched the conspirators, leaving them to wallow in a muddy pond. Prospero and Ariel send some spirit dogs after them and they run in terror. After Ariel releases the royal prisoners, Prospero thanks Gonzalo for his help and loyalty. As the rightful monarch, Prospero pardons Antonio and Sebastian for their attempt to murder the king.

Alonso blesses Ferdinand and Miranda's marriage. Ariel gathers the rest of the cast and crew, who are all astonished at the turn events have taken. Caliban realizes that Stephano isn't a god. "What a thrice-double ass / Was I to take this drunkard for a god, / And worship this dull fool," he says.

Kiss and Make Up

The King of Naples renounces any rights to the dukedom of Milan, and Antonio is silent. Prospero frees Ariel, as he had earlier promised. Prospero champions "virtue" over "vengeance" and abjures his magic.

> Though with their high wrongs I am strook to th' quick,
> Yet, with my nobler reason, 'gainst my fury
> Do I take part. The rarer action is
> In virtue than in vengeance. They being penitent,
> The sole drift of my purpose doth extend
> Not a frown further.

The play concludes when Prospero steps out of character to deliver an epilogue asking the audience to show its approval and forgive him. Since Prospero has thrown away his magic, he's powerless to return to Naples unless the good people of the audience put their hands together and show their approval.

Will Power

The Tempest is the only Shakespearean play that observes the three classical unities of time, place, and action. The unity of time specified that the action should be confined to a single day. The tempest arises on the ship at two o'clock in the afternoon; by six o'clock everything is over. The unity of place specified one setting: in *The Tempest*, virtually everything takes place on the island. The unity of action specified no subplots or digressions. There's a minor subplot involving Stephano, Trinculo, and Caliban, but these are all tied together by the plot against Prospero.

... Now I want
Spirits to enforce, art to enchant,
And my ending is despair,
Unless I be reliev'd by prayer,
Which pierces so, that it assaults
Mercy itself, and frees all my faults.
　　　As you from crimes would pardon'd be,
　　　Let your indulgences set me free.

The Medium Is the Message

Traditionally, *The Tempest* was read as Shakespeare's valedictory. As such, Prospero's final speech encompasses Shakespeare's own attitudes:

Sweets to the Sweet

The Tempest has also been read as a religious allegory.

Our revels now are ended. These our actors,
As I foretold you, were all spirits, and
Are melted into air, into thin air:
And, like the baseless fabric of this vision,
The cloud-capp'd towers, the gorgeous palaces,
The solemn temples, the great globe itself,
Yea, all which it inherit, shall dissolve,
And, like this insubstantial pageant faded,
Leave not a rack behind. We are such stuff
As dreams are made on; and our little life
Is rounded with a sleep.

Shakespeare did not write another complete play after *The Tempest*; instead, he retired at the height of his powers to his home in Stratford. In this interpretation, Prospero = Shakespeare and the soliloquy = Shakespeare's farewell to the London stage and the "magic" he had mastered.

Star Quality

The 1956 sci-fi epic *Forbidden Planet* grafts *The Tempest*'s plot to the '50s obsession with psychology, robots, and outer space. Prospero's island become planet Altair 4. Walter Pidgeon does the Prospero turn as Dr. Morbius, while Anne Francis becomes a lightly dressed Miranda.

Heart of Darkness

Recently, critics have looked at *The Tempest* another way—as a parable of colonialism. In this reading, Prospero is the colonizer, Ariel is the good native, and Caliban is the bad native. Ariel cooperates and serves his master, while Caliban (as in *cannibal*, get it?) recalls the colonial nightmare by trying to rape Miranda and kill Prospero. Prospero repeatedly invokes this incident to divert Caliban from his rightful claim to the island.

When read this way, *The Tempest* raises the question of the relationship of nature to civilization. Is nature superior to civilization and by extension, to art? And in which state—civilization or nature—are people more noble? Are you getting a headache yet?

Will Power

The headline story of 1609 was the storm that shipwrecked the flagship of a fleet sent to fortify John Smith's colony in Virginia. The tempest off the Isle of Devils in Bermuda blew "from out the North-east, which swelling, and roaring as it were by fits, some houres with more violence than others, at length did beate all light from heaven; which like an hell of darkenesse turned blacke upon us, so much the more fuller of horror."

An original and daring adaptation of The Tempest, *director Peter Greenaway's 1991 film* Prospero's Books *boasts an 87-year-old John Gielgud and an impressive amount of nudity. Photo courtesy of Miramax Films.*

Now You See It, Now You Don't

The Tempest also has the familiar Shakespearean theme of illusion and reality. From the moment the shipwrecked nobles set foot on Prospero's island, their senses are untrustworthy. Ariel deceives their eyes as well as ears with his magic.

Now, let's turn to another Shakespearean romance, *The Winter's Tale*.

Who's Who in *The Winter's Tale*

The Winter's Tale is even more magical and unbelievable than *The Tempest*: why would a wife turn into a statue for 16 years? (Don't answer that.)

Here's the cast:

➤ Leontes, *King of Sicilia*

➤ Mamillius, *young prince of Sicilia*

➤ Camillo, *lord of Sicilia*

➤ Antigonus, *lord of Sicilia*

➤ Cleomines, *lord of Sicilia*

➤ Dion, *lord of Sicilia*

➤ Polixenes, *King of Bohemia*

➤ Florizel, *prince of Bohemia*

➤ Archidamus, *a lord of Bohemia*

➤ Old Shepherd, *the reputed father of Perdita*

➤ Clown, *his son*

➤ Autolycus, *a rogue*

➤ Hermione, *Leontes' queen*

➤ Perdita, *daughter of Hermione and Leontes*

➤ Paulina, *Antigonus' wife*

➤ Emilia, *a lady attending on Hermione*

➤ Mopsa, Dorcas, *shepherdesses*

➤ Time, *as a chorus*

➤ Assortment of lords, gentlemen, officers, etc.

Fire at Will

The Winter's Tale has often been criticized because of its spectacular failure to observe the unity of time—all the action should take place within one day. There's a gap of 16 years between the events in Acts III and IV, for example. How dare *he*?

Midlife Crisis with a Vengeance

A man parked his car at the supermarket and was walking past an empty cart when he heard a woman ask, "Excuse me, did you want that cart?"

"No," he answered. "I'm only after one thing."

As he walked toward the store, he heard her murmur, "Typical male."

As the play opens, Polixenes, King of Bohemia, is visiting his boyhood friend, Leontes, King of Sicilia, and his wife, Hermione. The kings were good buddies in their childhood, but grew apart as each took over their family business. Polixenes thinks it's time to go home, but Leontes wants him to set a spell, so he enlists Hermione's help. She makes Polixenes feel so welcome that he decides to stay one more day.

Suddenly, without warning, Leontes becomes insanely jealous and suspicious, believing that Polixenes and Hermione are carrying on a love affair. He goes so far as to ask Camillo, his trusted advisor, to poison Polixenes. Shocked at the suggestion, Camillo warns Polixenes to chill.

Hermione is pregnant, and Leontes accuses her of carrying Polixenes' child. Unfortunately, the numbers add up, since Polixenes had indeed been at the Sicilian court for nine months. Leontes throws Hermione into prison to await trial. Facing her angry husband with dignity and love, Hermione goes to prison avowing her innocence.

Leontes sends messengers to the Oracle of Apollo at Delphos to find out the truth. It never occurs to Leontes that he might be wrong. And he is.

Sweets to the Sweet

To some scholars, the title *The Winter's Tale* suggests the play is an allegory of the seasons or a fertility myth. But for Shakespeare's audience it probably meant "a sad tale's best for winter."

The Big Chill

In prison awaiting trial, Hermione gives birth to a girl. The sight of the infant doesn't soften Leontes' heart.

Instead, he orders the baby to be burned. The lords exclaim in horror and finally Leontes offers to soften the sentence, but he makes Antigonus, Paulina's husband, swear that he will do whatever he is asked. To his horror, Antigonus learns that Leontes wants the child taken to a remote spot outside Sicily and exposed to the elements to live or die as the gods will. Antigonus believes that he must carry out the king's commands, however irrational they may be.

At the trial, Hermione defends herself with nobility and wisdom:

> Since what I am about to say must be but that
> Which contradicts my accusation, and
> The testimony on my part no other
> But that comes from myself, it shall scarce boot me
> To say "Not guilty." Mine integrity,
> Being counted falsehood, shall (as I express it)
> Be so received.

Nonetheless, Leontes is adamant, even though the oracle proclaims that "Hermione is chaste, Polixenes blameless, Camillo a true subject, Leontes a jealous tyrant, his innocent babe truly begotten." The oracle also predicts that the king will live without an heir "if that which is lost be not found." Leontes, however, dismisses the oracle's message and demands that sentence be passed on Hermione.

A Walk on the Wild Side

Word is brought announcing Mamillius' death. When Hermione faints and is carried from the courtroom, Leontes repents and says that he will take Hermione once more as his wife. But his good resolution comes too late; Hermione is dead.

Will Power

Act III, scene iii (baby and the bear) takes place on the sea coast of Bohemia—a land-locked country. Shakespeare flunked geography.

Antigonus had left the infant to die, but he had followed a dream to name the child "Perdita" and leave her on the coast. As he leaves, a great storm springs up, and his ship is sunk. He runs away pursued by a bear, which devours him. This results in one of the most famous (and oddest) stage directions in all of literature: "Exit pursued by a bear" (IV, i). Perdita is picked up by a shepherd and his father, who decide to take care of her.

What I Did for Love

Sixteen years pass. Perdita has now grown up, as has Prince Florizel, Polixenes' son. They are lovers. Polixenes and Camillo, disguised, come to spy on Florizel. When Perdita and Florizel are about to be engaged to each other, Polixenes threatens the girl with physical harm and his son with disinheritance. The couple flee to Sicilia.

Leontes and his court greet them happily. In the meantime, the shepherd and his son travel to Polixenes with the clothes and information concerning Perdita, which they found with her 16 years earlier.

In Sicilia, Leontes is completely changed, full of repentance for the irreparable harm he has done himself, his family, and his kingdom by his insane jealousy. When Florizel and Perdita arrive, Leontes looks on the young couple in grief when he realizes that his own lost son and daughter would have been about the same age as this young couple.

The King of Bohemia, the shepherd and his son, and Autolycus arrive in Sicilia. Perdita is terrified at what might happen to them, but Leontes agrees to speak to Polixenes in their behalf. No pleading is required, however, because the shepherd has revealed Perdita's identity to Polixenes, and the King and his companion have come to bless the marriage.

Chill with Will

When daffadils begin to peer,
    With height, the doxy over the dale!
Why, then comes in the sweet o' the year,
    For the red blood reigns in the winter's pale.

After a joyful reunion with his lost daughter, Leontes and the court go to Paulina's house to see the superb statue of the dead Hermione. The entire company is amazed at the brilliance of the likeness, especially since the statue seems to represent Hermione at the age she would have been had she lived. Perdita and Leontes both want to touch and kiss the statue, but Paulina refuses permission.

Leontes again expresses his repentance publicly. Paulina calls for music and the "statue" comes alive, revealing itself as Hermione, who has waited 16 years to return to her husband. The two embrace passionately. Paulina marries Camillo and everyone lives happily ever after.

Live and Learn

The play's theme arises from the conflict between good and evil, as Leontes is redeemed through a long period of mourning.

We also see the theme of forgiveness and mercy in Hermione.

She stays on ice until Leontes is worthy of a reconciliation. She forgives and shows mercy, even though she wouldn't have been off-base to smack him upside his face. Okay, so Leontes suffers for his sins, but not too much, since he finally has his wife and daughter restored to him.

Other important themes are those of time, growth, and regeneration, embodied in Perdita and Florizel. The theme of time pervades the play, because Time restores peace to Leontes.

Sweets to the Sweet

The subtitle of Shakespeare's main source, Greene's *Pandosto*, was *The Triumph of Time*. Shakespeare introduces his Chorus costumed as Time. Only Time can eventually bring forth truth and forgiveness.

The Least You Need to Know

➤ *The Tempest* and *The Winter's Tale* are romances, not tragedies.

➤ To get back at his throne-stealing brother and restore himself as the Duke of Milan, Prospero creates a storm that nets not only his brother but also Ferdinand, a suitor for his daughter Miranda. Prospero's magic shows everyone the error of their ways, and they all reconcile.

➤ *The Tempest* can be read as Shakespeare's farewell to the stage, a parable about colonialism, or an exploration of the interplay of illusion and reality.

➤ Both plays are tragedies in reverse: *The Tempest* opens with Ferdinand's "death" but ends with a happy reunion, everyone alive and well. *The Winter's Tale* opens with the death of Hermione and Perdita because of Leontes' insane jealousy but ends with their reunion, almost everyone alive and well.

➤ *The Winter's Tale*'s themes are good versus evil, forgiveness versus mercy, and the power of time to heal all wounds (and wound all heels).

Chapter 26

Pericles, Prince of Tyre and Cymbeline

> ## In This Chapter
>
> ➤ Who's who in *Pericles*
>
> ➤ The mismatched plot of *Pericles*
>
> ➤ Authorship of *Pericles*
>
> ➤ Who's who in *Cymbeline*
>
> ➤ *Cymbeline*'s unbelievable plot
>
> ➤ *Cymbeline*'s beautiful lyrics

One night a father overheard his son saying his prayers, "God bless Mommy and Daddy and Grammy. Good-bye Grampa."

The next day, the Grandfather died. About a month or two later, the father heard his son saying his prayers again, "God bless Mommy. God bless Daddy. Good-bye Grammy."

The next day the grandmother died. The father was getting more than a little worried about the whole situation. Two weeks later, the father once again overheard his son's prayers, "God bless Mommy. Good-bye Daddy."

The father nearly had a heart attack. To avoid a car accident in the heavy traffic, he got up early to go to work. He stayed at work all through lunch and dinner. Finally after midnight he went home—still alive! When he got home, he apologized to his wife. "I'm sorry, honey. I had a very bad day at work today."

"You think you've had a bad day? YOU THINK YOU'VE HAD A BAD DAY!" the wife yelled. "The mailman dropped dead on my doorstep this morning!"

So you think *you're* having a bad day, bunky? Add incest, a near-death experience, shipwrecks, abandonment, and a dash of death and what do you get? Pericles' life, that's what. But not to worry: Since it's a romance, everything ends happily.

Cymbeline features similar outrageous events: a headless corpse, abductions, mistaken identities, magic potions, disguises, and visions of Jupiter. At least with this romance, the poetry soars. Read on to get the inside scoop.

Who's Who in *Pericles*

Meet the cast:

➤ Gower, *as Chorus*

➤ Antiochus, *King of Antioch*

➤ Pericles, *Prince of Tyre*

➤ Helicanus and Escanes, *two lords of Tyre*

➤ Simonides, *King of Pentapolis*

➤ Cleon, *Governor of Tharsus*

➤ Lysimachus, *Governor of Mytilene*

➤ Cerimon, *a lord of Ephesus*

➤ Thaliard, *a lord of Antioch*

➤ Philemon, *Cerimon's servant*

➤ Leonine, *a murderer, Dionyza's servant*

➤ Marshal

➤ Pander

➤ Boult, *his servant*

➤ Antiochus' daughter

➤ Dionyza, *Cleon's wife*

➤ Thaisa, *Simonides' daughter*

➤ Marina, *daughter of Pericles and Thaisa*

➤ Lychorida, *Marina's nurse*

➤ Bawd

➤ Diana, *a goddess appearing to Pericles*

➤ The usual assortment of lords, ladies, knights, sailors, fishermen, and messengers

Riddle Me This

Antiochus, King of Antioch, refuses to let his daughter marry after the death of his wife. To make sure she stays by his side, he comes up with a riddle that each suitor must solve on his first attempt...or lose his head. Here's the riddle; try your hand:

> I am no viper, yet I feed
> On mother's flesh which did me breed.
> I sought a husband, in which labor
> I found that kindness in a father.
> He's father, son, and husband mild;
> I mother, wife—and yet his child.
> How they may be, and yet in two,
> As you will live, resolve it you.

Pericles, Prince of Tyre, solves the riddle and explains it to the king—Antiochus is guilty of incest with his daughter. "Great King," Pericles says, "Few love to hear the sins they love to act; / 'Twould braid yourself too near for me to tell it...It is enough that you know, and it is fit, / What being more known grows worse, to smother it. / All love the womb that their first love being bred, / Then give my tongue like leave to love my head."

Damage Control

When the King realizes that Pericles has solved the riddle, he tells him that the explanation is incomplete. Afraid that his secret will come out, Antiochus pretends to give Pericles extra time to work out the full solution—but he must remain in the palace. No dope, Pericles realizes that the King is ordering flowers for his funeral rather than his wedding, and so beats a hasty retreat.

To keep Pericles out of Antiochus' way for a while, his advisors in Tyre suggest that he take a nice, long cruise. Pericles agrees. In his absence, Helicanus will run the government. Ocean travel being what it was in the sixteenth century, Pericles is shipwrecked on a beach in Pentapolis, a land ruled by King Simonides. Three fishermen tell Pericles there's a tournament being held for the hand of the King's daughter, Thaisa.

Sweets to the Sweet

Pericles is often read as a symbol for a life that ends peacefully after being battered by misfortune.

Will Power

One of the 12 cities of the ancient Greek district of Iona, Ephesus is located in Turkey. A major departure point for trade routes to Asia Minor, Ephesus was also known in antiquity for its sacred shrines, especially a famous temple to the goddess Diana. This was one of the Seven Wonders of the Ancient World. The city was also an important center of early Christianity. Excavations at Ephesus, begun in 1863, have uncovered magnificent temples to Diana, public buildings, astonishing mosaics, works of the great Greek sculptors, a portrait of Alexander the Great, and some impressive ancient stone toilets.

Our hero enters the tournament and wins. (Bet you're shocked.) Simonides and Thaisa are impressed with Pericles' skill and learning and, soon after, Pericles and Thaisa are married.

Mike Gwilym plays Pericles on the lam in this PBS production. Photo courtesy of PBS.

Swimming with the Fishies

When Pericles hears a few months later that Antiochus and his daughter are dead, he decides it's safe to return to his kingdom of Tyre. During a severe storm at sea, Thaisa supposedly dies during childbirth. Pericles' farewell to his wife in the storm shows Shakespeare's characteristic touch:

> A terrible child-bed has thou had, my dear,
> No light, no fire. Th' unfriendly elements
> Forget thee utterly, nor have I time
> To give thee hallowed to thy grave, but straight
> Must cast thee, scarcely coffined, in the ooze,
> Where, for a monument upon thy bones,
> The e'er-remaining lamps, the belching whale
> And humming water must o'erwhelm thy corpse,
> Lying with simple shells.

Thaisa is buried at sea, and her coffin washes ashore at Ephesus. A doctor brings her back to life, and she decides to spend the rest of her life at the Temple of Diana in Ephesus. Why didn't she immediately decide to find her husband and baby daughter? Your guess is as good as everyone else's. Willie missed the boat on this one.

Pericles takes his baby daughter Marina to his friend Cleon, governor of Tarsus. There, Cleon's wife Dionyza promises to treat the child as her very own.

Time Flies When You're Having Fun

Fourteen years pass. Marina is more gifted and beautiful than Dionyza's daughter. Jealous, the queen orders Marina murdered when she's strolling by the seaside. As the murderers are trying to do their evil deed, two pirates seize Marina and sell her to the owners of a house of prostitution. Marina refuses to join the other girls in their reindeer games, and her virtue reforms the men who come for some nooky. Lysimachus, governor of Mytilene, is one such man. Through the aid of Boult, Pandar's servant, Marina is able to find work teaching sewing and painting.

Six Degrees of Separation

Meanwhile, Pericles decides it's time to check on Marina—hey, it's only been 14 years since he dropped her off. To his astonishment, child care proved inadequate, and Marina is rumored to be dead. Tormented, Pericles decides to refuse all visitors and live on a ship. When his yacht anchors at Mytilene, Lysimachus mans the Welcome Wagon.

Lysimachus suggests that a young woman he knows (Marina, of course) would be ideal to cheer up the despondent prince. During their conversation, Pericles discovers that she is his daughter.

> Tell thy story;
> If thine, considered, prove the thousand part
> Of my endurance, thou art a man, and I
> Have suffered like a girl. Yet thou dost look
> Like Patience gazing on kings' graves, and smiling
> Extremity out of act.

Back to the Future

Diana sends a vision, telling Pericles to make a sacrifice at her temple in Ephesus. He obeys the vision, taking Marina and Lysimachus along for company. Pericles and his wife, Thaisa, are reunited. In gratitude to Lysimachus, Pericles offers him anything he wants—even marriage to Marina. The couple marry, and Pericles throws in his kingdom as a wedding present. Thaisa's father Simonides has died, and Pericles goes to Pentapolis to rule his kingdom. Cleon and Dionyza die when their palace is burned to the ground.

Time takes its toll: Pericles at the temple of Diana. Photo courtesy of PBS.

Two Halves *Don't* Make a Whole

Now, you're not nuts; there *is* a definite difference between Acts I and II and the rest of the play. They don't match in style or tone. They're like two different plays slapped together. Various explanations have been offered to explain this incongruity:

Sweets to the Sweet

Renaissance dramatists excelled at play patching, a little nip-and-tuck to freshen an old play.

➤ Perhaps the split occurred when the text was first transcribed. *Pericles* is a "reported" text, not one based on a manuscript or play script. Maybe different writers copied down the script, and one wrote (or listened) better than the other.

➤ It could be that two people wrote the play, one being Shakespeare and the other being…? If so, didn't they ever talk to each other?

➤ Maybe Shakespeare revised someone else's play? In this scenario, he tarted up the first two acts but did some major body work on the last three.

Who's Who in *Cymbeline*

Cymbeline is a weak ruler, controlled by his Machiavellian queen. The day is saved by an old man and two boys—hardly the most ringing endorsement of Cymbeline's leadership skills. Here's the rest of the cast:

➤ Cymbeline, *King of Britain*

➤ Cloten, *the Queen's son by a former husband*

➤ Posthumus Leonatus, *a gentleman, Imogen's husband*

➤ Belarius, *a banished lord disguised under the name "Morgan"*

➤ Guilderius, *Cymbeline's son, disguised under the name "Polydore," supposed son to Morgan*

➤ Arviragus, *Cymbeline's son, disguised under the name "Cadwal," supposedly Morgan's son*

➤ Philario, *Posthumus' friend, an Italian*

➤ Jachimo, *Philario's friend, an Italian*

➤ Caius Lucius, *general of the Roman forces*

➤ Pisanio, *Posthumus' servant*

➤ Cornelius, *a physician*

➤ Philarmonus, *a soothsayer*

➤ Roman Captain

➤ Two British Captains

➤ Frenchman, *Philario's friend*

➤ Two Lords of Cymbeline's court

➤ Two Gentlemen of the same

➤ Two Jailers

➤ Apparitions

➤ Queen, *Cymbeline's wife*

➤ Imogen, *Cymbeline's daughter by a former queen*

➤ Helen, *a lady attending Imogen*

➤ Lords, Ladies, etc., etc., etc.

Fire at Will

We really can't judge *Pericles* fairly by the mangled text we've inherited; in its day, the play was tremendously successful.

Sweets to the Sweet

Take Jachimo as a cut-rate Iago, nasty but not wicked. Cymbeline emerges as a bargain-basement Lear, easily taken in by his lying wife.

Sweet Dreams Aren't Made of This

Cymbeline, the King of ancient Britain, was left with three children when his wife died. Belarius stole the boys, Guilderius and Arviragus, as revenge for being exiled for treason, and raised them in a far-off land as his own sons. When the play opens,

Cymbeline's daughter Imogen is nearly 20 years old. Cymbeline has married again, and his ambitious wife wants her wussy son Cloten to marry Imogen. Imogen, however, is in love with Posthumus, the King's ward and a commoner. Against her father's wishes, she marries him. Exiled, Posthumus goes to live in Rome.

Meanwhile, Cloten puts the moves on Imogen. Cloten may be stupid, but he's also determined: He refuses to understand that "No" really does mean "No." In Rome, Posthumus tells people about his nubile and noble wife. Jachimo, a Roman gentleman, bets Posthumus that he can seduce Imogen: after all, how can *any* woman be faithful?

Two's Company; Three's a Crowd

Jachimo travels to England and visits Imogen, but he finds her as chaste as her husband had claimed. Determined to get into her bedroom, the skunk hides in a trunk. Here's what he thinks as he spies on Imogen as she sleeps:

> 'Tis her breathing that
> Perfumes the chamber thus. The flame o' th' taper
> Bows toward her, and would under-peep her lids,
> To see th' enclosed lights, now canopied
> Under these windows, white and azure lac'd
> With blue of heaven's own tinct.

While Imogen snoozes, Jachimo takes her bracelet and glimpses a mole on her chest. With this circumstantial evidence, Jachimo convinces Posthumus that he has indeed seduced Imogen. In a fury, Posthumus writes to his servant Pisanio to murder Imogen. To ensure the murder, he sends a letter falsely advising her to meet him at Milford-Haven. The Queen also has murder on her mind: Since Imogen refused her son Cloten, she clearly deserves to die.

Disguised, Imogen sets off for Milford-Haven. Since Pisanio knows that Imogen is innocent, he refuses to murder her. Instead, he leaves her in the mountains with the suggestion that she wait for the Roman ambassador, Lucius, and offer herself as a page. Once she gets back to Rome, he reasons, she could explain that she'd been framed.

The Directionally Impaired

But Imogen gets lost and fails to connect with Lucius. Along the way, she becomes friends with Belarius and his supposed sons. Cymbeline and Cloten both hear that Imogen has run away. Cloten disguises himself in Posthumus' clothes and tries to head her off at the pass, but he also gets lost and finds himself at Belarius' cave. Imogen is ill and has taken a sleeping-potion, mistaking it for a mild medicine. Cloten gets in a fight with Guilderius/Polydore and is beheaded.

When Belarius and his sons can't wake Imogen up, they decide that she's dead. They lay her out on the ground next to the headless Cloten. When Imogen awakens, she mistakes Cloten's body for that of her husband Posthumus and throws herself over it. The head's gone; what can you expect?

We Feel Your Pain

Meanwhile, the Roman Emperor has declared war on Britain. Posthumus arrives with the Roman army to invade Britain. Filled with regret for ordering his wife's death, he decides to switch sides. With the aid of Belarius and his sons, Posthumus rescues Cymbeline. Along the way, they ambush and trounce the Romans. The Britons take him prisoner, assuming he's a poor Roman solider. Cymbeline orders him hanged.

Forsooth!

More for your money: People are **hanged**, pictures are **hung**.

The Queen has died of grief over her son Cloten's death. That's okay, since she was a louse. Since it's a romance, all the nice guys finish first: Cymbeline learns that Posthumus saved his life, so Posthumus is released. Belarius is pardoned, Cymbeline is delighted to have his sons back, Posthumus and Imogen are reunited, and even the Romans are forgiven. Peace breaks out.

Hidden Treasures

The plot's loose, the characters bland, but the poetry soars. Two of Shakespeare's most famous lyrics come from *Cymbeline*: "Hark, hark, the lark" and "Fear no more the heat o' th' sun." And here they are, for your reading enjoyment:

> Song
> Hark, hark, the lark at heaven's gate sings,
>   And Phoebus gins arise,
> His steed to water at those springs
>   On chalic'd flow'rs that lies;
> And winking Mary-buds begin to ope
>   their golden eyes;
> With every thing that pretty is, my lady
>   sweet, arise:
>   Arise, arise!

> Song
> Fear no more the heat o' th' sun,
> Nor the furious winter's rages,
> Thou thy worldly task hath done,
> Home art gone, and ta'en thy wages,
> Golden lads and girls all must,
> As chimney-sweepers, come to dust.

Fear no more the frown o' th' great,
Thou art past the tyrant's stroke;
Care no more to clothe and eat,
To thee the reed is as the oak.
The sceptre, learning, physic, must
All follow this and come to dust.

Fear no more the lightning-flash.
Nor th' all-dreaded thunder-stone.
Fear not slander, censure rash.
Thou hast finishe'd joy and moan.
All lovers young, all lovers must
Consign to thee and come to dust.

No exorciser harm thee.
Nor no witchcraft charm thee.
Ghost unlaid forbear thee.
Nothing ill come near thee.
Quiet consummation have,
And renowned be thy grave.

The Least You Need to Know

➤ *Pericles* is based on an ancient Greek play only partially rewritten by Shakespeare. It's a hodgepodge.

➤ *Pericles* shows a rough and violent world in which innocence miraculously survives and even triumphs.

➤ In *Cymbeline*, the new Queen of Britain is determined that her cloddish son Cloten marry King Cymbeline's daughter, Imogen. When Imogen marries Posthumus instead, the Queen orders her death. Along the way, Imogen meets her two long-lost brothers, Cymbeline defeats the invading Romans, and everyone lives happily ever after.

➤ No one's getting excited about *Cymbeline*'s plot or characters, but two of the lyrics are real humdingers.

Part 6
Histories

"The trouble with Shakespeare is that you never get to sit down unless you're a king."

—George S. Kaufman

Sit down a while as you enjoy Shakespeare's stories of kings. There are 10 in all:

King Henry VI, Part I
King Henry VI, Part II
King Henry VI, Part III
King Richard III
King Richard II

King John
King Henry IV, Part I
King Henry IV, Part II
King Henry V
King Henry VIII

Eight of Shakespeare's 10 history plays cover the political history of England, from the deposition of Richard II in 1399, to the defeat of Richard III at Bosworth Field, to the coronation of Henry VII in 1485. King John *and* Henry VIII *stand alone. But you'll like 'em all. I promise.*

Chapter 27

King Henry VI, Part I;
King Henry VI, Part II;
King Henry VI, Part III

In This Chapter

➤ The history of the history plays

➤ Who's who in *King Henry VI, Part I*

➤ The plot of *King Henry VI, Part I*

➤ Who's who in *King Henry VI, Part II*

➤ The plot of *King Henry VI, Part II*

➤ Who's who in *King Henry VI, Part III*

➤ The plot of *King Henry VI, Part III*

➤ What makes the plays confusing

Political history is far too criminal a subject to be fit to teach children, said the twentieth century poet W. H. Auden. It's fortunate, then, that Shakespeare aimed his history plays at big people like us. Shakespeare's 10 history plays recount the political story of England from the end of the 1300s to the coronation of Henry VIII in 1485.

Henry VI, Parts I, II, and *III* cover the events from the beginning of Henry VI's reign in 1422 until his death in 1471. By the end of *Henry VI, Part III,* Shakespeare has brought the saga halfway through the War of the Roses (1455–1487). Let's start with the basics—the history of the history plays.

The Backstory

The civil wars that took place in England on and off for almost a hundred years were known as the "War of the Roses." The Lancasters and the Yorks were the Hatfields and McCoys of medieval England except they knew the reason for their 100-year feud: each side wanted the big prize, the throne of England.

The war finally ended when Henry of Richmond, a Lancaster, defeated Richard III, a York, and married Elizabeth of York, thus uniting the two families. Henry VII founded the new Tudor dynasty and was succeeded by his son Henry VIII. His daughter Elizabeth began the last and most famous of the Tudor reigns. (That's "Elizabeth" as in the adjective "Elizabethan.")

Can't tell the players without a scorecard? Here's the rundown on the Kings and Queens of England of the era:

> **Forsooth!**
>
> The **War of the Roses** took its name from the red and white roses, symbols of the Lancasters and Yorks, respectively.

Richard II	1377–1399	Henry VII	1485–1509
Henry IV	1399–1413	Henry VIII	1509–1547
Henry V	1413–1422	Edward VI	1547–1553
Henry VI	1422–1461	Mary	1553–1558
Edward IV	1461–1483	Elizabeth	1558–1603
Richard III	1483–1485	James I	1603–1625

> **Sweets to the Sweet**
>
> No fool, Shakespeare intended the history plays to celebrate the Tudor dynasty, confirm its right to the throne, make rebellion a no-no, and thereby maintain peace in a land troubled by civil disunity. By showing the chaos of the previous dynasty, Shakespeare was underscoring Elizabeth's accomplishments.

Who's Who in *Henry VI, Part I*

Meet the gang (and it *is* a gang):

➤ King Henry the Sixth

➤ Duke of Gloucester, *King's uncle and Protector*

➤ Duke of Bedford, *King's uncle and Regent of France*

➤ Thomas Beauford, *Duke of Exeter*

➤ Henry Beauford, *Bishop of Winchester, then Cardinal*

➤ John Beauford, *Earl, then Duke of Somerset*

➤ Richard Plantagenet, *Richard's son, the Duke of York*

➤ Earl of Warwick, Earl of Salisbury, Earl of Suffolk

➤ Lord Talbot, *then Earl of Shrewsbury*

➤ John Talbot, *his son*

➤ Edmund Mortimer, *Earl of March*

➤ Sir John Falstaff

➤ Sir William Lucy

➤ Sir William Glansdale

➤ Sir Thomas Gargrave

➤ Mayor of London

➤ Woodville, *Lieutenant of the Tower*

➤ Vernon, *of the White Rose or York faction*

➤ Basset, *of the Red Rose or Lancaster faction*

➤ Lawyer, Jailers

➤ Charles, *Dauphin, then King of France*

➤ Reignier, *Duke of Anjou, titular head of Naples*

➤ Duke of Burgundy, *Duke of Alanson*

➤ Bastard Orleance

➤ Governor of Paris

➤ Master Gunner of Orleance, and his Son

➤ General of the French forces in Bordeaux

➤ French Sergeant

➤ Shepherd, *Joan de Pucelle's father*

➤ Margaret, *Reignier's daughter, then married to King Henry*

➤ Countess of Auvergne

➤ Joan de Pucelle, *AKA Joan of Aire, Joan of Arc*

➤ Fiends (*appearing to Joan de Pucelle*), lords, etc.

King Henry VI, Part I: Lifestyles of the Rich and Famous

> Brandish your crystal tresses in the sky,
> And with them scourge the bad revolting stars
> That have consented unto Henry's death:
> King Henry the Fift, too famous to live long!
> England ne'er lost a king of so much worth.
>
> —King Henry VI

The play opens with the funeral of King Henry V, once the celebrated "Prince Hal." A good King has died, and since there's no one to take his place (Henry VI is too young to rule—he's just King in name until he's "of age"), the kingdom is ripe for unrest and conquest. Sure enough, the English troops have suffered staggering losses in their pursuit of the French throne.

Forsooth!

The **dauphin** was the eldest son of a king of France. The term was used as a title from 1349 to 1830.

A messenger brings news that Charles, the French Dauphin, has been crowned king of France. Adding injury to insult, Lord Talbot, the English general, has been defeated and his men slaughtered. Bedford vows revenge by overthrowing the Dauphin. Winchester, meanwhile, plots to become head weenie at the roast.

Medieval Crystal Queen

At Orleans, the English have driven back the French troops. The Dauphin agrees to take Joan of Arc with him in battle; after all, she's allegedly been ordained by heaven to drive the English from France. And mysticism aside, she wields a mean sword.

Back in London, Gloucester accuses Henry Beauford, Bishop of Winchester of murdering Henry V. The battle lines are drawn: Winchester is driven by personal ambition to seize the throne; Gloucester, in contrast, is the rightful Protector of England, determined to shield Henry VI and the English people. Meanwhile, Joan of Arc retakes Orleans.

You Snooze, You Lose

When the Dauphin murders the Duke's father, Burgundy allies with the British. The British retake the city while the French nap, so Joan and the Dauphin hit the road. Talbot becomes the Countess of Auvergne's prisoner, but he succeeds in tipping off his men and winning the day.

Henry tries to break up a fight between Gloucester and Winchester, but he lacks the power of a true leader. "O, how this discord doth afflict my soul!" he kvetches. Nonetheless, Gloucester and Winchester call an uneasy truce.

Back in France, Joan of Arc enters the city of Rouen, assisted only by four soldiers. Charles and his men storm the city, and Talbot is forced to flee. Talbot and Burgundy retake Rouen from the French. Joan lures Burgundy back into the French camp.

Bridge Across Troubled Waters

While Winchester is crowning Henry, we learn that Burgundy has betrayed the English and that Falstaff is banished for deserting the English forces. (This is *not* the same Falstaff that is in *Henry IV, Parts I* and *II* and *The Merry Wives of Windsor*. His original name was Sir John Fastolfe.) The English are slaughtered at Bordeaux; Talbot and his son are victims of the carnage.

To bring peace, the Earl of Armagnac, a powerful Frenchman, has offered his daughter as Henry's wife. Henry agrees to the match. Winchester's moving up the ladder; he's now a cardinal—and he's playing for keeps: "I'll either make thee stoop and bend thy knee, / Or sack this country with a mutiny," he decides.

On the plains of Anjou, Joan's trusty spirits are out to lunch, and she is captured by York. She tries to bargain her way out of being the star of the marshmallow roast by claiming she's pregnant, but she comes off like a tramp for resorting to such a cheap trick. Suffolk decides to win the beautiful but poor Margaret of Anjou for Henry; her father agrees with the plan. Winchester announces a peace treaty between England and France. Henry decides to marry Margaret, rejecting the political match that had been set up for him. Why Margaret over politics? Because she may be poor and powerless, but she's pretty.

Fire at Will

The crafty Joan of Arc in this play is not the sainted Joan of Arc we're used to seeing. Why? As a French Catholic, Joan was considered the enemy in Protestant England. In this play, Shakespeare is giving us the correct Tudor spin on current events. As a result, Joan comes off as a slutty witch.

Who's Who in *Henry VI, Part II*

- ➤ King Henry the Sixth
- ➤ Humphrey, *Duke of Gloucester, his uncle*
- ➤ Cardinal Beauford, *Bishop of Winchester*
- ➤ Richard Plantagenet, *Duke of York*
- ➤ Edward and Richard, *his sons*
- ➤ Duke of Somerset, Duke of Suffolk, Duke of Buckingham
- ➤ Lord Clifford
- ➤ Young Clifford, *his son*
- ➤ Earl of Salisbury, Earl of Warwick
- ➤ Lord Scale, Lord Say
- ➤ Sir Humphrey Stafford and William Stafford, *his brother*
- ➤ Sir John Stanley
- ➤ Vaux
- ➤ Matthew Goffe
- ➤ Alexander Iden, *a Kentish gentleman*
- ➤ John Hume and John Southwell, *priests*
- ➤ Roger Bolingbrook, *a conjurer*

➤ Thomas Horner, *an armorer*

➤ Peter Thump, *his man (assistant)*

➤ Simpcox, *an imposter*

➤ Jack Cade, *a rebel*

➤ Margaret, *King Henry's Queen*

➤ Eleanor, *Duchess of Gloucester*

➤ Margery Jordan, *a witch*

➤ Lieutenant, Shipmaster, Master's Mate, Gentlemen, Clerk of Chartam, Major of Saint Albons, etc.

Sweets to the Sweet

Remember, Shakespeare penned the Hank trilogy very early in his career. As a result, we're not getting the lush poetry of his "mature" years.

King Henry VI, Part II: Swimming in the Gene Pool

Part II traces the mounting conspiracy against the noble Gloucester and the anarchy that results. Henry becomes a wussy ruler and the War of the Roses gets underway.

When the play opens, Suffolk has arrived with the new Queen, Margaret of Anjou. Henry falls in love with her instantly. Gloucester is very upset that Henry has chosen a marriage based strictly on physical attraction with no political or economic advantages. He also resents the wasted effort of his brothers, King Henry V and the Duke of Bedford, to conquer France. The other nobles, especially Buckingham and Beauford, plot against Gloucester. Here's your crib sheet:

Anti-Gloucester	Pro-Gloucester
Beauford	Salisbury
Buckingham	Warwick
Somerset	York
Suffolk	

Eleanor, the Duchess of Gloucester, lusts to be queen and doesn't hesitate to do whatever she can to get to that big gold throne. She even conjures a few spirits, but she ends up getting arrested for trying to overthrow the King and being banished to the Isle of Man.

Torn between his king and his wife, Gloucester joins his wife in her exile. Eleanor is furious rather than grateful.

Drew Snyder, Donald Madden, and Jeanne Hepple step back into history in this production of Henry VI, Part II. Photo courtesy of Zodiac Photographers.

Not Waving, but Drowning

By Act III, it's unmistakable that Gloucester is down for the count. Suffolk arrests him for treason and puts him under the control of his old enemy, Cardinal Beauford (who you might remember as "Winchester"). Henry is such a wimp that he makes no effort at all to defend his former Lord Protector.

Gloucester exposes his accusers' motivations, revealing his astute powers of judgment, which of course means that he *has* to be murdered. Suffolk and Beauford do the deed. Gloucester did not go gentle into that good night:

> His face is black and full of blood,
> His eyeballs further out than when he lived
> Staring full ghastly like a strangled man;
> His hair upreared, his nostrils stretch'd with struggling.

Fire at Will

Shakespeare's history plays are art, not history. The Bard distorts, rearranges, and invents facts. If you want a primer on fifteenth century politics, read a history book. If you want art, read Shakespeare.

London Bridge Is Falling Down

Beauford dies shortly thereafter. At his point, Gloucester, Eleanor, Suffolk, and Beauford are gone, so we're left with York, his supporters, the King, and his retinue.

The Queen caresses York's severed head as the rebels, called the "Cade Rebellion," slash and burn their way toward London. The rebels switch sides and decide to support the monarchy; the leader, Cade, is killed and dragged to a dunghill.

York asserts that he is king, which leads to the Battle of Saint Albons. York slays Clifford, Somerset is killed, and Henry beats a hasty retreat. The play ends with the Yorks ahead: They are the legitimate heirs to the throne and intend to get what's coming to them.

Sweets to the Sweet

The famous line "The first thing we do, let's kill all the lawyers" comes from *Henry VI, Part II.*

> After them! Nay, before them, if we can.
> Now, by my faith, lords, 'twas a glorious day.
> Saint Albons battle won by famous York
> Shall be eterniz'd in all ages to come.
> Sound drums and trumpets, and to London all,
> And more such days as these to us befall!

Who's Who in *Henry VI, Part III*

- ➤ King Henry the Sixth
- ➤ Edward, *Prince of Wales, Henry's son*
- ➤ Lewis the Eleventh, *King of France*
- ➤ Duke of Somerset, Duke of Exeter, Duke of Oxford
- ➤ Earl of Northumberland, Earl of Westmoreland
- ➤ Lord Clifford
- ➤ Richard Plantagenet, *Duke of York*
- ➤ Edward, *Earl of March, then King Edward IV*
- ➤ Edmund, George, Richard, *his sons*
- ➤ Duke of Norfolk
- ➤ Marquess of Montague
- ➤ Earl of Warwick, Earl of Pembroke

Forsooth!

The history plays are also known as the **chronicle** plays.

- ➤ Lord Hastings, Lord Stafford
- ➤ Sir John Mortimer, Sir Hugh Mortimer, *Duke of York's uncles*
- ➤ Henry, Earl of Richmond, *a child*
- ➤ Lord Rivers, *Lady Gray's brother*
- ➤ Sir William Stanley, Sir John Montgomery, Sir John Somerville
- ➤ Tutor to Rutland

➤ Mayor of York, Mayor of Coventry

➤ Queen Margaret

➤ Lady Grey, *then Edward IV's Queen*

➤ Bona, *the French Queen's sister*

➤ Lieutenant of the Tower, Noblemen, Huntsmen, etc.

Henry VI, Part III: Heir Today, Gone Tomorrow

In the last play of the Hank VI series, Henry gets his, the House of York triumphs, and Richard III is crowned. When the play begins, the Duke of York, his sons, and Warwick have returned to London to recount their triumphs on the battlefield. Warwick escorts York to the throne as Henry enters. It doesn't take Henry long to realize that York wants his job, but Henry claims that he has the inside track; after all, he *is* the son of King Henry V. They bicker.

Exeter suddenly switches sides and declares that York is the "lawful king." Henry begs to be allowed to remain king for the rest of his life. York agrees, but demands that Henry name him and his sons direct heirs. Henry's son Edward is less than delighted that his father has short-sheeted him; the Queen is equally incensed that her baby won't get the job. Both vow not to see Henry again until Edward York is restored to the throne.

Fire at Will

Don't get confused; Henry's son is named Edward, and York's son is named Edward. It's Eddie overload.

I Am Woman, Hear Me Roar

Margaret raises an army of 20,000 and takes York prisoner. To rub in his defeat, Margaret puts a paper crown on York's head and says, "Off with the crown; and with the crown, his head." Sure enough, York's head is impaled on the castle gates so that "it may overlook the town of York."

Richard demands Henry's throne, but Margaret wants the throne for her son. Margaret, Henry, and their son Edward arrive at York. At Margaret's urging, Henry knights their son. The York troops enter and York's son Edward challenges Henry to surrender the throne. They battle.

Days of Whine and Poses

Although he is the King, Henry sits out the battle, sobbing and moaning. Henry then high-tails it out of there with Margaret, Edward, and Exeter. The Yorks win and Edward is crowned. After the ceremony, he plans to go to France and marry Lady Bona, sister of the French queen. Henry is captured.

Turf Wars

While the wedding negotiations are underway, King Edward suddenly marries Lady Grey. Furious, Warwick returns to Henry's side. To show his anger, Warwick sends a fleet of French soldiers to England and gives his eldest daughter in marriage to Henry's son.

On the battlefield, Edward is outnumbered, and Warwick seizes his crown. Henry is freed from the Tower of London. Warwick announces that since he saved the day, he'll rule the government, but Henry gets to wear the gold party hat. Meanwhile, Edward escapes, and Gloucester proclaims him King. Edward, Gloucester, and their supporters seize Henry and order him back to the Tower. Don't these people have any reliable guards? And who has the crown now?

Warwick and Montague die on the battlefield. Somerset is beheaded; Oxford is locked up. The captured Prince Edward is killed. At the Tower, Gloucester stabs Henry to death with a great slam:

> Down, down to hell, and say I sent thee thither—
> [*Stabs him again...*]
> I'll throw the body in another room,
> And triumph, Henry, in thy day of doom.

Sweets to the Sweet

The Hundred Years' War is old news to us today, but to Shakespeare's audience, it was fresh. Everyone knew the characters and the outcome. As a result, they could cheer the hero, hiss the villain, and enjoy the irony.

They Walk Alike, They Talk Alike, You Could Lose Your Mind

Yes, *King Henry VI, Parts I, II,* and *III* are confusing. You're not the first to ask, "What's the plot?" "Who's the hero?" "What the heck is going on?"

Shakespeare's history plays are notoriously confusing—even Shakespeare sharpies have trouble keeping them straight. Here are some reasons you're likely to be pulling your hair out right about now:

➤ Everyone in the play seems to have the same name. You're not crazy; English kings have a real name shortage. All we get are Henry, Richard, Margaret, and Edward. There's not an Irving or Esmerelda in the bunch.

➤ If that's not bad enough, each character has a series of names—their surname, place of their inherited seat, their title, their first name.

Sweets to the Sweet

In Shakespeare's history plays, good wins over evil. Good = English, Tudor, Protestant. Evil = French, Italian, Roman Catholic.

➤ Just when you figure out who's who, the characters change their names as they get promoted.

Take this quiz to test your knowledge of the players:

Question: What do King Henry IV, Bolingbroke, Hereford, Lancaster, and Henry have in common?

Answer: They're all the same person.

Stick with it; eventually it all falls into place.

The Least You Need to Know

➤ *Henry VI, Part I*: Henry V dies while his heir Henry VI is still a child; the uncles jockey for power; France is lost.

➤ *Henry VI, Part II*: Henry grows up but doesn't mature. He's a weak ruler and the War of the Roses starts.

➤ *Henry VI, Part III*: Henry goes down in flames; the House of York triumphs; Richard of Gloucester's brother is crowned Richard III.

➤ Overall, *Henry VI, Parts I, II*, and *III*, describes the problems created by a weak king who has a dubious claim to his throne.

➤ It's not you: *Everyone* finds the history plays confusing.

Chapter 28

King Richard III, King Richard II

In This Chapter

➤ Richard III's rotten character

➤ Who's who in *King Richard III*

➤ The plot of *King Richard III*

➤ Richard II's weak character

➤ Who's who in *King Richard II*

➤ The plot of *King Richard II*

Now is the winter of our discontent
Made glorious summer by this son of York;
And all the clouds that low'r'd upon our house
In the deep bosom of the ocean buried.
Now are our brows bound with victorious wreaths,
Our bruised arms hung up for monuments,
Our stern alarums chang'd to merry meetings,
Our dreadful marches to delightful measures.
Grim-visag'd War hath smooth'd his wrinkled front;
And now, in stead of mounting barbed steeds
To fright the souls of fearful adversaries,
He capers nimbly in a lady's chamber
To the lascivious pleasing of a lute.

And so *The Tragedy of Richard III* begins, and we continue our journey through England's history. In today's installment, ladies and gentlemen, we'll see what happens when Richard steps into the shoes of Edward. In *Richard II*, we'll follow the story of the abdication and murder of Richard II.

Who's Who in *Richard III*

> But I, that am not shap'd for sportive tricks.
> Now made to court an amorous looking-glass;
> I, that am rudely stamp'd, and want love's majesty
> To strut before a wanton ambling nymph;
> I, that am curtail'd of this fair proportion,
> Cheated of feature by dissembling nature,
> Deform'd, unfinish'd, sent before my time
> Into this breathing world, scarce half made up,
> And that so lamely and unfashionable
> That dogs bark at me as I halt by them—
> Why I, in this weak piping time of peace,
> Have no delight to pass away the time,
> Unless to see my shadow in the sun
> And descant on mine own deformity.

Richard may have been a king, but he wasn't a looker. Thomas More described him as "little of stature, ill-featured of limbs, crook-backed, his left shoulder much higher than his right." And if that wasn't bad enough, he was also "malicious, wrathful, and envious, close and secret, lowly of countenance, arrogant of heart." As "his advantage grew, he spared no man's death whose life withstood his purpose." Richard himself wasn't shy about his motives:

> And therefore, since I cannot prove a lover
> To entertain these fair well-spoken days,
> I am determined to prove a villain
> And hate the idle pleasure of these days.
> Plots I have laid, inductions dangerous,
> By drunken prophecies, libels, and dreams,
> To set my brother Clarence and the King
> In deadly hate against one another...

Here's the complete cast:

➤ King Edward the Fourth

➤ Edward, *Prince of Wales, then King Edward V*

➤ Richard, *Duke of York, the King's son*

➤ George, *Duke of Clarence, the King's son*

➤ Richard, *Duke of Gloucester, then King Richard III*

➤ Edward Plantagenet, *Earl of Warwick, Clarence's son*

➤ Henry, *Earl of Richmond, then King Henry VII*

➤ Cardinal Bourchier, *Archbishop of Canterbury*

➤ Thomas Rotherham, *Archbishop of York*

➤ John Morton, *Bishop of Ely*

➤ Duke of Buckingham

➤ Duke of Norfolk

➤ Earl of Surrey, *his son*

➤ Earl Rivers *(Anthony Woodvile), Queen Elizabeth's brother*

➤ Marquess of Dorest, *Queen Elizabeth's son*

➤ Lord Grey, *Queen Elizabeth's son*

➤ Earl of Oxford, *Queen Elizabeth's son*

➤ Lord Hastings

➤ Lord Stanley, *also called Earl of Derby*

➤ Lord Lovel

➤ Sir Thomas Vaughn, Sir Richard Ratcliffe, Sir William Catesby, Sir James Tyrrel, Sir James Blunt, Sir Walter Herbert

➤ Sir Robert Brakenbury, *Lieutenant of the Tower*

➤ Sir William Brandon

➤ Christopher Urswick, *a priest*

➤ Hastings, *a pursuivant (a heraldic officer of the lowest class, ranking below a herald)*

➤ Tressel and Berkeley, *gentlemen attending Lady Anne*

➤ Elizabeth, *Queen to King Edward IV*

➤ Margaret, *widow of King Henry VI*

➤ Duchess of York, *mother of King Edward IV, Clarence, and Gloucester*

➤ Lady Anne, *widow of Edward, then married to Richard, Duke of Gloucester*

➤ Margaret Plantagenet, *Countess of Salisbury, Clarence's young daughter*

➤ Ghosts, lords, gentlemen, etc.

Star Quality

Laurence Olivier's 1955 *Richard III* is the model: All following portrayals of Richard come from Olivier's wonderfully accessible performance. Camp as well as chilling, Olivier was the first to see that Richard had a comic side beneath his murderous exterior. It's a glittering cast, too: John Gielgud is Clarence, Claire Bloom is Lady Anne, and Ralph Richardson is Buckingham.

Richard III: **Dick Lit**

It's 1477. Richard, Duke of Gloucester, lusts to become King of England after the death of his sickly brother, King Edward IV. The rightful successor is George, Duke of Clarence, the second son. What to do? Richard solves the problem with a swipe of the ax and has his brother murdered in the Tower of London. A few years later, Edward dies, and Richard is appointed Royal Protector for Edward's two young sons, Edward, Prince of Wales, and Richard, Duke of York.

Richard Burton does Richard III on a really bad hair day. Photo courtesy of Fox.

In his scheme to gain the Crown, Richard separates the children (two boys) from their mother and her family. To prevent the persistent relatives from stopping by for holiday meals and advancement, Richard has the adults beheaded. When Lord Hastings refuses to let Richard take the throne over Edward's children, Hastings' body is also separated from his head.

Spin City

In an impressive PR coup, the Duke of Buckingham spins public opinion in favor of Richard. Buckingham starts a rumor that the King was illegitimate, so that his young sons are ineligible for the Crown. Gathering a large group of citizens led by the Lord Mayor and his entourage, Buckingham finally "convinces" Richard to accept the throne. Shortly thereafter, the two children who really should get the crown are murdered.

To strengthen his hold on the Crown, Richard decides to marry his brother Edward's daughter, Elizabeth. He sends out rumors that his wife Anne is gravely ill. She dies soon after (arsenic, anyone?). Richard turns on Buckingham, who then raises an army to fight him. Buckingham is captured and—are you ready?—beheaded. "Off with his head!" So much for Buckingham.

Fire at Will

The line "Off with his head!" has become indelibly linked to Shakespeare, but he didn't write it—Colley Cibber did. Never heard of him? Don't worry; no one else has either.

Off with his head! Photo courtesy of BBC.

Make My Day

Richard's rule is next threatened by the exiled young Duke of Richmond. At the decisive battle of Bosworth Field, Richard courageously continues fighting, even after his horse has been killed. "My kingdom for a horse," he screams.

In a duel with Richmond, Richard III is stabbed to death. His crown is placed on Richmond's head, who as King becomes Henry VII. Richmond marries Elizabeth, Edward's daughter, the woman Richard had wanted to marry but obviously never did. Richmond promises peace with the union of the White and the Red Rose of the Houses of York and Lancaster.

Sweets to the Sweet

Richard can be charming as well as cruel. Nonetheless, he is so driven by ambition that despite his intelligence and charisma, he becomes the agent of his own downfall.

The brother blindly shed the brother's blood,
The father rashly slaughter'd his own son,
The son, compell'd, been butcher to the sure.
All this divided York and Lancaster,
Divided in their dire division,
O now let Richmond and Elizabeth,
The true succeeders of each royal house,
By God's fair ordinance conjoin together!
And let their heirs (God, if thy will be so)
Enrich the time to come with smooth-fac'd peace,
With smiling plenty, and fair prosperous days!

The first play in the tetralogy, *Richard II*, offers more about England's history. Let's look at it now.

Who's Who in *Richard II*

The historical Richard II or Richard of Bordeaux (named after the town where he was born) became King of England as a boy of 10. Despite some early promise, Richard turned out to be a lousy king. He was imprisoned first in the Tower of London and later at Pomfret Castle, where he died. Historians are convinced that he was murdered, probably by starvation. Richard has come down through history as a weak, perhaps at the end even insane, king. Shakespeare's re-creation of the King was pretty close to the real thing, but he does stir up some sympathy for Richard.

Here's the whole court and kingdom:

➤ King Richard II

➤ John of Gaunt, *Duke of Lancaster, King's uncle*

➤ Edmund of Langley, *Duke of York, King's uncle*

➤ Henry Bolingbroke, *then King Henry IV*

➤ Duke of Aumerle, *Duke of York's son*

➤ Thomas Mowbray, *Duke of Norfolk*

➤ Duke of Surrey

➤ Earl of Salisbury

➤ Lord Berkeley

➤ Sir John Bushy, Sir John Bagot, Sir Henry Green, *King Richard's favorites*

➤ Earl of Northumberland

➤ Henry Percy, *surnamed Hotspur, his son*

➤ Lord Ross, Lord Willoughby, Lord Fitzwater

➤ Bishop of Carlisle

➤ Abbot of Westminster

➤ Lord Marshall

➤ Sir Stephen Scroop

➤ Sir Pierce of Exton

➤ Captain of a band of Welshmen

➤ Queen to King Richard

➤ Duchess of York

➤ Duchess of Gloucester, *widow of Thomas Woodstock, Duke of Gloucester*

➤ Lady attending on the Queen

➤ Usual assortment of lords, gentlemen, etc.

Will Power

The Tower of London is the historic fortress on the north bank of the Thames River used as a prison and a royal residence. Built about 1078, the interior retains much of its original Norman character. The inner fortifications (Ballium Wall) have 12 towers, including the Bloody Tower, which got its name from being the site of the murder of the children of King Edward V and Richard Plantagenet in 1483. The Tower was used as a prison until the nineteenth century, with executions held in the central courtyard or outside the Tower on Tower Hill. Today, the Tower holds England's crown jewels and is one of the country's greatest tourist attractions.

Richard II: You Don't Know Dick

King Richard II ruled England from 1377 to 1399. The play begins in the last year of his reign. Richard has not been a successful king, and the powerful nobility of the land, especially his own relatives, have had enough. A capricious king, his court is packed with flunkies and favorites. A monarch who would be far happier roaming a mall with a platinum AmEx, Richard ignores the day-to-day realities of running a country. Even worse than his neglect of his duties, however, is his abuse of power; Richard taxes his subjects unmercifully.

Henry Bolingbroke accuses Thomas Mowbray of treason. As gentlemen, Bolingbroke and Mowbray agree to settle their quarrel by trying to make shishka-bob out of each other. But during the duel, King

Fire at Will

Although not a great play, *Richard II* is a good one. It poses a recurring political problem and presents a complex hero. It also gives evidence of Shakespeare's powers at a crucial stage in his dramatic development.

Richard intervenes and sends both men into exile. Why? He's afraid that Bolingbroke will kill his favorite, Mowbray. Besides, he's thrilled to get rid of Bolingbroke, who's not only heir to chunks of England, but who's also very popular with the great un-washed. The common people send Bolingbroke off with the medieval equivalent of a ticker-tape parade, which annoys Richard.

Buy High, Sell Low

Shortly thereafter, a rebellion breaks out in Ireland. Richard needs cash to put down the revolt, but he's already leveraged to the max so he decides to continue the brutal taxation and other unsound fiscal policies that have made his subjects angry. In the midst of his departure plans, he hears that Gaunt is seriously ill. Richard visits him, hoping that Gaunt will die.

Sure enough, Gaunt checks out, but not before giving one of the most quoted passages in all of Shakespeare, a last shot at Richard and an elegy for an England long past:

> This royal throne of kings, this sceptred isle,
> This earth of majesty, this seat of Mars,
> This other Eden, demi-paradise,
> This fortress built by Nature for herself
> Against infection and the hand of war,
> This happy breed of men, this little world,
> This precious stone set in the silver sea,
> Which serves it in the office of a wall,
> Or as a moat defensive to a house,
> Against the envy of less happier lands;
> This blessed plot, this earth, this realm, this England...

Before the body's cold, Richard seizes the Lancaster properties that should go to Bolingbroke. The nobles are furious. When Bolingbroke hears what has happened, he scurries back to England. As he marches south, he is joined by the Earl of Worcester and Harry Hotspur, Northumberland's son. The common people also rally to Bolingbroke, a noble and heroic figure to them.

The multiplex hit in 1955: Laurence Olivier's Richard III. *Photo courtesy of UA London.*

You'll Miss Me When I'm Gone

Richard's Queen fears trouble. Her feelings are validated as the conspiracy gathers strength. Richard is called back to court, but he is delayed. The nobles—including Richard's closest advisors—defect to Bolingbroke. The Earl of Northumberland and Bolingbroke join forces and add a key troop of Welsh soldiers. They capture Bristol Castle, Richard's stronghold, and execute its occupants.

Richard finally arrives in England, close to the rebels' camp. He flips from foolish confidence to utter despair, showing how unfit he is for leadership.

Richard and Bolingbroke meet. Bolingbroke wants Richard to revoke his exile sentence and return his property. Richard realizes that in so doing he is abdicating his power to Bolingbroke. Nonetheless, he quickly agrees to Bolingbroke's demands. His lines are Shakespeare at his best:

> For God's sake let us sit upon the ground
> And tell sad stories of the death of kings—
> How some have been deposed, some slain in war,
> Some haunted by the ghosts they have deposed,
> Some poisoned by their wives, some sleeping killed,
> All murdered. For within the hollow crown
> That rounds the mortal temples of a king
> Keeps death his court.

Fire at Will

Richard is a bad king, but he *is* the King. From the Elizabethan viewpoint, Bolingbroke's usurping of the throne was more than an act of power politics, it was an act of metaphysical violence. That Richard deeply believed in this doctrine is revealed in the desolation he feels once he has given up his crown, and he becomes a man "with no name, no title," a half-man searching for wholeness.

313

The King Is Dead, Long Live the King

Bolingbroke sends everyone to London and Westminster. The Queen gets the scoop and decides to go to London. At Westminster, Bolingbroke reopens Gloucester's murder and hears Richard's formal abdication. Richard steps down, but not without pointing out that it's risky to mess with God's special deputy, a sitting king. The Bishop of Carlisle, the Abbot of Westminster, and Aumerle plot a revolt against Bolingbroke.

Bolingbroke decides that the Queen must return to her native France and Richard must be locked up in northern England. Once there, Richard is attacked but fights back bravely before being killed. While he's still self-obsessed and discontented, he has nonetheless earned some dignity in his misfortune, as the following speech shows:

> Of comfort no man speak.
> Let's talk of graves, of worms, and epitaphs,
> Make dust our paper, and with rainy eyes
> Write sorrow on the bosom of the earth.
> Let's choose executors and talk of wills—
> And yet not so; for what can we bequeath
> Save our deposed bodies to the ground?

Richard's body is brought to Bolingbroke, who announces a period of mourning for the court and vows that he will make a pilgrimage to the Holy Land. *Richard II* is the tragedy of a man forced into a position for which he wasn't fit. It's also a tragedy for England, forced to choose between lawful incompetence and unlawful competence.

The Least You Need to Know

➤ Richard III was a deformed, malicious monarch.

➤ *Richard III*: Edward II dies, Richard steps to the head of the line and is crowned. He is killed at the Battle of Bosworth by Henry Richmond, later Henry VII (Elizabeth's grandfather, the first Tudor king).

➤ Richard II was a wimp, but Shakespeare manages to whip up some sympathy for him.

➤ *Richard II* is the story of the abdication and murder of Richard II. It features his usurper, Henry Bolingbroke (later Henry IV).

Chapter 29

King John; King Henry IV, Part I

In This Chapter

➤ Who's who in *King John*

➤ The plot of *King John*

➤ The message of *King John*

➤ King Henry's character

➤ Who's who in *King Henry IV, Part I*

➤ The plot of *King Henry IV, Part I*

➤ The play's real focus

➤ Falstaff

> Peace be to England, if that war return
> From France to England, there to live in peace.
> England we love, and for that England's sake
> With burden of our armor here we sweat.
>
> —*King John* (II, i)

One thing about the history plays: Those monarchs (and monarch wannabes) sure loved their country. But love aside, they all wanted power, power, and more power. King John coveted his brother's throne—and went after it full-throttle. What about *King Henry IV, Part I*? If *King Lear* is about the decaying of a king, and *Richard II* about the "unmaking" of a king, *Henry IV, Part I* is about the making of a king. Read on, fans, to see how the story unfolds.

Who's Who in *King John*

➤ King John

➤ Prince Henry, *the King's son*

➤ Arthur, *Duke of Britain, the King's nephew*

➤ Earl of Pembroke

➤ Earl of Essex

➤ Earl of Salisbury

➤ Lord Bigot

➤ Hubert de Burgh

➤ Robert Faulconbridge, *Sir Robert Faulconbridge's son*

➤ Philip the Bastard, *his half-brother (also called Richard)*

➤ James Gurney, *Lady Faulconbridge's servant*

➤ Peter of Promfret, *a prophet*

➤ Philip, *King of France*

➤ Lewis, *the Dauphin*

➤ Lymoges, *Duke of Austria*

➤ Cardinal Pandulph, *the Pope's legate*

➤ Melune, *a French lord*

➤ Chatillion, *ambassador from France to King John*

➤ Queen Elinor, *widow of Henry II, King John's mother*

➤ Constance, *Geffrey's widow, Arthur's mother*

➤ Blanch of Spain, *King of Castile's daughter, King John's niece*

➤ Lady Faulconbridge, *widow of Sir Robert Faulconbridge*

➤ Assorted lords, citizens, sheriff, heralds, officers, executioners

Star Quality

In what was surely a strange choice, *King John* was the first Shakespearean film ever made, in 1899. The movie was directed by Sir Herbert Beerbohm Tree, who also played the title role.

Heeeeere's Johnny!

When the play opens, King Philip of France has sent an ambassador to King John of England to demand the surrender of his crown to his nephew, young Arthur, the son of John's elder brother Geffrey. John indignantly refuses and prepares to invade France. The King appoints Philip Faulconbridge as one of the leaders of the expedition. Philip is the illegitimate son of his brother, the late King Richard Coeur-de-lion, popularly known as "The Bastard Faulconbridge." Don'tcha just love those Old English nicknames?

In Act II, the English and the French armies meet at Angiers. (Today it is called Angers.) When the citizens refuse to acknowledge either John or Arthur as their ruler, the two kings fight an indecisive skirmish for control of the city. At the Bastard's suggestion, the two kings plan to unite their forces against the stubborn town but the burghers (well-to-do middle-class citizens) convince them to settle their differences by agreeing to a marriage between Lewis the Dauphin and the Lady Blanch, daughter of John's sister. The Bastard and Lady Constance, Arthur's mother, find this shameful peace hateful.

Lady Constance, "as fond of grief as of [her] child," gets some appalling lines to show her feelings:

> But that which ends all counsel, true redress:
> Death, death. O amiable lovely death!
> Thou odoriferous stench! sound rottenness!
> Arise forth from the couch of lasting night,
> Thou hate and terror to prosperity,
> And I will kiss thy detestable bones,
> And put my eyeballs in thy vaulty brows,
> And ring these fingers with thy household worms,
> And stop this gap of breath with fulsome dust,
> And be a carrion monster like thyself.
> Come, grin with me, and I will think thou smil'st
> And buss thee as thy wife. Misery's love,
> O, come to me!

Sweets to the Sweet

King John had a weak claim to his brother Richard Coeur-de-lion's throne. Prince Arthur, the son of John's elder brother Geffrey, had no less strong a claim, which was upheld by his mother, Constance, and by King Philip of France. The futility of the consequent war between power-hungry leaders is satirically demonstrated in the dispute over the French town of Angiers.

Peace in Our Time?

At you probably predicted, the false peace doesn't last long, as Pandulph, the Pope's legate, excommunicates John for his refusal to bow to the will of the Church. He also orders the French to break the new compact and wage war against the English. In a

Fire at Will

King John is rarely performed because it's a static and talky play.

Sweets to the Sweet

Arthur becomes the play's touchstone of humanity as he persuades John's agent, Hubert, to disobey John's orders to blind him, only to kill himself while trying to escape. .

battle near Angiers, the French are defeated, and the Bastard kills the Duke of Austria. Arthur falls into the hands of his uncle, who orders his chamberlain, Hubert de Burgh, to kill the young Prince. Meanwhile, Pandulph persuades the Dauphin to claim England's crown and invade its rainy shores.

In an English prison, King John has ordered Hubert de Burgh to burn out Arthur's eyes. Moved by the boy's pleas, de Burgh spares him. It's a short reprieve, however; in an attempt to escape from the castle, the Prince leaps from the walls and is killed on the stones below. The nobles wail:

> This is the very top,
> The heighth, the crest, or crest unto the crest,
> Of murther's arms.

After finding Arthur's broken body, the three English noblemen who have suspected the King's evil purposes are convinced that Hubert has murdered the child at the King's orders, and they break their allegiance to John. They join the Dauphin who has meanwhile landed in England with a large army.

What Me, Worry?

John surrenders his crown to the papal legate and so secures Pandulph's aid against the French. But Pandulph's attempts to persuade the Dauphin to return to France are in vain. The French, assisted by the English traitors who have joined them, fight an indecisive battle with the English under the Bastard. The noblemen are warned that the Dauphin intends to execute them as soon as he has gotten what he wants. No fools, they return their allegiance to the English king, but it's too late—he's dying, apparently from poison.

After John's death, Pandulph succeeds in bringing about an honorable peace between the French and English, and the crown of England passes to John's son Henry.

My Hero

The Bastard Faulconbridge becomes the hero of the play, for he is true to his country and his king. And he's noble, loyal, and brave. When his wicked wuss of a king falters, he says:

...why look you so sad?
Be great in act, as you have been in thought,
Let not the world see fear and sad distrust
Govern the motion of a kingly eye.
Be stirring as the time, be fire with fire,
Threaten the threat'ner, and outface the brow
Of dragging horror; so shall inferior eyes,
That borrow their behaviors from the great,
Grow great by your example, and put on
The dauntless spirit of resolution.
Away, and glister like the god of war
When he intendeth to become the field.
Show boldness and aspiring confidence.

What's the play's final message? It's a corker:

This England never did, nor never shall,
Lie at the proud foot of a conqueror,
But when it first did help to wound itself.
Now these her princes are come home again,
Come the three corners of the world in arms,
And we shall shock them. Nought shall make
us rue,
If England to itself do rest but true.

Sweets to the Sweet

King John is set about two centuries earlier than the rest of the history plays.

From King John to Henry IV. Let's pick up the story with *King Henry IV, Part I*.

Who's Who in *King Henry IV, Part I*

A shrewd politician and capable warrior, King Henry IV is nonetheless suffering the aftershocks of usurping the throne and murdering Richard. He is haunted by the fear that his oldest son, who should succeed him to the throne, will be the same kind of wastrel that Richard was, and he is distraught to think that Northumberland's son Henry (Hotspur) is more truly "honorable" and worthy of the throne than his own Henry. Henry IV *is* a little smarmy, but he does have the cold and arrogant manner of a king.

➤ King Henry the Fourth

➤ Henry, *Prince of Wales, the King's son*

➤ Prince John of Lancaster, *the King's son*

➤ Earl of Westmerland

➤ Sir Walter Blunt

➤ Thomas Percy, *Earl of Worcester*

➤ Henry Percy, *Earl of Northumberland*

➤ Henry Percy, *surnamed Hotspur, his son (called "Hotspur" in the play)*

➤ Edmund Mortimer, *Earl of March*

➤ Richard Scroop, *Archbishop of York*

➤ Archibald, *Earl of Douglas*

➤ Owen Glendower

➤ Sir Richard Vernon

➤ Sir John Falstaff

➤ Sir Michael, *a friend to the Archbishop of York*

➤ Edward Poins, *gentleman-in-waiting to Prince Henry*

➤ Gadshill

➤ Peto

➤ Bardolph

➤ Lady Percy, *Hotspur's wife, Mortimer's sister*

➤ Lady Mortimer, *Glendower's daughter, Mortimer's wife*

➤ Mistress Quickly, *hostess of the Boar's Head Tavern in Eastcheap*

➤ Lords, officers, sheriff, vintner, chamberlain, drawers, two carriers, travelers, attendants, and an ostler

Fire at Will

The label "history play" is almost a misnomer when used to describe these plays, not only because Shakespeare played fast and loose with the facts but also because the term calls forth the image of a dry historical documentary. Nothing could be further from the truth. *Henry IV* has been called "the broadest, the most varied, and in some ways the richest campaign in Shakespeare's extensive empire."

Cruisin' for a Bruising

On the surface, *Henry IV* is the story of Henry's struggle to keep the throne against the Percys, but the play really revolves around Prince Henry and his maturation from a medieval frat boy into a king.

When the play opens, King Henry is celebrating a momentary lull in the civil war by reviving his plan to see the Holy Land. Henry Percy (Hotspur) has defeated Douglas but won't ransom his prisoners until King Henry promises to ransom Mortimer. King Henry is annoyed with Hotspur, but even more annoyed with his wastrel son Henry, who could use a little of Hotspur's moxie. Daddy's on to something: The Prince *is* very busy carousing with Falstaff through London, planning a robbery. But Henry Jr. has a plan up his sleeve.

The King has summoned the Percy group, the Earl of Northumberland, his son Hotspur, and his brother Worcester.

Hotspur claims that he refused to release the prisoners because he didn't like the messenger the King sent. They still refuse to release the prisoners, and the King threatens reprisals. They decide to revolt.

Liar, Liar, Pants on Fire

Gadshill, one of the thieves, scopes out the travelers at an inn in Rochester. Soon after, the robbery takes place and the Prince and Poins steal the loot from Falstaff and the others, who scatter. Later, Falstaff loudly denounces Henry Jr. and Poins as cowards for missing the robbery. They lead him on, and he tells a dazzling lie about the "hundred" men who attacked them and took their booty. Faced with the facts, he pretends he knew it was the Prince all along. The sheriff arrives, looking for Falstaff, and the Prince dismisses him, promising to send Falstaff to him the next day. Falstaff snoozes behind a tapestry.

Party Like It's 1499

In Wales, Hotspur, Mortimer, and Glendower divide the kingdom into the three parts they'll take after their revolt. Back at the palace, Henry chides his son for becoming a "companion to the common streets." The Prince promises to reform, and Henry promises him a command.

At the Boar's Head Tavern, Falstaff exercises his wit at the expense of Bardolph and the hostess until the Prince and Poins come in with the news that they are all off to the wars—Falstaff as captain of an infantry troop. Soon after, Henry Jr. banishes Falstaff:

> Swearest thou, ungracious boy? henceforth ne'er look on me. Thou art violently carried away from grace, there is a devil haunts thee in the likeness of an old man, a tun of man is thy companion.

"Banish plump Jack, and banish all the world," Falstaff pleads. Nonetheless, the Prince replies, "I do, I will." This shows that the Prince is maturing and rejecting the idle pursuits of his youth.

Beating a Dead Horse

In the rebel camp, Hotspur rallies the rebels after they learn that Northumberland and Glendower are pulling out.

Blunt approaches with an offer of pardon if they will disband. Hotspur violently condemns the King but promises to think the offer over.

Hotspur and Prince Hal square off.

In the King's camp, the Prince offers to settle the issue by fighting mano a mano with Hotspur. King Henry refuses to allow this, but in the rebel camp, Hotspur vows to hold the contest. On the battlefield, Douglas kills Blunt. After some comic relief, the Prince kills Hotspur. The Prince makes a speech over his body extolling his bravery:

> For worms, brave Percy. Fare thee well, great heart!
> Ill-weav'd ambition, how much art thou shrunk!
> When that this body did contain a spirit,
> A kingdom for it was too small a bound,
> But now two paces of the vilest earth
> Is room enough. The earth that bears thee dead
> Bears not alive so stout a gentleman…
> Adieu, and take thy praise with thee to heaven!
> Thy ignominy sleep with thee in the grave,
> But not rememb'red in thy epitaph!

Meanwhile, Falstaff plays 'possum to escape from Douglas. Prince Henry assumes that Falstaff has died and delivers this farewell:

> What, old acquaintance, could not all this flesh
> Keep in a little life? Poor Jack, farewell!
> I could have better spar'd a better man,
> O, I should have a heavy miss of thee
> If I were much in love with vanity!
> Death hath not strook so fat a deer to-day,
> Though many dearer, in this bloody fray.
> Enbowell'd will I see thee by and by,
> Till then in blood by noble Percy lie.

When the Prince leaves, Falstaff rises, brushes himself off, and says, "The better part of valor is discretion, in which the better part I have sav'd my life." To look heroic, Falstaff stabs Hotspur's dead body and raises it to his shoulders. See where this is going? Falstaff tries to convince the Prince he took Hotspur out. "This is the strangest tale that ever I heard," says Prince Henry's brother Lancaster.

The King sentences Worcester and Vernon to death. The Prince gives Douglas his freedom, and the play ends with Henry's speech determining to do equivalent justice on Northumberland and Glendower.

> Rebellion in this land shall lose his sway,
> Meeting the check of such another day.
> And since this business so fair is done,
> Let us not leave till all our own be won.

Sweets to the Sweet

Orson Welles claimed that Hotspur's murder was the death of medieval chivalry and that Falstaff's was the end of merrye olde England.

The Second Fiddle Holds the First Chair

Don't be misled by the title *Henry IV*: King Henry is usually not on stage. Instead, most of the action revolves around the story of Prince Henry and Falstaff.

Henry IV, Part I charts Prince Henry's odyssey from profligate prince to chivalrous heir. At the beginning of *Henry IV, Part I*, Prince Henry is Falstaff's degenerate cohort; indeed, he appears more comfortable in the taverns and on the highways of London than at court. His father bemoans his behavior, comparing him unfavorably with Hotspur and suggesting that he'd be happier if the two boys had been switched at birth.

But reading a little closer, we see that although Prince Henry parties with the profligates, he remains apart from them in temperament. His soliloquy at the end of Act I, scene ii leaves no doubt that he is only biding his time before stepping up to claim his destiny:

> So when this loose behavior I throw off
> And pay the debt I never promised,
> By how much better than my word I am,
> By so much shall I falsify men's hopes;
> And, like bright metal on a sullen ground,
> My reformation, glitt'ring o'er my fault,
> Shall show more goodly and attract more eyes
> Than that which hath no foil to set it off.

Sweets to the Sweet

Falstaff's supporters see him as the real hero of the play; his detractors, in contrast, see him as a bad influence.

During the first three acts he moves from the tavern to the court, learning the value of responsibility from his father and earning the older man's respect and affection.

Hal's destiny lies between Falstaff and Hotspur, who stand at extreme ends of the same pole. Both knights corrupt the chivalric code in different ways—Falstaff in a comically pathetic manner, Hotspur in a tragic pursuit of misguided ambition. Prince Henry proves himself gracious and forgiving, honorable, and just.

More to Love

Henry IV, Part I has always been one of Shakespeare's most popular history plays, largely because of Falstaff. Even literary criticism of the play has tended to concentrate on Falstaff. The famous eighteenth century literary critic Samuel Johnson gushed: "Falstaff, how shall I describe thee? Thou compound of sense and vice...a character loaded with faults, and with faults which naturally produce contempt...a thief, a glutton, a coward, and a boaster, always ready to cheat the weak and prey upon the poor; to terrify the timorous the insult and defenseless."

Orson Wells was such a cute Falstaff. Sort of like a dissolute Santa Claus? Photo courtesy of UA/Turner.

Shakespearean critics rarely agree on much, but they *do* agree on this: Falstaff is the most superbly rendered comic figure in all of Shakespeare. (Only Chaucer's Wife of Bath gets anywhere near the same number of great lines.) Here's a sample of Falstaff's skill with swearing:

> 'Sblood, you starveling, you eel-skin, you dried neat's tongue, you bull's pizzle, you stock-fish! O for breath to utter what is like thee! you tailor's yard, you sheath, you bowcase, you vile standing tuck—...

The Least You Need to Know

➤ In *King John*, King John is the villain; the Bastard Faulconbridge, son of Richard the Lion-Hearted, is the hero.

➤ *King John* is more rhetoric than poetry, especially about the rights of kings, the wisdom of primogeniture, and the relation of secular rulers to spiritual ones.

➤ In *Henry IV, Part I*, Prince Henry matures from party boy to true prince.

➤ *Henry IV, Part I* has always been one of Shakespeare's most popular history plays, largely because of Falstaff. *Everyone* loves the fat, funny Falstaff.

Chapter 30

King Henry IV, Part II; King Henry V; King Henry VIII

In This Chapter

➤ Who's who in *King Henry IV, Part II*

➤ The plot of *King Henry IV, Part II*

➤ Henry V's character

➤ Who's who in *King Henry V*

➤ The plot of *King Henry V*

➤ Who's who in *King Henry VIII*

➤ The plot of *King Henry VIII*

Harry the Fift is crown'd! Up, vanity!
Down, royal state! All you sage counsellors, hence!
For the fift Harry from curb'd license plucks
The muzzle of restraint, and the wild dog
Shall flesh his tooth on every innocent.
O my poor kingdom, sick with civil blows!
When that my care could not withhold thy riots,
What wild thou do when riot is thy care?
O, thou wilt be a wilderness again,
Peopled with wolves, thy old inhabitants!

—*Henry IV, Part II*

And you thought *your* kids were driving you crazy? In these three plays, you'll see how Henry V and Henry VIII drive *their* fathers nuts.

Who's Who in *King Henry IV, Part II*

Henry IV is a regular Rubik's cube. Both Falstaff and the King recognize his many-sided character. Falstaff explains that "the cold blood he did naturally inherit of his father he hath...manured, husbanded and tilled with...fertile sherry, that he is become very hot and valiant." The King warns his other sons that though Prince Henry is gracious, merciful, and charitable, he is also hard, moody, and quick-tempered. Meet the rest of the crew:

- ➤ Rumour, *the Presenter*
- ➤ King Henry the Fourth
- ➤ Prince Henry, *then King Henry the Fifth*
- ➤ Prince John of Lancaster
- ➤ Humphrey, *Duke of Gloucester*
- ➤ Thomas, *Duke of Clarence*
- ➤ Earl of Northumberland
- ➤ Richard Scroop, *Archbishop of York*
- ➤ Lord Mobray
- ➤ Lord Hastings
- ➤ Lord Bardolph
- ➤ Travers, Morton, *retainers of Northumberland*
- ➤ Sir John Colevile
- ➤ Earl of Warwick
- ➤ Earl of Westmerland
- ➤ Earl of Surrey
- ➤ Sir John Blunt
- ➤ Gower, Harcourt, *Lord Chief Justice*
- ➤ Edward Poins
- ➤ Sir John Falstaff
- ➤ Bardolph, Pistol, Peto
- ➤ Shallow, Silence, *both country justices*
- ➤ Davy, *Shallow's servant*

➤ Fang and Snare, *two sergeants*

➤ Mouldy, Shadow, Wart, Feeble, Bullcalf, *country soldiers*

➤ Northumberland's wife

➤ Lady Percy, *Percy's widow*

➤ Mistress Quickly, *hostess of the Boar's Head Tavern in Eastcheap*

➤ Doll Tearsheet

➤ Assorted extras

Forsooth!

Richard II, the two parts of *Henry IV*, and *Henry V* are also known as the **Lancastrian tetralogy**, because it's the history of the Lancaster family.

King Henry IV, Part II: Local Boy Makes Good

Rumour, an allegorical character, gives us the 60-second recap: The royal party has just won the Battle of Shrewsbury, Hotspur is dead, and Douglas is a prisoner.

In a burst of grief, the Earl of Northumberland vows revenge. The Archbishop of York, Lord Mowbray, and Lord Hastings see their chance to attack Henry in the east.

Cut to London: The Lord Chief Justice is curious about Falstaff's part in the Gadshill robbery (from *Henry IV, Part I*). Falstaff asserts that his commission to join Prince John against the Yorkist rebels has made him immune to arrest. Falstaff may have wiggled free, but he's still flat broke.

The Archbishop holds a council of war with Mowbray, Hastings, and Bardolph. They decide they have enough support to defeat the King.

Sweets to the Sweet

What's the connection between *Henry IV, Part I* and *Henry IV, Part II*? According to the venerable critic Samuel Johnson, Shakespeare separated the plays "only because they are too long to be one." Of course, it's not that simple—or is it?

Meanwhile, the police try to arrest Falstaff for debt—he's run up quite at tab at the tavern. Falstaff manages to placate Mistress Quickly, who invites him to dinner and promises to float him still another loan. Prince Henry and Poins disguise themselves as waiters to spy on Falstaff at the tavern. They hear Falstaff trash the Prince to Doll. When the disguised waiters reveal their identities, Falstaff claims he has disparaged the young heir to spare him from unworthy followers.

Measuring Up

As he is dying, King Henry IV muses on the responsibilities of leadership: "Then happy low, lie down! / Uneasy lies the head that wears a crown." News of the King's waning strength sends the Prince flying to his side.

Prince Henry muses on his father's crown as a symbol of care and worry. Seeing his father in a stupor, he concludes that he is dead and places the crown on his own head:

> Lo where it sits,
> Which God shall guard; and put the world's whole strength
> Into one giant arm, it shall not force
> This lineal honor from mee. This from thee
> Will I to mine leave, as 'tis left to me.

The King awakens, sees the crown and his son are gone, and assumes that Prince Henry is too eager to step into his shoes:

> See, sons, what things you are!
> How quickly nature falls into revolt
> When gold becomes her object!

In an emotional speech, he accuses his son of not loving him and bemoans how the lad's years of partying have led to this:

> Dost thou so hunger for mine empty chair
> That thou wilt needs invest thee with my honors
> Before thy hour be ripe? O foolish youth,
> Thou seek'st the greatness that will overwhelm thee.

Star Quality

Chimes at Midnight is Orson Welles' 1967 combination of *Henry IV, Parts I* and *II*; *Henry V*; and *The Merry Wives of Windsor*. The movie focuses on Falstaff, the part Welles was born to play (yes, along with Charles Foster Kane). A dark comedy, Welles has often been identified with the part of the rotund high roller who frittered away his genius.

Once more Hal promises to reform. Soon after, the King dies.

Meanwhile, the Archbishop learns of Northumberland's retreat so he is eager to negotiate a peace. Still in Gaultree Forest, Prince John promises to remedy the rebels' grievances if they will disband their armies and return their allegiance to the King. As soon as they have done so, the Archbishop and his cohorts are seized and executed for treason. Meanwhile, Falstaff captures Sir John Coleville, a rebel knight.

Bet you never expected to see the great Italian heart throb Marcello Mastroianni play Henry IV. In this 1984 version of Pirandello's brilliant satirical play, a nobleman falls off his throne and comes to believe he's Henry IV. Photo courtesy of Orion Classics.

Bye, Bye Buddy

When news of the King's death reaches Falstaff, he hurries to court, confident of special favors now that his friend the Prince is King Henry V. He is deeply disappointed, however, when the younger Henry shows that he intends to keep his promise to his dying father. As soon as he ascends the throne, King Henry V renounces "vanity" for majesty and sets about organizing a stable government. In a public scene, the new King turns away from Falstaff and his former companions:

> I know thee not, old man, fall to thy prayers.
> How ill white hairs becomes a fool and jester!
> I have long dreamed of such a kind of man,
> So surfeit-swell'd, so old, and so profane;
> But, being awaken'd, I do despise my dream.

Hal has transformed from a juvenile delinquent to the ideal king, Henry V. The march of British history continues with *King Henry V*.

Sweets to the Sweet

King Henry V's rejection of Falstaff is the moral center of the play.

Who's Who in *King Henry V*

Henry V is clearly the main man—and he does get top billing. He's the ideal king. Even before he appears in person, the churchmen declare their unbounded admiration for him, and in the course of the play their judgment is confirmed. A political genius, he sets up the Archbishop of Canterbury as the fall guy in case the war with France fails. Henry is also an outstanding general. Fearless, he even fights in the forefront of the army and refuses to save himself by ransom. Here's the complete cast and crew:

➤ King Henry the Fifth
➤ Humphrey Duke of Gloucester
➤ John Duke of Bedford
➤ Duke of Clarence
➤ Duke of Exeter, *the King's uncle*
➤ Duke of York, *the King's cousin*
➤ Earl of Salisbury
➤ Earl of Westmerland
➤ Earl of Warwick
➤ Archbishop of Canterbury
➤ Bishop of Ely
➤ Earl of Cambridge
➤ Lord Croop
➤ Sir Thomas Grey
➤ Sir Thomas Eppingham, Gower, Fluellen, MacMorris, *officers in King Henry's army*
➤ Jamy, Bates, Court, Williams, *soldiers in the army*
➤ Pistol
➤ Nym, Bardolph, Boy, Herald
➤ Charles the Sixth, *King of France*
➤ Lewis, the Dauphin
➤ Duke of Burgandy
➤ Duke of Orleance
➤ Duke of Burbon
➤ Duke of Britain
➤ Duke or Berri
➤ Duke of Beaumont
➤ Constable of France

➤ Rambures, Grandpre, *French lords*

➤ Governor of Harfleur

➤ Montjoy, *a French herald*

➤ Ambassadors to the King of England

➤ Isabel, *Queen of France*

➤ Katherine, *Charles and Isabel's daughter*

➤ Alice, *her attendant*

➤ Hostess of the Boar's Head Tavern in Eastcheap, *formerly Mistress Quickly, now married to Pistol*

➤ Assorted extras

Laurence Olivier's 1944 version of Henry V *is one of the most enjoyable Shakespearean movies ever made. Filmed at the request of Winston Churchill to boost war morale, the film has great pride and swagger. Don't miss this one. Photo courtesy of UA/Turner.*

King Henry V: Oh, Henry!

> But pardon, gentles all,
> The flat unraised spirits that hath dar'd
> On this unworthy scaffold to bring forth
> So great an object. Can this cockpit hold
> The vasty fields of France? Or may we cram
> Within this wooden O the very casques
> That did affright the air at Agincourt?
>
> —King Henry VI

Soon after King Henry decides to make war on France, the French ambassador arrives with a case of tennis balls and a contemptuous message from the French dauphin:

> …the prince our master
> Says that you savor too much of your youth,
> And bids you be advis'd: there's nought in France
> That can be with nimble galliard won;
> You cannot revel into dukedoms there.
> He therefore sends you, meeter for your spirit,
> This tun of treasure; and, in lieu of this,
> Desires you let the dukedoms that you claim
> Hear no more of you.

The King sends word to the dauphin that he will answer this affront in the forthcoming war on France:

> When we have match'd our rackets to these balls,
> We will in France, by God's grace, play a set
> Shall strike his father's crown into the hazard.

As the King prepares to invade France, he uncovers a plot against his life. He has the assassins arrested and executed.

I Came, I Saw, I Conquered

Pompous and foolish, the French seriously underestimate the threat posed by Henry's invasion. The dauphin in particular refuses to believe that Henry the King is different from the wild and crazy prince.

The English troops land in France and storm the town of Harfleur, which goes belly-up when the citizens realize they've been hung out to dry. Humiliated by the loss of Harfleur, the French are determined to force an encounter immediately. Henry refuses to retreat or surrender.

The Three Stooges Ride Again

The comic subplot involves three rogues: Bardolph, Pistol, and Nym. They're in it strictly for the money, not glory or honor. Before they can leave for the war, Falstaff dies, which briefly dampens their spirits. In France they avoid fighting as much as possible. Bardolph is hanged for stealing from a church, and Nym also comes to a bad end.

Night Moves

Outnumbered five to one, the English soldiers are jumpy about the battle. Through the long night, the King goes among his men, trying to cheer them with his own confidence. They talk about the duty a subject owes to his sovereign and about the responsibility the King must bear. Henry tells them he thinks the King is a man just as they are. Henry and a soldier named Williams exchange gloves as tokens by which they can recognize and so meet each other after the battle.

Before the battle starts, Henry encourages his men with a rousing (and very famous) "Saint Crispin's Day" speech:

> We few, we happy few, we band of brothers;
> For he to-day that sheds his blood with me
> Shall be my brother; be he ne'er so vile,
> This day shall gentle his condition;
> And gentlemen in England, now a-bed,
> Shall think themselves accurs'd they were not here;
> And hold their manhood cheap whiles any speaks
> That fought with us upon Saint Crispin's Day.

Now, who wouldn't march into battle after a bracing speech like that?

The English win a glorious victory, and the French are forced to surrender. The French have lost 10,000 men; the English, 25. Henry gives thanks to God and promises his troops a speedy return to England. He reveals his true identity to the soldier Williams and rewards him for his courage and dignity.

The King and his followers return to France to conclude the peace. Henry woos the French princess, and it is decided that he shall marry her and be heir to France upon the death of the present French king. France and England are reconciled, and the play ends on a happy and hopeful note, although the Chorus reminds the audience that England lost France in the troubled reign of Henry VI.

Will Power

Some critics and scholars consider *Henry V* the most obscene of all the history plays. There's a lot of male bonding, which lends itself to some bawdy word play and some great piggy puns thrown in for their sheer entertainment value. If you're looking for an educated cheap thrill, why not check out Act III, scene iv, where Princess Katherine receives an English lesson from her attendant, Alice. Just don't read it aloud if there are children present. (What *am* I saying? They know more dirty words than we do!)

Art meets life as King Henry V, Kenneth Branagh, woos the princess Emma Thompson. Photo courtesy of Goldwyn.

Who's Who in *King Henry VIII*

Meet the cast:

- ➤ King Henry the Eighth
- ➤ Cardinal Wolsey
- ➤ Cardinal Campeius
- ➤ Capuchius, *ambassador from the Emperor Charles V*
- ➤ Cranmer, *Archbishop of Canterbury*
- ➤ Duke of Norfolk
- ➤ Duke of Buckingham
- ➤ Duke of Suffolk
- ➤ Earl of Surrey
- ➤ Lord Chamberlain

- ➤ Lord Chancellor
- ➤ Gardiner, *the King's secretary, then Bishop of Winchester*
- ➤ Bishop of Lincoln
- ➤ Lord Aburgavenny
- ➤ Lord Sands *(also called Sir Walter Sands)*
- ➤ Sir Henry Guilford
- ➤ Sir Thomas Lovell

Sweets to the Sweet

Henry VIII takes place from 1520 to 1533.

- ➤ Sir Anthony Denny
- ➤ Sir Nicholas Vaux
- ➤ Cromwell, *Wolsey's servant*
- ➤ Secretaries to Wolsey
- ➤ Griffith, *gentleman usher to Queen Katherine*
- ➤ Doctor Butts, *the King's physician*
- ➤ Garter King-at-Arms
- ➤ Surveyor to the Duke of Buckingham
- ➤ Brandon and a Sergeant-at-Arms
- ➤ Doorkeeper at the Council-chamber
- ➤ Porter and his Man
- ➤ Queen Katherine, *King Henry's wife, afterward divorced*
- ➤ Anne Bullen, *her Maid of Honor, afterward Queen*
- ➤ Old Lady, *Anne Bullen's friend*
- ➤ Patience, *woman to Queen Katherine*
- ➤ Spirits and assorted bishops, lords, ladies, etc.

King Henry VIII: I'm Henry the Eighth I Am, I Am

Although of humble birth, Cardinal Wolsey has managed through clever political maneuvering to become one of Henry VIII's most trusted advisors. But the coast isn't clear to total access: The Duke of Buckingham stands in the way. What to do? Wolsey charges the Duke with treason. Unfortunately for the Cardinal, Henry's wife Katherine has taken the Duke's side.

To make his case stick, the Cardinal produces a surveyor who once worked for the Duke and is willing to claim that the Duke wanted to kill the King. As a result of this testimony, the Duke is executed, and his son-in-law, the Earl of Surrey, is packed off to Ireland. Duke down, Queen to go.

Fire at Will

Shakespeare's part in *Henry VIII* has long been in dispute. Some critics claim he wrote all of it; others, that he penned about half. Try this issue when you're sick of arguing about politics, religion, or sex.

Sweets to the Sweet

Can't remember the fate of Henry VIII's six wives? Use this rhyme, popular with generations of British schoolchildren: "Divorced, beheaded, died; divorced, beheaded, survived." That's Katherine of Aragone, Anne Boleyn, Jane Seymour, Anne of Cleves, Catherine Howard, Catherine Parr.

The First Wives' Club

To get Katherine out of the way, the Cardinal raises Henry's suspicions about his wife and gets him to look at Anne Bullen, the Queen's maid of honor. Since Katherine hasn't provided Henry with any male heirs, Henry has an additional reason to look for a new honey. Katherine isn't ready to pack her bags just yet, however, so she begs Henry for a reconciliation:

> Sir, I desire you do me right and justice,
> And to bestow your pity on me; for
> I am a most poor woman, and a stranger,
> Born out of your dominions; having here
> No judge indifferent, nor more assurance
> Of equal friendship and proceeding. Alas, sir!
> In what have I offended you? What cause
> Hath my behavior given to your displeasure,
> That thus you should proceed to put me off,
> And take your good grace from me?

Her plea fails and the Cardinal asks the Pope to provide a royal divorce. Cardinal Campeius arrives in England. Shortly thereafter, Katherine is thrown out of court. Are we shocked yet?

John Stride poses as Henry VIII. Don't cross this monarch, baby. Photo courtesy of PBS.

Return to Sender

The Cardinal should be a happy man, but he's greedy. Even though he's got a pile of money as well as a pile of power, he starts shooting himself in the foot. Afraid that the King will marry Anne Bullen instead of seeking a marriage with a French princess and thus cementing the alliance with a country that makes good bread, the Cardinal writes a letter to the Pope asking that the King's marriage be put off.

Through one of those cosmic errors, the letter is delivered to the King instead of the Pope. (That's what happens when you don't write your zip code clearly, kids.) Shocked that his trusted advisor would take such an action, Henry gives the Cardinal the old heave-ho. Later, the Cardinal is arrested and dies before he can be tried.

Splitsville

Henry divorces Katherine, marries Anne Bullen, and gets a new advisor, the Archbishop of Canterbury, Cranmer. But people are still hot for power and so Gardiner, the Bishop of Winchester, tries to destroy Cranmer by accusing him of heresy. The King, on Cranmer's side, offers him the royal signet ring, which he can use to show the King's support.

In court, Cranmer is found guilty, but when he produces the ring, the nobles realize their goof and apologize; after all, it's rarely a good idea to cross a king or someone he protects. Henry condemns the nobles for their mistakes, but then blesses them. He asks them to play nice and share their toys.

Henry and Anne have a daughter, whom they name Elizabeth. Cranmer predicts that she will have a long and blessed reign:

> This royal infant—heaven still move about her!—
> Though in her cradle, yet now promises
> Upon this land a thousand thousand blessings,
> Which time shall bring to ripeness. She shall be
> (but few now living can behold that goodness)
> A pattern to all princes living with her,
> And all that shall succeed.

Hindsight *is* 20-20.

Will Power

Henry VIII (1491–1547), King of England from 1509–1547, did indeed marry his brother's widow Katherine of Aragon. In 1528, Henry tried to divorce Katherine because she hadn't produced a male heir, and he had fallen in love with Anne Boleyn, the queen's comely lady-in-waiting called "Anne Bullen" in Shakespeare's play. In 1528, the Pope appointed Cardinal Wolsey to try the case, but the matter dragged on. In 1529, Henry fired Wolsey and appointed Sir Thomas More, who wasn't that keen on the divorce. Finally, Henry decided to make a break from the papacy and in 1532 succeeded in getting named the head of the English church. In 1533 he married Anne; three years later, Henry charged her with incest and adultery and had her beheaded.

Will Power

This is the ultimate in sucking up. Henry wanted a boy, but Elizabeth was born. Shakespeare shows him to be so delighted. Right.

The Least You Need to Know

➤ *King Henry IV, Part II* shows the maturation of Prince Hal from party boy par excellence to King.

➤ *King Henry V* describes the historical events leading up to and following the battle of Agincourt. Prince Hal, now a hero–king, conquers France.

➤ *King Henry V* shows King Henry V as the ideal monarch. He conquers France and gets the princess, too.

➤ In *King Henry VIII*, Cardinal Wolsey maneuvers to get to the head of the class, but his lust for power causes his downfall. Henry divorces Katherine and marries Anne Bullen (commonly known as "Anne Boleyn").

➤ *King Henry VIII* is a play about power and the struggle to get it.

Part 7
Poems and Sonnets

Choice #1: "Sonnet 116"

> *Let me not to the marriage of true minds*
> *Admit impediments; Love is not love*
> *Which alters when it alteration finds,*
> *Or bends with the remover to remove.*
> *O no! it is an ever-fixed mark*
> *That looks on tempests and is never shaken;*
> *It is the star to every wandering bark,*
> *Whose worth's unknown, although his height be taken.*
> *Love's not Time's fool, though rosy lips and cheeks*
> *Within his bending sickle's compass come,*
> *Love alters not with his brief hours and weeks,*
> *But bears it out even to the edge of doom.*
> *If this be error and upon me proved,*
> *I never writ, nor no man ever loved.*

Choice #2: "Sonnet 130"

> *My mistress' eyes are nothing like the sun;*
> *Coral is far more red than her lips' red;*
> *If snow be white, why then her breasts are dun;*
> *If hairs be wires, black wires grow on her head.*
> *I have seen roses damask'd, red and white,*
> *But no such roses see I in her cheeks,*
> *And in some perfumes is there more delight*
> *Than in the breath that from my mistress reeks.*
> *I love to hear her speak, yet well I know*
> *That music hath a far more pleasing sound;*
> *I grant I never saw a goddess go,*
> *My mistress, when she walks, treads on the ground.*
> *And yet, by heaven, I think my love as rare*
> *As any she belied with false compare.*

As you'll learn in this section, Shakespeare has love sonnets for all tastes. I'll help you pick the ones that suit your fancy.

Chapter 31

The Battle of the Sexes Told in Rhyme

In This Chapter

➤ "Venus and Adonis"

➤ "The Rape of Lucrece"

➤ "A Lover's Complaint"

➤ "The Phoenix and the Turtle"

Shakespeare knew that women speak in estrogen and men listen in testosterone. The four poems in this chapter—"Venus and Adonis," "The Rape of Lucrece," "A Lover's Complaint," and "The Phoenix and the Turtle"—provide a window on the age-old battle of the sexes.

"Venus and Adonis"

Snap quiz: What was the most popular work Shakespeare published during his lifetime?

Answer: "Venus and Adonis." I kid you not. Shakespeare hit pay dirt with his very first published poem, which appeared in 1593. The poem was reprinted at least nine times during his life and had scores of imitators.

In "Venus and Adonis," Shakespeare threw his poetic glove into the ring. He designed the piece to display his talents and announce his intention of becoming one of the big boys in the rhyme racket. The dedication to his patron, the Earl of Southampton, shows his intention:

Sweets to the Sweet

During Shakespeare's lifetime, he was probably best known for "Venus and Adonis" and his play *Titus Andronicus*—another runaway hit—more than for any other works.

Will Power

According to the classical myth, Venus was struck by Cupid's arrow, glanced at Adonis, and fell in love with him instantly. She gave up all her old friends and followed Adonis over hill and dale, dressed as the huntress Diana. After warning Adonis to steer clear of wolves and boars, Venus mounted her chariot and headed to Cyprus. Adonis ignored her warning and so ended up getting wounded by a wild boar he had attacked. Venus heard Adonis' dying gasps and hurried back. As she saw his lifeless body bathed in blood, she reproached the Fates and transformed Adonis into a flower, the Anemone.

RIGHT HONORABLE,

I KNOW not how I shall offend in dedicating my unpolished lines to your lordship, nor how the world will censure me for choosing so strong a prop to support so weak a burden only, if your honour seem but pleased, I account myself highly praised, and vow to take advantage of all idle hours, till I have honored you with some graver labor. But if the first heir of my invention prove deformed, I shall be sorry it had so noble a god-father, and never after ear so barren a land, for fear it yield me still so bad a harvest. I leave it to your honorable survey, and your honour to your heart's content; which I wish may always answer your own wish and the world's hopeful expectation.

Your honor's in all duty,

WILLIAM SHAKESPEARE

Not Now, Dear, the Game Is on

The poem describes Venus, the Queen of Love, putting the moves on a bashful hunter, Adonis. In erotic and funny passages, Venus courts Adonis, trying to convince him to make love. Unmoved by lust, Adonis prefers to go hunting. The following morning, Venus finds Adonis' dead body—he has been killed by a wild boar. The poem ends with her lament.

Think of "Venus and Adonis" as a poetic week in the country: The poem is packed with vivid imagery, especially of birds, beasts, the hunt, and the weather. In between the burbling brooks and bounding deer, Shakespeare squeezed in some birds and bees: The poem contains remarkably erotic love scenes.

Vital statistics:

➤ The story is based on a classic myth from Ovid.

➤ The poem describes the love affair of two mythical creatures. They're not hard on the eyes, but Adonis is certainly naive.

➤ Shakespeare used a six-line stanza verse form.

➤ The poem is meant as entertainment; there's no deep message here.

Fire at Will

As presented by Shakespeare, Adonis comes off as a Stratford–upon–Avon hayseed.

Sneak Peak

Scan the opening stanzas to get the flavor of the whole poem:

> Even as the sun with purple-color'd face
> Had ta'en his last leave of the weeping morn,
> Rose-cheek'd Adonis hied him to the chase;
> Hunting he lov'd, but love he laugh'd to scorn;
>> Sick-thoughted Venus makes amain unto him,
>> And like a bold-fac'd suitor gins to woo him.
>
> "Thrice-fairer than myself," thus she began,
> "The field's chief flower, sweet above compare,
> Stain to all nymphs, more lovely than a man,
> More white and red than doves or roses are;
>> Nature that made thee, with herself at strife,
>> Saith that the world hath ending with thy life.
>
> "Vouchsafe, thou wonder, to alight thy steed,
> And rein his proud head to the saddle-bow;
> If thou wilt deign this favor, for thy meed
> A thousand honey secrets shalt thou know:
>> Here come and sit, where never serpent hisses,
>> And being set, I'll smother thee with kisses;
>
> "And yet not cloy thy lips with loathed satiety,
> But rather famish them amid their plenty,
> Making them red and pale with fresh variety,
> Ten kisses short as one, one long as twenty:
>> A summer's day will seem an hour but short,
>> Being wasted in such time-beguiling sport."
>
> With this she seizeth on his sweating palm,
> The precedent of pith and livelihood,
> And trembling in her passion, calls it balm,
> Earth's sovereign salve to do a goddess good:
>> Being so enraged, desire doth lend her force
>> Courageously to pluck him from his horse.

Over one arm the lusty courser's rein,
Under her other was the tender boy,
Who blush'd and pouted in a dull disdain,
With leaden appetite, unapt to toy;
    She red and hot as coals of glowing fire,
    He red for shame, but frosty in desire.

The studded bridle on a ragged bough
Nimbly she fastens:—O, how quick is love!—
The steed is stalled up, and even now
To tie the rider she begins to prove:
    Backward she push'd him, as she would be thrust,
    And govern'd him in strength, though not in lust.

"The Rape of Lucrece"

A little more than a year after "Venus and Adonis," Shakespeare published "The Rape of Lucrece." It's a far more serious poem than "Venus and Adonis" in that it describes a tragic rape rather than a comic courtship. Nonetheless, "The Rape of Lucrece" was nearly as popular as "Venus and Adonis." It was reprinted at least six times during Shakespeare's life.

The poem retells the ancient Latin story of the sexual assault of Lucrece, a high-ranking Roman woman, by Tarquin (Sextus Tarquinius), the son of the Roman king. Even though he is aware of his own evil, Tarquin rapes Lucrece. Before her death, Lucrece tells her husband and others of Tarquin's crime and makes them promise to exact vengeance. In the last stanza, we learn that the men drove Tarquin and his father out of Rome.

Sweets to the Sweet

"The Rape of Lucrece" is most similar to Shakespeare's *Titus Andronicus* (see Chapter 16). Both works describe rapes, contrast good and evil, and are crude and unsubtle.

Vital statistics:

➤ "The Rape of Lucrece" was written in a popular art form of the time called a "complaint poem" that reflected the hardships of life or of a particular event.

➤ The moral of the poem: Disaster will result from a serious moral transgression.

➤ Shakespeare used a seven-line rhyme stanza called "royal rhyme," considered appropriate for such a serious subject.

➤ The images suggest what Shakespeare would later accomplish in the tragedies.

The Argument

The poem starts with the argument:

Lucius Tarquinius, for his excessive pride surnamed Superbus, after he had caused his own father-in-law Servius Tullius to be cruelly murdered, and, contrary to the Roman laws and customs, not requiring or staying for the people's suffrages, had possessed himself of the kingdom, went, accompanied with his sons and other noblemen of Rome, to besiege Ardea. During which siege the principal men of the army meeting one evening at the tent of Sextus Tarquinius, the King's son, in their discourses after supper every one commended the virtues of his own wife: among whom Collatinus extolled the incomparable chastity of his wife Lucrece. In that pleasant humor they posted to Rome; and intending, by their secret and sudden arrival, to make trial of that which every one had before avouched, only Collatinus finds his wife, though it were late in the night, spinning amongst her maids: the other ladies were all found dancing and reveling, or in several disports. Whereupon the noblemen yielded Collatinus the victory, and his wife the fame. At that time Sextus Tarquinius being inflamed with Lucrece's beauty, yet smothering his passions for the present, departed with the rest back to the camp; from whence he shortly after privily withdrew himself, and was, according to his estate, royally entertained and lodged by Lucrece at Collatium. The same night he treacherously stealeth into her chamber, violently ravished her, and early in the morning speedeth away. Lucrece, in this lamentable plight, hastily dispatcheth messengers, one to Rome for her father, another to the camp for Collatine. They came, the one accompanied with Junius Brutus, the other with Publius Valerius; and finding Lucrece attired in mourning habit, demanded the cause of her sorrow. She, first taking an oath of them for her revenge, revealed the actor, and whole manner of his dealing, and withal suddenly stabbed herself. Which done, with one consent they all vowed to root out the whole hated family of the Tarquins; and bearing the dead body to Rome, Brutus acquainted the people with the doer and manner of the vile deed, with a bitter invective against the tyranny of the King: wherewith the people were so moved, that with one consent and a general acclamation the Tarquins were all exiled, and the state government changed from kings to consuls.

Dip a Toe in the Water

Shakespeare's skill as a dramatist is evident in the poem's opening: He starts at a dramatic point in the story to grab the reader from the very start:

> From the besieged Ardea all in post,
> Borne by the trustless wings of false desire,
> Lust-breathed Tarquin leaves the Roman host,
> And to Collatium bears the lightless fire
> Which, in pale embers hid, lurks to aspire
> And girdle with embracing flames the waist
> Of Collatine's fair love, Lucrece the chaste.

Haply that name of 'chaste' unhappily set
This bateless edge on his keen appetite;
When Collatine unwisely did not let
To praise the clear unmatched red and white
Which triumph'd in that sky of his delight,
Where mortal stars, as bright as heaven's beauties,
With pure aspects did him peculiar duties.

For he the night before, in Tarquin's tent,
Unlock'd the treasure of his happy state;
What priceless wealth the heavens had him lent
In the possession of his beauteous mate;
Reckoning his fortune at such high-proud rate,
That kings might be espoused to more fame,
But king nor peer to such a peerless dame.

O happiness enjoy'd but of a few!
And, if possess'd, as soon decay'd and done
As is the morning's silver-melting dew
Against the golden splendor of the sun!
An expired date, cancell'd ere well begun:
Honour and beauty, in the owner's arms,
Are weakly fortress'd from a world of harms.

Beauty itself doth of itself persuade
The eyes of men without an orator;
What needeth then apologies be made,
To set forth that which is so singular?
Or why is Collatine the publisher
Of that rich jewel he should keep unknown
From thievish ears, because it is his own?

Perchance his boast of Lucrece' sovereignty
Suggested this proud issue of a king;
For by our ears our hearts oft tainted be:
Perchance that envy of so rich a thing,
Braving compare, disdainfully did sting
His high-pitch'd thoughts, that meaner men should vaunt
That golden hap which their superiors want.

But some untimely thought did instigate
His all-too-timeless speed, if none of those:
His honour, his affairs, his friends, his state,
Neglected all, with swift intent he goes

To quench the coal which in his liver glows
O rash false heat, wrapp'd in repentant cold,
Thy hasty spring still blasts, and ne'er grows old!

"A Lover's Complaint"

"A Lover's Complaint" is not a major work by any means, so don't obsess if you've never heard of it. You don't even have to memorize it; just appreciate its beauty. Here's how it starts:

From off a hill whose concave womb reworded
A plaintful story from a sistering vale,
My spirits to attend this double voice accorded,
And down I laid to list the sad-tuned tale;
Ere long espied a fickle maid full pale,
Tearing of papers, breaking rings a-twain,
Storming her world with sorrow's wind and rain.

Upon her head a platted hive of straw,
Which fortified her visage from the sun,
Whereon the thought might think sometime it saw
The carcass of beauty spent and done:
Time had not scythed all that youth begun,
Nor youth all quit; but, spite of heaven's fell rage,
Some beauty peep'd through lattice of sear'd age.

The poem is primarily a monologue delivered to an old shepherd by a distraught young woman who has been betrayed by her lover. The woman met a hot young man, handsome and intelligent. She soon realized by the number of his illegitimate children that he had a taste for the ladies and an inability to commit. But his line was so good—he cried and claimed that only she could teach him true love—that she gave in.

Mama was right: Men never buy the cow when they can get the milk for free. Sure enough, the young woman's lover splits soon after their affair, leaving her in disgrace. Nonetheless, some kids never learn: He was such a hunk that she's not sure she wouldn't fall for him all over again.

Vital statistics:

➤ The poem has 329 lines.

➤ It was first published with the sonnets in their first edition (1609).

➤ It's characteristically Elizabethan, with lots of high-flown emotion and heavy embellishment.

➤ Scholars aren't sure it was written by Shakespeare.

"The Phoenix and the Turtle"

Truth may seem, but cannot be,
Beauty brag, but 'tis not she,
Truth and Beauty buried be.
To this urn let those repair
That are either true or fair;
For these dead birds sigh a prayer.

"The Phoenix and the Turtle," as with the mythical phoenix itself, is unique. As there was only one phoenix at a time, so there is no other work in Shakespeare's canon like this poem.

The poem describes the funeral of two lovers: the phoenix, a mythological bird that symbolized immortality, and the turtledove, a symbol of faithfulness in love. To be united for eternity, the two birds have burned themselves to death. The allegorical poem celebrates ideal love and devotion.

Vital statistics:

Forsooth!

The turtle in the poem's title refers to a bird, not a reptile—the **turtle** is the **turtledove**.

Sweets to the Sweet

According to the legend, the phoenix lived in a nest of spices and perfumes, died in its own flames, and was reborn. Sounds like a modern rock star.

➤ The poem has 67 lines, arranged in 13 quatrains (four-line stanzas) followed by five triplets (three-line stanzas), all in iambic tetrameter.

➤ The first five stanzas are a funeral procession. Birds that represent evil, such as the owl, are not admitted to the funeral, while those associated with death, such as the crow and swan, do make the cut.

➤ The next eight stanzas are an anthem in which the lovers are praised for having defied reason and achieved eternal union.

➤ The final section (in a different verse form) is a lament for the dead. The phoenix and the turtle represent truth and beauty. Through their death, they have conveyed these values to us.

➤ The title characters might represent Queen Elizabeth (the phoenix) and the Earl of Essex (reputed to be her sweetcakes, the turtledove).

The Least You Need to Know

➤ Shakespeare's first published poem, "Venus and Adonis," was a smash hit. It describes Venus, the Goddess of Love, putting the moves on a bashful hunter, Adonis.

➤ "The Rape of Lucrece" describes the tragic rape of Lucrece, a high-ranking Roman woman, by Tarquin, the son of the Roman king. It was nearly as popular as "Venus and Adonis."

➤ "A Lover's Complaint," a minor work, describes a young woman's seduction and betrayal.

➤ "The Phoenix and the Turtle" is an allegorical poem about the funeral of two lovers: the phoenix, a mythological bird that symbolized immortality, and the turtledove, a symbol of faithfulness in love.

Chapter 32

The Sonnets

In This Chapter

➤ Definition of a sonnet

➤ Italian and English sonnets

➤ The Shakespearean sonnet

➤ Shakespeare's sonnet sequence

➤ Sex and the single sonnet

Sonnet 116

Let me not to the marriage of true minds
Admit impediments; love is not love
Which alters when it alteration finds,
Or bends with the remover to remove:
O, no, it is an ever-fixed mark,
That looks on tempests and is never shaken;
It is the star to every wandering bark,
Whose worth's unknown, although his highth be taken.
Love's not Time's fool, though rosy lips and cheeks
Within his bending sickle's compass come;
Love alters not with his brief hours and weeks,
But bears it out even to the edge of doom.
    If this be error and upon me proved,
    I never writ, nor no man ever loved.

Why can't we all talk like this—and *feel* like this? Ahhh…

Forsooth!

A **sonnet** is a 14-line poem written in iambic pentameter. The term sonnet comes from an Italian word that means "little song."

Forsooth!

An **iamb** is an unstressed syllable followed by a stressed one. The word "deceive" is an iamb. **Pentameter** just tells you how many of these stressed beats occur in one line. "Penta" means five, so pentameter means five beats to a measure, or line.

In addition to all those famous plays, William Shakespeare also wrote 154 sonnets, first published in 1609. Next to *Hamlet*, the sonnets have sparked more commentary and stirred up more controversy than any other Shakespearean work. Why all the analysis and argument? Read on to find out!

For Better or Verse: The Sonnet

"Sonnet" is a fancy word, but it's an easy concept. A *sonnet* is a lyric poem of 14 lines, written in iambic pentameter, a meter with five accents in each line.

Originated by Italian poets in the thirteenth century, the sonnet form reached perfection a century later in the works of Francesco Petrarch, the famous Italian poet and scholar. Not surprisingly, it came to be known as the "Italian" or "Petrarchan" sonnet. The 14 lines of the Petrarchan sonnet have a rigid rhyme scheme: The first eight lines, called the *octave*, rhyme *a-b-b-a-a-b-b-a* and present the poem's subject; the concluding six lines, the *sestet*, rhyme *c-d-e-c-d-e* and resolve the problem set forth in the octave.

Here's a Petrarchan sonnet by the American poet Henry Wadsworth Longfellow (1807–1882).

Nature

As a fond mother, when the day is o'er,	a
Leads by the hand her little child to bed,	b
Half willing, half reluctant to be led,	b
And leave his broken playthings on the floor,	a
Still gazing at them through the open door,	a
Nor wholly reassured and comforted	b
By promises of others in their stead,	b
Which, though more splendid, may not please him more;	a
So Nature deals with us, and takes away	c
Our playthings one by one, and by the hand	d
Leads us to rest so gently, that we go	e
Scarce knowing if we wish to go or stay,	c
Being too full of sleep to understand	d
How far the unknown transcends the what we know.	e

When sixteenth century English poets discovered the Italian sonnet, they decided to alter the rhyme scheme to a-b-a-b, c-d-c-d, e-f-e-f, g-g. In the English sonnet, the poet describes the problem in the first 12 lines and resolves it in the final couplet. With the exception of Sonnets 99, 126, and 145, Shakespeare used the English sonnet form. Of course, after his death the English sonnet was renamed the "Shakespearean sonnet," a bow to his mastery of the form. Shakespeare succeeded in doing for the love sonnet what Godiva did for chocolate.

Hooked on Sonnets

Sonnet cycles (or groups of sonnets) were all the rage in Europe during the Elizabethan and Jacobean age. In the sixteenth century, candy wasn't dandy and liquor wasn't quicker: Any gentleman with his finger on the pulse of the times sent a sweet sonnet to his lady love.

Everybody who was anybody was writing sonnets, but Shakespeare's sonnets were a cut above the crowd. Here's why:

➤ Many of the poems address a man rather than a woman.

➤ The "Dark Lady" (the subject of many Shakespeare's sonnets) is very different from the usual subject of sonnets since she's a hot babe.

➤ Most important, the sonnets reveal an uncommon depth of feeling and artistic craft.

No one knows if Shakespeare arranged the sonnets in the order in which they were printed. However, every time an editor tries to rearrange them, it doesn't stick, and so the original order remains. None of the sonnets have formal titles. Therefore, the order is shown by numbers (i.e., Sonnet 1, Sonnet 2, Sonnet 3, etc.) or by the sonnet's first line.

Love Is a Many Splendored Thing

Many sonnet sequences were autobiographical, charting the trajectory of a love affair. Shakespeare's sonnets are a sensational story of love, lust, and disloyalty. Don't assume, however, that Shakespeare was baring his soul for all to see. We'll never know if Shakespeare's sonnets were inspired by an actual love affair. Of course, that hasn't stopped critics from assuming that they do spring from his own

Sweets to the Sweet

To find a poem's rhyme, assign a letter to each new sound at the end of the line. For example, if line #1 ends with "o'er," give it the letter *a*. If line #2 ends with "bed," assign the letter *b*. If line #3 ends with "led," assign *b*, because "led" and "bed" have the same sound. And so on.

Forsooth!

A **couplet** is two successive, rhyming lines of poetry.

Fire at Will

Sonnets were regarded as personal art; as such, it was considered tacky to publish them. Before their unauthorized publication, Shakespeare's sonnets were widely circulated in manuscript form.

private passions. That said, let's look at what the sonnets *do* suggest about Shakespeare's concerns.

The sonnets can be divided into two main groups:

➤ Sonnets 1–126 seem to address a handsome man, whom the speaker loved.

➤ Sonnets 127–156 are less unified. Some address a mysterious "Dark Lady," seductive and sexy.

Remember, this is all conjecture: we don't know exactly when the sonnets were written or to whom, or even if they were indeed written to anyone at all. That said, let's look at a representative sonnet or two from each grouping.

Love Is in the Air

In Sonnets 1–17, the older poet speaks to a young nobleman blessed with glamour and grace. The speaker wants his friend to marry and reproduce so he can pass his beauty on. The tone is affectionate, not sexually passionate. Here's a famous example:

Sonnet 15

When I consider every thing that grows
Holds [1] in perfection but a little moment,
That this huge stage presenteth naught but shows
Whereon the stars in secret influence comment; [2]
When I perceive that men as plants increase,
Cheered and checked [3] even by the self-same sky,
Vaunt [4] in their youthful sap, at height decrease,
And wear their brave state out of memory; [5]
Then the conceit [6] of this inconstant stay
Sets you most rich in youth before my sight,
Where wasteful Time debateth [7] with Decay,
To change your day of youth to sullied [8] night;
   And, all in war with Time, for love of you,
    As he takes from you, I engraft [9] you new.

[1] *Remains*
[2] *The stars influence human actions*
[3] *Encouraged and stopped*
[4] *Display themselves*
[5] *Wear out their showiness and are forgotten*
[6] *Conception*
[7] *Discusses*
[8] *Dirtied*
[9] *Implant beauty again through the verse*

The message: I would like you to marry and have kids, but if that's not in the cards, don't worry: My verse will preserve your youth and beauty eternally.

Living on Love

In "Sonnet 18," the poet decides to immortalize his friend in verse.

Sonnet 18

Shall I compare thee to a summer's day?
>Thou art more lovely and more temperate:
>Rough winds do shake the darling buds of May,
>And summer's lease hath all too short a date:
>Sometime too hot the eye of heaven shines,
>And often is his gold complexion dimmed;
>And every fair from fair sometime declines,
>By chance, or nature's changing course, untrimmed; [1]
>But thy eternal summer shall not fade,
>Nor lose possession of that fair thou ow'st; [2]
>Nor shall Death brag thou wander'st in his shade,
>When in eternal lines to time thou grow'st: [3]
>>So long as men can breathe, or eyes can see,
>>So long lives this, and this gives life to thee. [4]

[1] *Stripped of beautiful clothes*
[2] *Owns*
[3] *You become even with time, thanks to this poetry*
[4] *The poetry will make you immortal; poetry is permanent*

The message: You are more beautiful than a summer's day and your beauty will last forever since it is being preserved in my verse.

The speaker's feelings are strong and true, as this famous sonnet shows:

Sonnet 29

When, in disgrace [1] with fortune and men's eyes,
I all alone beweep my outcast state,
And trouble deaf heaven with my bootless [2] cries,
And look upon myself, and curse my fate,
Wishing me like to one more rich in hope,
Featured like him, like him with friends possessed,
Desiring this man's art, and that man's scope,
With what I most enjoy contented least;
Yet in these thoughts myself almost despising,
Haply I think on thee, and then my state, [3]
Like to the lark at break of day arising
From sullen earth, sings hymns at heaven's gate;
>For thy sweet love remembered such wealth brings,
>That then I scorn to change my state with kings.

[1] *Not in favor*
[2] *Futile*
[3] *State of mind; also a pun on the word chair of state, i.e., throne*

The message: When I am depressed and jealous of others, the thought of your love always brings me joy.

Sometimes Love Hurts

In "Sonnet 42," it appears that the young man has stolen the poet's mistress.

Sonnet 42

That thou hast her, it is not all my grief,
And yet it may be said I loved her dearly;
That she hath thee, is of my wailing chief,
A loss in love that touches me more nearly.
Loving offenders, thus I will excuse ye:
Thou dost love her, because thou know'st I love her;
And for my sake even so doth she abuse me,
Suffering my friend for my sake to approve her.
If I lose thee, my loss is my love's gain,
And losing her, my friend hath found that loss;
Both find each other, and I lose both twain,
And both for my sake lay on me this cross:
    But here's the joy; my friend and I are one;
    Sweet flattery! then she loves but me alone.

The message: Both my lovers have betrayed me, but since my friend and I are one, my mistress loves me alone. This sonnet is rationalization raised to art.

Their love is tempered by the realization that life is tragically brief:

Sonnet 73

That time of year thou mayst in me behold
When yellow leaves, or none, or few, do hang
Upon those boughs which shake against the cold,
Bare ruined choirs, where late the sweet birds sang.
In me thou see'st the twilight of such day
As after sunset fadeth in the west;
Which by and by black night doth take away,
Death's second self, that seals up all in rest.
In me thou see'st the glowing of such fire,
    That on the ashes of his youth doth lie,
    As the death-bed whereon it must expire,
    Consumed with that which it was nourished by. [1]
    This thou perceivest, which makes thy love more strong,
      To love that well which thou must leave ere long.

[1] *Choked by the ashes of that which once nourished the flame.*

The message: You will love me more when you realize that I'm going to die soon. Probably the first version of "You'll be sorry when I'm gone."

Sweets to the Sweet

The phrase "Bare ruined choirs" has become very famous.

Duke It Out

In Sonnets 78–86, the speaker bemoans a competitor for his friend's affection. His friend appears to have fallen for a more successful poet. Here's a sample sonnet from this grouping:

Sonnet 80

O, how I faint when I of you do write,
Knowing a better spirit doth use your name,
And in the praise thereof spends all his might,
To make me tongue-tied, speaking of your fame!
But since your worth, wide as the ocean is,
The humble as the proudest sail doth bear,
My saucy bark, inferior far to his,
On your broad main doth willfully appear.
Your shallowest help will hold me up afloat,
While he upon your soundless deep doth ride;
Or, being wracked, I am a worthless boat,
He of tall building and of goodly pride:
    Then if he thrive, and I be cast away,
    The worst was this; my love was my decay.

The message: You may like the other guy better, but I still have a place in your heart because of my verse. Besides, my love for you was the cause of my downfall in the first place.

An Affair to Remember

In "Sonnet 127," we meet the Dark Lady, who ensnares the poet in her seductive web. Here's where things start to really heat up.

Sonnet 127

In the old age black was not counted fair. [1]
Or is I were it bore not beauty's name;
But now is black beauty's successive heir, [2]
And beauty slandered with a bastard shame, [3]
For since each hand hath put on nature's power,
Fairing the foul with art's false borrowed face, [4]
Sweet beauty hath no name, no holy bower, [5]
But is profaned, if not lives in disgrace.
Therefore my mistress' eyes are raven black,
Her eyes so suited, [6] and they mourners seem
At such who, not born fair, no beauty lack, [7]
Slandering creation with false esteem:
    Yet so they mourn, becoming of [8] their woe,
    That every tongue says beauty should look so.

¹ *Beautiful*
² *Heir in line of succession*
³ *To be declared illegitimate*
⁴ *Makeup*
⁵ *Shrine*
⁶ *Also black*
⁷ *Nonetheless look beautiful*
⁸ *Gracing*

The message: An ironic and teasing look at love.

Notice the cynical tone of "Sonnet 151," the knowing ruminations of an experienced lover. Then check out the risqué sexual pun in the final couplet:

Sonnet 151

Love is too young to know what conscience is,
Yet who knows not conscience is born of love?
Then, gentle cheater, urge not my amiss,
Lest guilty of my faults thy sweet self prove:
For thou betraying me, I do betray
My nobler part of my gross body's treason;
My soul doth tell my body that he may
Triumph in love; flesh strays no farther reason,
But rising as thy name doth point out three,
As his triumphant prize. Proud of this pride,
He is contented thy poor drudge to be,
To stand in thy affairs, fall by thy side.
    No want of conscience hold it that I call
    Her "love" for whose dear love I rise and fall.

The message: Let's make whoopee. The soul is described as a military commander goading the body to success on the battlefield of sexual intercourse.

Shove Over

In the final sonnets, it appears that the speaker's friend has an affair with the Dark Lady, descending into a twisted threesome. Things are getting a little crowded in that bed, as the following sonnet shows:

Sonnet 152

In loving thee thou know'st I am forsworn,
But thou art twice forsworn, to me love swearing;
In act thy bed-vow broke, and new faith torn
In vowing new hate after new love bearing.
But why of two oaths' breach do I accuse thee,
When I break twenty? I am perjured most;
For all my vows are oaths but to misuse thee,
And all my honest faith in thee is lost:

For I have sworn deep oaths of thy deep kindness,
Oaths of thy love, thy truth, thy constancy;
And, to enlighten thee, gave eyes to blindness,
Or made them swear against the thing they see;
For I have sworn thee fair; more perjured I,
To swear against the truth so foul a lie!

The message: After we reconciled, you were unfaithful again. I'm ready to walk off in disgust. Indeed, this is the last sonnet in the "Dark Lady" sequence. So there!

The sonnets become filled with images of disease and decay.

Sonnet 147

My love is as a fever, longing still [1]
For that which longer nurseth [2] the disease,
Feeding on that which doth preserve the ill, [3]
Th' uncertain sickly appetite [4] to please.
My reason, the physician to my love,
Angry that his prescriptions are not kept,
Hath left me, and I desperate now approve
Desire is death, which physic did except. [5]
Past cure I am, now reason is past care, [6]
And frantic mad with evermore unrest;
My thoughts and my discourse as madmen's are,
At random form the truth vainly expressed; [7]
For I have sworn thee fair, and thought thee bright,
Who art as black as hell, as dark as night.

[1] *Without break*
[2] *Nourishes*
[3] *Maintain the illness*
[4] *Desire for food; lust*
[5] *Learn by experience that desire is death*
[6] *Medical cure*
[7] *Nonsense*

The message: Reason has been overthrown by passion, thus enraging my sexual desire for you, which is the essence of evil itself.

Death Takes a Holiday

It really doesn't matter if the sonnets are "about" a man, a woman, or a French poodle because their ultimate theme is art, not love. As a result, the poems go beyond their time and place and so manage to defeat time. Here are three famous examples:

Sonnet 19

Devouring Time, blunt thou the lion's paws,
And make the earth devour her own sweet brood;
Pluck the keen teeth from the fierce tiger's jaws,
And burn the long-lived phoenix in her blood; [1]
Make glad and sorry seasons as thou fleets,
And do whate'er thou wilt, swift-footed Time,
To the wide world and all her fading sweets;
But I forbid thee one most heinous crime:
O, carve not with thy hours my love's fair brow,
Nor draw no lines there with thine antique [2] pen;
Him in thy course untainted [3] do allow
For beauty's pattern to succeeding men.
      Yet, do thy worst, old Time: despite thy wrong,
      My love shall in my verse ever live young.

[1] *A hunting term that means in full strength*
[2] *Old, fantastic*
[3] *Undefiled*

The message: Don't spoil my lover's beauty, Time, but even if you do, my love will live forever in my poetry. (And so it has.)

Sonnet 55

Not marble, nor the gilded monuments
Of princes, shall outlive this powerful rime;
But you shall shine more bright in these contents
Than unswept stone, besmeared with sluttish time. [1]
When wasteful war shall statues overturn,
And broils root out the work of masonry,
Nor Mars his [2] sword nor war's quick fire shall burn
The living record of your memory.
      'Gainst death and all-oblivious enmity [3]
Shall you pace forth; your praise shall still find room
Even in the eyes of all posterity
That wears this world out to the ending doom. [4]
      So till the judgment that yourself arise, [5]
      You live in this, and dwell in lovers' eyes.

[1] *Time wears away a tomb*
[2] *Mars' sword*
[3] *Being forgotten*
[4] *Judgment Day*
[5] *Until you rise from the dead on Judgment Day*

The message: Until the Day of Judgment, you will live in my verse.

Sonnet 60

Like as the waves make towards the pebbled shore,
So do our minutes hasten to their end;
Each changing place with that which goes before,
In sequent toil all forwards do contend. [1]
Nativity, once in the main [2] of light,
Crawls to maturity, wherewith being crowned,
Crooked eclipses 'gainst his glory fight,
And Time that gave doth now his gift confound.
Time doth transfix the flourish set on youth,
And delves the parallels [3] in beauty's brow;
Feeds on the rarities of nature's truth,
And nothing stands but for his scythe to mow:
　　　And yet, to times in hope [4] my verse shall stand,
　　　Praising thy worth, despite his cruel hand.

[1] *Following each other, as the waves do*
[2] *Broad expanse*
[3] *Makes the wrinkles parallel*
[4] *The future*

The message: Nothing can withstand time's call to death, but my verse will praise your virtue forever.

I've Looked at Love from Both Sides Now

No one knows who Shakespeare addressed in the sonnets. All we have are the initials *W.H.* Those on the short list include William Herbert, Henry Wriothesley, William Harte, Willie Hughes, William Hathaway, William Hall, and William Harvey.

A group of scholars stump vigorously for Henry Wriothesley, Third Earl of Southampton, who was 20 years old in 1593, the year in which many of the sonnets to the youth were probably written. Wriothesley was handsome and younger than Shakespeare, and reversing his initials is a nice transparent disguise. He's still the front-runner, but the field is very crowded. One scholar even believes that the initials stand for Shakespeare himself, a printer's error for "W. Sh."

Notice that no women are included in this scavenger hunt. That's because we're pretty certain that the sonnets were addressed to a man (yes, even the "Dark Lady" ones). This suggests to many that Shakespeare was gay or bisexual. You can find the strongest evidence in critic Joseph Pequigney's landmark study *Such Is My Love*. Dr. Pequigney, a meticulous scholar and brilliant teacher, was one of my professors at The State University of New York at Stony Brook.

Sweets to the Sweet

Shakespeare addressed 126 passionate sonnets to a man. A few scholars get around the dilemma by claiming that Shakespeare was really addressing the sonnets to Queen Elizabeth since she was often considered a man for her vigorous leadership.

In the final analysis, what matters are the sonnets themselves. Enjoy this gem:

Sonnet 30

When to the sessions of sweet silent thought
I summon up [1] remembrance of things past,
I sigh the lack of many a thing I sought,
And with old woes new wail [2] my dear time's waste:
Then can I drown an eye, unused to flow,
For precious friends hid in death's dateless [3] night,
And weep afresh love's long-since-canceled woe,
And moan the expense [4] of many a vanished sight:
Then can I grieve at grievances foregone,
And heavily from woe to woe tell [5] o'er
The sad account of fore-bemoaned moan,
Which I new pay as if not paid before.
    But if the while I think on thee, dear friend,
    All losses are restored, and sorrows end.

[1] *Courtroom metaphor*
[2] *Bewail again*
[3] *Endless*
[4] *Loss*
[5] *Count*

The message: When I am alone with my thoughts, I cry over past sorrows, but thoughts of you immediately end my anguish.

The Least You Need to Know

➤ Shakespeare wrote 154 sonnets, first published in 1609.

➤ Next to *Hamlet,* the sonnets have sparked more commentary and stirred up more controversy than any other Shakespearean work.

➤ A sonnet is a lyric poem of 14 lines, written in iambic pentameter, a meter with five accents in each line.

➤ The Shakespearean or English sonnet rhymes a-b-a-b, c-d-c-d, e-f-e-f, g-g. The poet describes the problem in the first 12 lines and resolves it in the final couplet.

➤ Shakespeare's sonnets are a sensational story of love, lust, and disloyalty that may or may not have been inspired by his own experiences.

➤ No one knows whom Shakespeare addressed in the sonnets. It appears to have been a man, which raises the issue of Shakespeare's sexual orientation.

Elizabethan English

Shakespeare's English	Contemporary English
anon	until later
aroint	away
aside	a speech in which the actor turns away from the other performers and reveals his feelings to the audience
assail (verb) and assault (noun)	laying siege to a lady's chastity
aye/yea	yes
banns	notice of an intended marriage
bed trick	the surreptitious substitution of a virgin wife for another woman who is sinfully desired; it occurs in *Measure for Measure* and *All's Well That Ends Well*
blank verse	unrhymed iambic pentameter (10 syllables in each line, in which an unaccented syllable is followed by an accented one); blank verse has five feet, or beats, per line and every other syllable is stressed; blank verse can be smooth and dignified, but it can also mimic the pattern of natural speech more effectively than any other metrical pattern; as a result, it is one of the most versatile and flexible verse forms, a favorite not only of the Renaissance poets but also of many later poets
braggart soldier	a stock character, the comic figure drawn from ancient Roman comedy: Falstaff (*Henry IV, Parts I and II*) is Shakespeare's most famous use of this character
broadside	a single folio sheet (half the size of a regular sheet), printed on one side only; broadsides were used to publish ballads, proclamations, and other announcements

continues

continued

Shakespeare's English	Contemporary English
bum	buttocks
cock	penis; God
concordance	a reference book that lists every word that an author used; the *Harvard Concordance* is the authoritative Shakespeare concordance; it is especially useful for authenticating Shakespeare's works
edition	all copies of a book printed from the same setting of type (allowing for differences between copies resulting from press-corrections)
e'en	even/evening
enow	enough
fare-thee-well	good-bye
fie	a curse
foil	a minor character used as a contrast to a main character—Banquo, for example, serves as a foil to Macbeth
folio	a book format in which each individual sheet has been folded once, across the middle of the longer side, creating two leaves for each sheet; the sheets vary from 15 by 10 inches to 12 by 8inches—with many sizes in between
grammarcy	thank you
humors	the fluids of the human body: bile, phlegm, choler, and blood; according to Elizabethan medical theory, disease and emotion were caused by the balance of the humors
iamb	a poet foot or unit with one unstressed syllable followed by one stressed syllable, as in the word "a/fraid"
iambic pentameter	10 syllables or beats in each line (*see* iamb)
mayhap/perchance/belike	maybe
miles gloriosis	*see* braggart soldier
morrow	day
nay	no
ne'r	never
octavo	a book format in which the individual sheets have been folded three times, creating eight sheets; the measurements of an octavo are a fourth of that of a folio
oft	often

Shakespeare's English	Contemporary English
prithee/pray	please
quarto	a book format in which the individual sheets have been folded twice, creating four sheets; recto the front of a leaf, always the right-hand page
setpiece	an elaborate poetic passage that follows the rules of dramatic oratory; setpieces do not move the action forward and are often filled with quotations that become memorable; Hamlet's famous soliloquy "To be, or not to be" is a setpiece
sheet	a page; in Shakespeare's day, the size of a sheet varied a great deal, from 20 by 15 inches to 16 by 12 inches
soliloquy	a speech in which a character is alone with his private thoughts; it tells the audience what the character is thinking
sonnet	a 14-line poem written in iambic pentameter
stock character	a standard character who appeared in many plays and thus would be instantly recognizable to members of Shakespeare's audience
terminus ad quem	the time after which a play could not have been written (Latin)
thane	a Scotch title equal to "earl"
tribunes	officers appointed to protect the interests of the people from possible injustice at the hands of patrician magistrates
verily	very/truly
verso	the back of a leaf, always the left-hand page
wherefore	why

Further Reading

Bentley, Gerald Eades. *Shakespeare: A Biographical Handbook*. New Haven: Yale University Press, 1961.

Bloom, Harold. *Shakespeare: The Invention of the Human*. Riverhead Books, 1998.

Bradley, A. C. *Shakespearean Tragedy*. St. Martins Press, 1992.

Cartwright, Kent. *Shakespearean Tragedy and Its Double: The Rhythms of Audience Response*. Pennsylvania State University Press, 1991.

Charney, Maurice. *All of Shakespeare*. Columbia University Press, 1993.

Engle, Lars. *Shakespearean Pragmatism: Market of His Time*. University of Chicago Press, 1993.

Frye, Northrop. *A Natural Perspective: The Development of Shakespearean Comedy and Romance*. Columbia University Press, 1995.

Garner, Shirley Nelson. *Shakespearean Tragedy and Gender*. Indiana University Press, 1996.

Graham-White, Anthony. *Punctuation and Its Dramatic Value in Shakespearean Drama*. University of Delaware Press, 1995.

Granville-Barker, Harley. *Prefaces to Shakespeare*. Princeton: Princeton University Press, 1946.

Greenblatt, Stephen, Walter Cohen, Jean E. Howard, and Katharine Eisman Maus, eds. *The Norton Shakespeare Based on the Oxford Edition*. Norton, 1997.

Lewis, Anthony J. *The Love Story in Shakespearean Comedy*. University Press of Kentucky, 1992.

"Looking for Shakespeare: Two Partisans Explain and Debate the Authorship Question," *The Atlantic Monthly*, October 1991.

McDonald, Russ. *The Bedford Companion to Shakespeare: An Introduction with Documents.* St. Martin's Press, 1996.

Schoenbaum, Samuel. *Shakespeare His Life, His Language, His Theater.* Signet, 1990.

Schoenbaum, Samuel. *Shakespeare's Lives.* Clarendon, 1991.

Schoenbaum, Samuel. *William Shakespeare: A Documentary Life.* Oxford University Press, 1975.

"The Shakespeare Mystery," a Frontline TV program broadcast by PBS on April 18, 1987, and December 22, 1992.

Shapiro, Michael. *Gender in Play on the Shakespearean Stage: Boy Heroines and Female Pages.* University of Michigan Press, 1996.

Tobin, J. J. M., Herschel Baker, and G. Blakemore Evans, eds. *The Riverside Shakespeare.* Houghton Mifflin, 1997.

Wells, Stanley, ed. *The Cambridge Companion to Shakespeare Studies.* The Cambridge University Press, 1986.

Wells, Stanley. *Shakespeare a Life in Drama.* W.W. Norton, 1995.

Young, David. *The Action to the Word: Structure and Style in Shakespearean Tragedy.* Yale University Press, 1990.

Index

Q